A CO
SMITH vs. SMITH, 1944

HOLLAND M. SMITH—His explosive temper had justly
earned him the nickname "Howlin' Mad." He had spent
over forty years in the Marine Corps, but until Saipan he
had never been in action, never been a "fighting Marine."
Was he a bully, "tactically a chowderhead," as an Army
historian described him? Or a fierce defender of the Corps
and the honor of his men?

RALPH SMITH—An Army intellectual, soft-spoken,
compassionate, he was popular with his men and superiors
alike . . . except for "Howlin' Mad." As a combat veteran
with twenty-five years of unblemished service behind him,
would he have allowed the Marines to take the brunt of
enemy action to reduce casualties to the Army's 27th Division? Or was he just a scapegoat in a struggle for power and
prestige?

HARRY A. GAILEY'S INTRIGUING, LUCID STUDY
BRINGS YOU ALL THE FACTS FOR THE FIRST
TIME. NOW YOU CAN BE THE JUDGE. WAS THE
RELIEF OF RALPH SMITH JUSTIFIED? WAS IT A
PERSONALITY CONFLICT? OR WAS IT POLITICS
AFTER ALL?

HOWLIN' MAD
vs. THE ARMY

Conflict in Command:
Saipan 1944

Harry A. Gailey

A DELL BOOK

*For those officers and men of all the
services who fought on Saipan.*

When a general makes no mistakes in war, it is because he has not been at it long.
Marshal Henri Vicomte de Turenne

CONTENTS

PREFACE

AN INTEREST IN THE MANY PROBLEMS OF COM-
mand on the higher levels led me to consider investigating the
Marianas campaign. I was concerned initially with familiariz-
ing myself with the details of planning for and carrying out the
invasion of all three Japanese-held islands and relating these to
Admiral Spruance's decisions which led to the great naval victory in the Philippine Sea. The more I read in the few books
available on the subject, the more fascinated I became with
Saipan and the debate engendered by the actions of Marine
Corps Lt. Gen. Holland M. Smith in relieving his subordinate
of command of the Army 27th Infantry Division. Perhaps this
was because almost 35 years earlier I had read Gen. H. M.
Smith's apologia in the *Saturday Evening Post* and somewhat
later his memoir *Coral and Brass.* I am certain that at that time I
was no different from most who read these remembrances—I
believed them. There seemed no reason not to. I had, and still
retain, a great respect for the men of the Marine Corps, and
until I began investigating the Saipan affair had no suspicion
that what H. M. Smith had written about Saipan, and what had
been repeated almost by rote by several other authors, might
be suspect.

The first voice I heard raised in the defense of the Army's
actions on Saipan came from a colleague, Benjamin Hazard,
who had been in charge of a prisoner of war interrogating

team on Saipan. Long before I began a serious investigation of the conflict he was stating vociferously that much of what had been reported was pure myth. The next step in my education about Saipan was reading Edmund Love's works defending the 27th Division. My doubts as to the accuracy of the accepted version of events grew as I met and talked extensively with Gen. Ralph Smith, the officer who had been relieved. By the time I received a copy of Norman Cooper's dissertation on the military career of Gen. H. M. Smith, I had already concluded that the accepted version of what had occurred was deeply flawed. Reading Cooper's well-researched biography only confirmed my opinion, since much of what he wrote about H. M. Smith's personality and earlier decisions began to confirm Smith's detractors. However informative Cooper's work is, he tends to evade certain very pertinent questions concerning his subject, particularly the obvious evidence of Smith's dislike for Army units and the 27th Division in particular.

Exhaustive research on interservice relations on Saipan eventually led me to conclusions different from what has normally been accepted by historians of the War in the Central Pacific. I have attempted to base my conclusions on the written and oral evidence available, and to survey the background as well as those developments that occurred on Saipan. I had never intended this work to be a type of legal brief presenting Gen. Ralph Smith and the 27th Division's case by refuting on a point by point basis what H. M. Smith had written earlier. I hope it does not appear so to the reader. Inevitably, though, the many accusations made by the Marine general and his stated reasons for certain actions had to be confronted, and wherever these conflicted with the evidence, I attempted to ascertain the facts. One disclaimer is absolutely necessary. Although I fault many of the decisions and actions of Gen. H. M. Smith and his staff, this should not be taken to be in any way a condemnation of the Marine Corps or the actions of Marine units on Saipan. My admiration for these elite troops remains unchanged. I agree with the Army battalion commander who commented about the Marines on Saipan, "They were classy troops." To point out the injustices done to the Army units by a Marine commander should not be construed as an attack upon the Corps. It must be emphasized, however, that the

Army also fought bravely on Saipan. The officers and men of the 27th Division performed extremely well as they too bled and died attacking perhaps the strongest Japanese defenses on the island. These men and their commander, Maj. Gen. Ralph C. Smith, deserve better from posterity than to be remembered as their actions on Saipan have been portrayed in previous accounts.

In putting together the pieces of such a complex puzzle as the Saipan controversy, one contracts many debts. Although it is not possible to give credit to all who aided me, a few names should be mentioned. Chief among these are Gen. Ralph Smith, still vital and active in his ninth decade of life, who gave selflessly of himself in a number of time-consuming interviews and who allowed me access to his private files. Edmund Love, the historian of the 27th Division, trained by Gen. S. L. A. Marshall in the methodology of combat history, also contributed much. His excellent, detailed history of *The 27th Infantry Division in World War II,* utilized in conjunction with archival sources and the official service histories, was the source for the battle accounts. He also was most hospitable in allowing me an extensive interview. I must express my gratitude to Stephen Prusky, who unknown to me was also researching this topic and who unselfishly shared with me much of what he had learned.

The directors and staff of the various archives were most helpful. One could not expect better or more efficient service than I received from all. The National Archives at Washington, D.C. and Suitland, Maryland were indispensable in providing the primary materials related to the actions of the 27th Division. As usual, the staffs of the Marine Corps and Navy Archives in Washington, D.C. were courteous and provided me with all the pertinent files I requested. The Hoover Institution, although their holdings are not large in this subject area, did have very important papers without which this study would not have been complete. Finally, I must note my appreciation to all those who gave so willingly of their time in the many interviews I conducted during the research phase of this topic. Space does not allow me to express my gratitude individually to all. Their names are listed in the Bibliography and

I wish each to know how valuable were his recollections and insights. I thank them all for their assistance.

Harry A. Gailey
Los Gatos, California
February 1985

1 | THE MEDIA

DURING THE AFTERNOON OF 24 JUNE 1944, LT. Gen. Holland M. (Howlin' Mad) Smith, the Marine Corps Commander of V Amphibious Corps then assaulting Saipan, made a decision that, although serious, was not unique. He relieved a subordinate, the commander of the Army 27th Division. The 2nd and 4th Marine Divisions which made the landings had suffered such heavy initial casualties that the 27th Division had been hastily landed and literally thrown into the center of the line advancing eastward across the waist of the island. Once his forces had captured Aslito Airfield and secured the central part of the island, Smith's plan called for a pivoting movement to change the axis of attack northward in the final drive to eliminate a still numerous and dangerous enemy. For this he assigned the 2nd Marine Division to advance up the coast west of Mt. Tapotchau; the 4th Marine Division was simultaneously to move north along the eastern coastal plain. In order to complete his line across the island, he also committed the bulk of the 27th Division to the center facing the main highland areas. He left only two battalions of the 27th, one of which was considerably understrength, to complete the secondary objective of destroying the enemy in the southeastern part of the island adjacent to Nafutan Point. H. M. Smith ordered the two regiments of the 27th, the

165th and 106th, to take their positions between the two
Marine divisions, confronting some of the worst terrain on the
island. The Japanese, who were dug into caves on both sides
of the attacking army units, slowed their advance. H. M.
Smith, without any reconnaissance by members of Corps staff,
decided that it was not the entrenched Japanese who were
responsible for the Army attack lagging behind the Marine
advance on either flank; it was the fault of this particular Army
division with which he had had previous firsthand experience.
Narrowing the blame further, he concluded that the 27th's
commander, Maj. Gen. Ralph Smith, was primarily the cause
of the Army's lack of drive. So, like the owner of a baseball
team that was not performing up to expectations, H. M. Smith
fired the manager. He relieved Gen. Ralph Smith, replacing
him with an older Army general, Sanderford Jarman, who had
been scheduled to become base commander when the island
was secured.[1]

The relief of subordinate commanders during World War II,
while not commonplace, occurred quite often. Sometimes the
relief appeared justified by the situation, while in other cases it
was probably caused by personality conflicts, disagreement
over policy, or simple politics. Generals Eisenhower, MacArthur,
McNair, and Bradley had all faced the problem of telling
one of their senior commanders that he was not performing
adequately and was being replaced. These changes were an
accepted fact of military life and even if a dismissed officer felt
he had been unjustly treated, he would not complain publicly
of his treatment. The relief was contained within the closed
world of the military at war. The aftermath of Gen. H. M.
Smith's decision to replace Gen. Ralph Smith did not follow
this usual course. It became known almost immediately to the
American public and touched off a controversy within the military
establishment that, had it not been contained, could have
seriously impaired cooperation—so necessary for the successful
termination of the Pacific War—between Marine and Army
units.

Why was the Smith relief on Saipan so different from all the
others, enough so that it caused an immediate furor involving
many of the senior United States commanders in the Central
Pacific and Washington? One obvious reason was that H. M.

Smith had reopened an argument that, if not settled, had at least become quiescent by mid-1944. Army leaders from Gen. George C. Marshall down to divisional commanders had argued that Marine officers had never been trained to command large bodies of troops. Without descending to the level of calling Marines the Navy's policemen, Army spokesmen had pointed to the small pre-war size of the Marine Corps and had drawn the conclusion that in any operation calling for more than one division, the overall ground command should be reserved for an Army general. Lt. Gen. Robert Richardson, commander of all U.S. Army troops in the Central Pacific, was one of the more vocal proponents of relegating Marine generals to the level of divisional command.[2] Aside from the possible merits of his arguments, it was obvious that General Richardson had a personal stake in downgrading the Marines. He was in an ambivalent position in Hawaii. Ostensibly, he occupied a similar position to that held by Gen. Douglas MacArthur in the Southwest Pacific area, with one major exception. The actual command decisions affecting the utilization of Army personnel in combat areas were made by Adm. Chester Nimitz, COMCINCPAC. Nimitz favored the use of Marines in the amphibious attacks in the Central Pacific and the use of Marine generals under the direct control of Naval commanders to operate, if necessary, as corps commanders. Thus, long before Saipan, there had been considerable debate on this subject which tended to ruffle the feelings of senior Naval, Marine, and Army commanders. Gen. H. M. Smith did nothing to ease the rivalry after arriving in Hawaii in September, 1943. Rather, he exacerbated it. By the testimony of his own book, he saw not only a conspiracy by the Army, but also by the Navy, to deprive the Marines of their share of glory in reducing the Japanese redoubts in the Central Pacific and more specifically to restrict him to an advisory, non-combat role.[3]

Although apparent, such divisions in the senior military command were contained within the complex hierarchy in Washington and Hawaii. It was another matter with the mainland press. William Randolph Hearst had long taken the position that a supreme commander should be appointed with authority over the entire Pacific area. His choice for that commander was General MacArthur. The logic of Hearst's position dictated that, wherever possible without directly impairing the war effort, stories and editorials lauding MacArthur and the Army should be complemented by those indicating how the Naval command in the Central Pacific fell short of the ideal. Thus the story of the relief of Ralph Smith by his Marine superior appeared to the managers of Hearst papers to be a golden opportunity to embarrass Naval high command.

Gen. Ralph Smith had absolutely nothing to do with launching the media debate over his relief on Saipan. Nor would he take part in any such debates over the next few years. Only recently, after the passage of forty years, has Smith decided to speak candidly of what had occurred on Saipan. He had accepted his relief stoically, reported to his superior in Hawaii, and complied with General Richardson's request to provide a written account of the events leading up to his dismissal. This task occupied the better part of a week, and after the report had been turned over to General Richardson, it was classified as Top Secret.[4] There was no leakage of either the relief or Gen. Ralph Smith's report to the press from Army or Navy headquarters in Hawaii. The first news to reach the mainland came from an Army officer who had been on Saipan and was being rotated back to the United States. Without understanding how potentially explosive the subject was, and no doubt believing that his commanding officer and the 27th Division had been treated unfairly, he gave out the basic information as he understood it to a reporter.

Hearst's San Francisco newspaper, the *Examiner*, broke the story on 8 July. Their report was not a small informational item neatly tucked away in the back pages. Rather, front page headlines proclaimed, "Army General Relieved in Row over Marine Losses." An article authored by Ray Richards then amplified the headline. Since this story would continue to be the basis of charge and countercharge, certain key excerpts need to be quoted. Richards wrote:

Allegedly excessive loss of life attributed to Marine Corps impetuosity of attack has brought a breach between Marine and Army commanders in the Pacific.

General Ralph Smith's opinion that the attacking forces should conserve lives to a greater extent is said to have been openly expressed when a late casualty report showed 1289 Marine dead . . . and only 185 Army dead in the same length of time.[5]

The article was a bad one, particularly since it was not buried deep inside the paper. Richards had made an article out of rumor and innuendo, a type of journalism more in keeping with a scandal sheet than a reputable major urban newspaper. As will be shown later, little in the article was true. Alleging that Gen. Ralph Smith had "openly expressed" an opinion concerning tactics gave the impression there had been a simmering disagreement between the two commanders on this issue, resulting in Gen. H. M. Smith being relieved of his Army subordinate. If such had been the truth, the dismissal would have been raised to a higher plane than the actual facts of the case indicated when later discovered. Despite the inaccuracy of the article, its main theme that the relief was due to an open quarrel between the two generals over tactics would persist, and is openly believed even today.

Gen. H. M. Smith was reportedly infuriated when he saw a copy of the *Examiner* article. That, taken with the actions of General Richardson in appointing Ralph Smith to command the 98th Division and his subsequent visit to Saipan and confrontation with H. M. and Admiral Turner, must have made even "Howlin' Mad" wonder at the furor that had been created over what seemed to him a simple action. More was yet to come. Hearst's *New York Journal-American* on 17 July continued the attack upon H. M. Smith's competence and editorialized that Americans were shocked at the "staggering casualties" on Saipan following similar heavy losses by Marine commanders at Tarawa and Kwajalein.[6] It then presented Gen. Ralph Smith as having viewed the Marine general's strategy as a "reckless and needless waste of American lives" and indicated that this characterization had led to his dismissal. The editorial tied Ralph Smith's allegedly more cautious approach into its argument for appointing General MacArthur as Supreme Commander of the Pacific Theater. The obvious conclusion to be drawn was that such an appointment would result in fewer losses of America's fighting men. The *Journal-American* of the following day returned to the subject, reiterating its position against the Navy and Marine policies that had resulted in very high casualties.[7]

The decision made in Washington and adhered to by Admiral Nimitz and all subordinate commanders restricting any type of statement from official sources kept the debate in the lower echelons of the military in the Pacific to the level of rumor and innuendo. While this might have been necessary for the war effort, it allowed all kinds of stories to circulate that had no basis in fact. Depending upon one's branch of service, the replacement of Ralph Smith was seen either as necessary because the Army would not fight, or as a gross injustice by a Marine general who was a butcher. The Hearst newspapers' accounts were picked up by many others throughout the country and reported as factual. However, the main concern of most newspapers and editors in July and August of 1944 was to report on the successes of the Allied armies in Europe and most specifically with the fighting in Normandy. The Smith controversy was dropped and the concluding phases of the battle for Saipan were given only cursory treatment. Even in reports from the Pacific theater, the invasion of Guam took precedence. Then in September the controversy was given new life by a press conference given by Gen. H. M. Smith, who was in Washington, D.C. on an official visit, and following this was a short article in *Time* authored by Robert Sherrod.

Time reported that Gen. H. M. Smith, by then commander of Fleet Marine Force Pacific, was persuaded to meet the press in order to reiterate the concept of "unity of command" in the Pacific. When asked about the affair on Saipan, he was very restrained in his replies. He stated that he had been "forced" to relieve Gen. Ralph Smith, but gave no reason; he avoided doing so by stating, "I am not given to passing the buck, but as you seek details concerning this incident, I remind you that General Smith is an Army officer and I must refer you to the War Department."[8] He must have been aware that the War Department had decided to downplay the issue and would not make any statement which might exacerbate the problem further. Spokesmen at the War Department simply referred all questions back to the Marine general with the comment that since the decision for relief was his, "the reasons for that change should properly be given by him."[9] The reporter for the *New York Times* covering this interview was not content, however, with the no comment position of H. M. Smith and the War Department. He closed his report by repeating the by now familiar statement that the reason for the change was because "the Marine favored quick hard drives to end it as promptly as possible. The Army man advocated a slow more cautious campaign."[10]

The author of the long *New York Herald-Tribune* article, Don Cook, was even more inventive than his *Times* counterpart. After he had noted H. M. Smith's brief comments to the press corps, he launched into a long dissertation on the reasons for Ralph Smith's dismissal based upon a Congressional source "thoroughly familiar" with what went on after the Saipan landings. The article had the debate over tactics between the two generals beginning on the beach where the Army was "responsible for the center of the beachhead." As the troops pushed inland there was a "cloud of disagreement at the command level." The columnist then went on to reconstruct a hypothetical battle in which the Army in the center did not advance quickly enough, which gave the Japanese who had been "thrown all the way back" a chance to recover; they quickly found "the soft spot" and "plunged" through, "hacking the flanks of the two Marine units." Gen. H. M. Smith supposedly then "ordered the Army troops out altogether and sent in some of his Marine reserves who promptly cleared out the enemy pouring into the center."[11]

This description of what was supposed to have happened on the battlefield with the 27th Division was fanciful enough, but nothing as compared to Cook's account of an acrimonious meeting between the two generals during the height of this imaginary crisis. Presumably this confrontation took place at Corps Headquarters where Ralph Smith had continued his criticism of Marine Corps tactics. Thereupon, Lt. Gen. Smith "turned upon his subordinate and told him he could take his troops and go back to Pearl Harbor for guard duty as far as he was concerned."[12] Needless to say, no such meeting ever took place, not even at the height of the fictitious battle that Cook had conjured up. The only accurate statement in the body of the article was Cook's statement that it was obvious that H. M.

Smith had made no attempt to handle the situation diplomatically.

The highly publicized article of 18 September 1944 in *Time*, according to author Robert Sherrod, was prompted by his belief that Gen. H. M. Smith was getting a raw deal in the press and that the record should be set straight. Unfortunately, he did not do so. Rather, he added to the controversy and indeed became a part of it. Sherrod, a distinguished correspondent, landed on Saipan and attached himself to the 2nd Marine Division. Although he did move into the 27th's sector briefly after the fall of Aslito Airfield, he admitted later that he had spent most of his time with the Marines, generally at divisional or corps level. Later, in 1945, Sherrod would publish a portion of his diary kept during that period in his book, *On to Westward*. In that work he gives a very balanced view of the Marine-Army actions on Saipan with no implied accusations of Gen. Ralph Smith or his successor, Gen. George Griner, or the 27th Division. He did report what he observed of Gen. H. M. Smith after he had relieved the Army commander.[13] However, the article he had written for *Time* was not so restrained and produced a surprising reaction that almost led to his loss of accreditation to the Pacific theater.

Sherrod, like so many Americans, was an unabashed admirer of the Marine Corps. He later quoted an excerpt from a letter from Gen. Julian Smith to his wife which best expressed Sherrod's feelings toward the Corps. Julian Smith had written, "I can never again see a United States Marine without experiencing a feeling of reverence."[14] In the case of the *Time* article, Sherrod appeared to have allowed that feeling and his admiration of Gen. H. M. Smith to overpower his duty as an objective reporter. Although Sherrod's article appeared to give both sides of the controversy, some of the phrases were poorly chosen and appeared to favor the "Marine version." It is necessary to quote this article at length because it, along with H. M. Smith's reminiscences, form the basis of what later came to be accepted as fact. Sherrod wrote:

By the eighth day of the Saipan battle the Second and Fourth Marine Divisions had advanced rapidly on each side of the island. Then they had to wait because two regiments of the 27th Army division—with battalions faced in three directions unable even to form a line—were hopelessly bogged down in the center. The third regiment of the 27th meanwhile had failed dismally to clean out a pocket of Japs in the southeast corner of the island.

Although terrific artillery barrages were laid down in front of them, Ralph Smith's men froze in their foxholes. For days these men, who lacked confidence in their officers, were held up by handfuls of Japs in caves.[15]

The article went on to state that all might have been lost had not elements of the Fourth Marines "moved in front of the sector to save it." It then said that the new Army commander, Sanderford Jarman, had fired several officers and "thereafter the 27th performed fairly well until its greenest regiment broke and let some 3000 Japs through in a suicide charge which a Marine artillery battalion finally stopped, at great cost to itself."[16]

Whether Sherrod had intended to vilify the 27th and its officers or was merely trying to present the Marine case is largely irrelevant, given how damaging his choice of words was. The Marines had to "wait," according to Sherrod, because despite "terrific artillery barrages," the Army troops "froze" in their foxholes. This was partially because the men "lacked confidence" in their officers and Gen. Ralph Smith had been relieved because his chief fault was that "he had long ago failed to get tough enough to remove incompetent subordinate officers." General Jarman had come in, cleaned house, and the 27th had then performed very well until one of their regiments "broke" and let 3000 Japanese through on a suicide mission before they were stopped by the heroic action of only one battalion of Marine artillerymen. To *Time*'s millions of subscribers, it appeared obvious why Gen. H. M. Smith had relieved a softhearted commander of troops who were reluctant to fight. They could breathe a sigh of relief that there were Marines such as that lone artillery battalion which could stop the maddened *banzai* charge of 3000 suicidal Japanese troops.

None of the major points in Sherrod's article appeared among the official reasons given for the relief of Gen. Ralph Smith. However one views the Army board convened by General Richardson to investigate events on Saipan, one thing is clear—Gen. H. M. Smith never made any such official charges against his Army subordinate or the 27th Division.[17] What Sherrod had done was to pick up on rumor and possibly the intemperate talk of H. M. Smith and other Marine officers. He then presented such scuttlebutt as fact, using it to explain why it had been H. M. Smith's duty to get rid of an incompetent officer who could not "get tough" enough with subordinates to get them to move into an area lightly defended by the Japanese even after "terrific artillery" barrages had cleared the way.

Time, one of the major news magazines in the country, had reintroduced some old "facts" embellished by what appeared to be a number of new charges. The editors had obviously not checked the story's accuracy. They submitted it to the Army Bureau of Public Relations, which withheld the formal stamp of clearance. Although no security matters were involved, the Director, Maj. Gen. Alexander Surles, called *Time's* Washington Bureau and strongly recommended that the article not be printed until all its allegations could be thoroughly checked. Surles pointed out what an adverse effect such an article would have upon the men of the 27th Division and their families, and even the general population of New York (the 27th had been a New York National Guard Division).[18]

The article was published nonetheless and, as General Surles had warned, it had a devastating effect upon the 27th Division. On 24 September, that issue of *Time* reached the division on Espirito Santo in the New Hebrides, where it had been ordered after the conclusion of the Saipan campaign. So deep was the resentment against the rumors, now compounded by Sherrod's negative article, that General Griner communicated directly to General Richardson his reluctance to lead the division into combat once again unless steps were taken to clear the division's good name. He pointed out that it would be impossible, given wartime censorship, to refute the accusations in detail, but he felt that someone in authority should attempt to repair the damage.[19] General Richardson concurred and in October presented Admiral Nimitz with a point by point refutation of the article. He asked that Sherrod's credentials as a war correspondent be revoked and that an official statement by the War Department be given the widest circulation in the United States. All the documents were then forwarded to Washington with Admiral Nimitz's recommendation for favorable action. Eventually the materials reached General Marshall's desk; Marshall made the key decision that ultimately forced the men of the 27th to live with the accusations and innuendos of the Sherrod article. Marshall believed that the whole affair had been blown out of proportion and did not want to continue the questionable debate in the American press. To do so, he felt, would only lead to more disunity in the Pacific command structure. Thus, with the concurrence of Admiral King, the Chief of Naval Operations, nothing was done to rectify the errors of the *Time* article.[20] The best the 27th could get was a personal letter from Admiral Nimitz to General Griner expressing his full confidence in the division's past actions. This was little comfort to the officers and men of the 27th who, despite the loss of over a thousand on Saipan, would go into the bloody Okinawa campaign bearing a stigma of a division that would not fight. Given the rivalry in the Pacific, one can be certain the Marines never let the Army troops forget it.

Except for stories spread by Marines within the limited confines of the Central Pacific zone of action, there the Saipan controversy rested until after the war. Newspapers and magazines had much more important and interesting stories to report during the closing months of World War II. In all probability, the so-called Smith vs. Smith clash would have been completely forgotten, except as a minor footnote to the Pacific War or in the minds of aging Marine and Army troops, had not Gen. H. M. Smith decided, like so many other senior military commanders, to write his memoirs. His decision was perhaps triggered by the debates then current at the highest levels regarding the fate of the Marine Corps. The proposed unification of the services deeply disturbed most Marines—given H. M. Smith's combative personality, it would have been strange if he had not seen in Edmund Love's article in the September, 1946 issue of *Infantry Journal* a further attack upon the Marine Corps.[21]

Actually, Love's article, entitled "The 27th's Battle for Saipan," was a spinoff from the work he was then doing on the

official divisional history. Love had been a member of Col.
S. L. A. Marshall's team of historians and had been assigned to
the Saipan operation. In the five years after World War II, he
became the most informed and vocal defender of the 27th
Division, although he had only a limited audience—the general public does not include divisional histories or the *Infantry
Journal* among its favorite evening reading. An article in August 1946 in *Harper's,* which had many thousands more readers than the *Journal,* had actually reopened the debate. The
article added little to what had already been presented by the
popular press. One additional snippet, however, was interesting; it was reported that Admiral Spruance had based some of
his decisions on the fleet movement on 16 June 1944 because
of the poor showing of the 27th Division.[22] Although it was
later pointed out to the editors of *Harper's* that the 27th was
not even ashore on the 16th, they did nothing to correct the
implications of the largely erroneous article. In the case of the
1946 *Journal* article, Love had no idea he would be the indirect cause of a series of articles and a book ostensibly written
by Gen. H. M. Smith. A three-part article appeared in *Saturday
Evening Post* in November 1948, and, in the following year,
Charles Scribner's Sons published *Coral and Brass.* These set
the seal upon Gen. H. M. Smith's version of what happened
on Saipan, and soon became accepted by not only the general
public, but also most historians and journalists who later
would write of the Pacific War.

Even the most ardent admirer of Gen. H. M. Smith would
admit that the old general was no writer. If he was going to
present his story, he would need the assistance of a professional writer. He chose as his collaborator Percy Finch, an
Australian who had been a correspondent in the Pacific during
the war. Unfortunately, Finch was not the man to curb Smith's
intemperate language or to carefully research those items
which he must have known would be questioned not only by
the Army, but also by Smith's companions in arms in the Navy
and Marine Corps.[23] It may not have been possible to restrain
the general; if so, Finch probably should have withdrawn from
the project which was what Smith's old friend and defender
Robert Sherrod, who had initially agreed to write the foreword to the book, had done. Instead, the *Post* articles and the

book were filled with sensational revelations and frank but damaging personal opinions concerning almost everyone with whom H. M. Smith had served, including Admirals Nimitz, Spruance, Turner, and Hill.

There is every indication that, long before he retired, H. M. Smith was a very bitter man. His pugnacious personality had alienated many and he was obviously difficult to work with. Even his closest associates had to put up with a great deal. After Saipan, he believed that the Army was out to get him and that he was not being defended properly by Admiral Nimitz. Nimitz had become, in his eyes, a man who could no longer be trusted and whose direction of the Pacific War was therefore suspect. Smith had wanted the command of the 10th Army on Okinawa, but was bypassed in favor of the Army's Lt. Gen. Simon B. Buckner, the same officer who had chaired the board examining the dismissal of Ralph Smith. H. M. Smith had relinquished command of V Corps to Maj. Gen. Harry Schmidt in order to take up the newly created position of commander of the Fleet Marine Corps Pacific. Although ostensibly a promotion, his new job was largely titular, somewhat similar to that held by his nemesis, Army General Richardson. Nevertheless, Admirals Spruance and Turner insisted that H. M. Smith be present during the invasion of Iwo Jima. Although the effective overall command of the Marines there was General Schmidt's, Smith was involved along with Adm. Turner in overruling the request that the 3rd Marine Regiment, which had been held in reserve, should be committed.[24] Generals Schmidt and Graves Erskine, Commander of the 3rd Marine Division, were both openly critical of this decision. Much of the newspaper accounts, particularly those of the Hearst papers, placed a large share of the blame for the heavy casualties on Iwo to the Marine methods and General Smith.

There is no doubt that H. M. Smith, during this period of his career, was very depressed. His old friend Admiral Hill later recalled his fear that Smith's depression was so deep Smith might even harm himself. Hill and the doctor on board the *Auburn* kept a close watch on the general while Smith was on board.[25] Whether suicide was ever a possibility is questionable. Without a doubt, however, H. M. Smith was bitterly resentful, and if his outbursts were often misdirected, he was

nonetheless correct in thinking that much of his trouble
stemmed from his decision on Saipan to dismiss Ralph Smith.
The critics who claimed that he had wasted lives also wounded
the general, who had always had a near-mystic affection for the
Corps and a deep awe and admiration for the many thousands
of young Marines who had died. H. M. Smith was tired, and
his statements were increasingly embarrassing. As a result, his
superiors decided to bring him home to rest, and on 3 July
1945, Smith turned over his command to Gen. Roy Geiger.
Later Smith was appointed commander of the Marine Training
and Replacement Command. A further disappointment was in
store, however. Despite their major role in the Central Pacific,
only one Marine representative had been invited to be on
board the *Missouri* when the Japanese surrendered. And that
Marine was not H. M. Smith, but Roy Geiger. H. M. Smith
correctly interpreted this as an obvious shortchanging of the
Marines and a direct personal snub.[26]

When H. M. Smith retired in August 1946, even the fourth
star granted him on retirement did not assuage his feelings of
isolation and betrayal. Thus when it appeared that his beloved
Corps was to be done away with, or at best merged with the
Army, and that there were renewed attacks on his Saipan decisions, he decided to act. He provided Percy Finch with a few
letters and documents and Finch, without exerting himself
very much, pieced together details abstracted from them, in-
terspersed with opinions solicited from the General on specific
incidents. Even before Finch had completed the manuscript,
rumors circulated that it would be a bombshell. Secretary of
Defense James Forrestal was concerned that the book would
reopen many of the interservice wounds not yet completely
healed during the unification debates. It was at this juncture
that the new Marine Commandant, Clifton Cates, gave Lt. Col.
Robert Heinl permission to "unofficially" proof the work. He
did not want the Corps to appear in any way as the sponsor of
Smith's book. Robert Sherrod was also brought in to suggest
modifications to the book and the articles contracted by the
Saturday Evening Post.[27]

Heinl and Sherrod must have been appalled by what they
read. They corrected the many technical errors of spellings,
names, and dates. They met with Smith a number of times and

got him to agree to many changes. One of these concerned his accusation against the 3rd Marine Division's performance on Guam which, in his opinion, placed them on the same level as the 27th Division. The General refused to moderate some of his statements about his fellow Naval and Marine commanders, or to withdraw his claim that Tarawa had been a mistake. The veracity of the future *Coral and Brass* could be challenged on many counts other than statements referring to Gen. Ralph Smith or the Army. One of the most obvious errors is the general's statement about Tarawa. General Smith was unmoved in his attitude, even though he was shown documents clearly indicating that he had approved of the invasion at the time.[28]

The behind-the-scenes attempt to either modify Smith's memoirs or delay publication went on during the early fall of 1948. The Secretary of the Navy, John Sullivan, was disturbed by all the rumors and demanded to see advance copies of the *Post* articles. Sullivan even asked Smith to come to Washington for conferences over the proposed publications. By this time Smith was disenchanted with Finch and was more than willing to accept help from any source, but his stubbornness got in the way of accepting the best advice, that given by his old friend, Robert Sherrod, who wrote:

My honest opinion is that you should start all over with a new writer . . . Your life-long reputation is more important than the manuscript as it now exists.[29]

Sherrod did not, however, volunteer to be that new writer. Specifically why H. M. Smith did not heed Sherrod's advice is not known. It may have had to do with his perception of undue pressure being directed at him from the highest levels of Naval and Marine command. He also must have known that the *Infantry Journal* was planning an article on Saipan, written by Edmund Love, which would be very critical of his actions.

During his visit to Washington in late October, H. M. Smith met with General Cates, who felt that the publication of *Coral and Brass* as it then stood would not be in the Corps' best interests. He wanted Smith to agree not to publish the work, but shied away from ordering the old general to cancel his contracts. General Cates later recalled that, among the arguments he used was that Gen. Roy Geiger, Smith's good friend, would not want the book published. At that, General Cates remembered, "The tears started coming down General Smith's cheeks and he looked at me and all of a sudden he jumped at me and I thought he was going to hit me. He said, 'God damn it, don't hit me below the belt.' I said, 'All right, go ahead and publish it.' "[30]

Gen. H. M. Smith decided soon after this conversation to allow both publications to go forward, although it was obvious by this time that he was sick of the whole affair. The first installment of the *Post* articles—excerpts from the book that would later be published—had the general title "Howlin' Mad's Own Story" and was subtitled "Tarawa was a Mistake"; it appeared in the issue of 6 November 1948, and was followed by the remaining sections in the following two issues. The second installment was titled "My Troubles with the Army on Saipan" and the final one was called "Iwo Jima Cost too Much."[31] By this time both Sherrod and Heinl had disassociated themselves from the project.

Coral and Brass came off the press early in 1949. Smith's book was replete with errors and half-truths when describing events in Washington and the Pacific unrelated to the Army. It brought on immediate negative comments from men who had been closest to Smith in both the Navy and Marine Corps. Among those who made statements to the press regarding more controversial sections of the book were Admirals Nimitz, Spruance, and Turner. Smith's old associates, Gen. Julian Smith and Adm. Harry Hill, both wrote him scathing letters of criticism. Hill even threatened to sue if certain statements attributed to him were not removed from the book. Norman Cooper, who much later thoroughly researched the life and career of H. M. Smith and whose doctoral dissertation remains the best source of information about the general, concluded:

Undoubtedly, however, the book with its extravagant claims and its wild charges, did serious harm to Smith's reputation. Thenceforth, he was remembered more for his criticisms of the Army and Navy at Tarawa, Saipan, and Iwo Jima than for his very important contributions to those victories. *Coral and Brass* was a mistake.[32]

The next publication to focus on the controversy was a long article entitled "Smith Vs. Smith" by Edmund Love published in the *Infantry Journal* of November 1948.[33] In it Love presented the case for the Army and Gen. Ralph Smith. There were no wild accusations or denigrating statements about the Marine Corps. Love theorized that the reasons for Ralph Smith's relief, while possibly grounded in a difference in philosophy and tactics, were technical and related primarily to a misunderstanding between the two generals regarding one particular order. H. M. Smith had removed his subordinate for a very specific reason, one not at all related to the presumed differences between the two generals. Love attempted to prove that this was petty and the relief was based more on H. M. Smith's ignorance of the true state of affairs on the front line than anything else. The article went beyond the controversy and also dealt with the Sherrod story in *Time* (which for the benefit of Love's readers was reprinted in the *Journal*).

Love's article resulted in a response from Robert Sherrod titled "An Answer and Rebuttal to 'Smith Vs. Smith, The Saipan Controversy' " which was published in the *Infantry Journal* in January 1949.[34] Sherrod argued in some detail for the correctness of his *Time* article with specific reference to those points about the Smith relief, Nafutan Point, and the *banzai* charge. Although nothing was added to the controversy, Sherrod's response was a much more reasoned presentation of the Marine Corps position than *Coral and Brass* had been. The editors of the *Journal* placed a series of statements by participants in the Makin and Saipan invasions throughout the Sherrod rebuttal. These boxed statements attacked not only some of Sherrod's arguments, but also refuted many of H. M. Smith's allegations. Included were statements by Army Generals Griner, Jarman, Colloday, and Harper, as well as eyewitness accounts of many of the events reported by General Smith in his articles.

Although obviously the *Journal* was biased in favor of the Army position, it allowed Sherrod space for a long rebuttal. Any reader of the two articles familiar with the controversy could form an informed opinion of what had happened on Makin and Saipan. The media controversy, in which Gen. Ralph Smith had taken no part, was for all practical purposes at an end. But the misunderstanding and bitterness engendered by the media accounts lingered on. Most of the men of the 27th Division still felt injured and were convinced that they had not been adequately defended by the Army. General Marshall's decision not to rebut the charges, and the later reluctance of Defense Department officials to disturb the fragile unity achieved in the latter 1940s, had given H. M. Smith's version credence. The public had accepted Smith's version, just as they had accepted the authenticity of Joe Rosenthal's photo of the flag-raising on Mount Surabachi. The *Infantry Journal* articles had a restricted circulation, generally reaching only those readers who did not need to be convinced that the Army had been treated badly. In this manner, the myths created by the popular media and Gen. H. M. Smith became reality.

That the feeling by members of the 27th Division of having been maligned is not merely collective paranoia can be seen in William Manchester's book, *Goodbye Darkness,* published in 1979, thirty-five years after Saipan. Manchester, a writer of popular history and biography and himself a Marine veteran of the Pacific campaign, while reporting on a long trip to visit the battlefields of the Pacific wrote an extremely interesting "Memoir of the Pacific War." As with most of Manchester's books, it soon appeared on the best seller list. What he wrote of the Saipan controversy would, presumably, be read by many thousands of people with no reason to question his credibility. Did Manchester have anything to add? No, he simply repeated the conventional wisdom abstracted from H. M. Smith's account. He wrote:

Both Marine divisions moved well; Mt. Tipo Pale was taken, riflemen began their agonizing ascent of Tapotchau, and the Second marines battled their way into the outskirts of Garapan. But Ralph Smith's GIs seemed impotent. Their jump-off was fifty-five minutes late; they edged forward cautiously, then stopped altogether. Because the Marines continued to pick up momentum, fighting the Japs in caves with grenades and pole charges and the terrain with bulldozers, the American front formed a shallow U, exposing the Marines' flanks. Ralph Smith reprimanded his regimental commanders. He himself received a gruff message from

Holland Smith informing him that Howlin' Mad was 'highly displeased' with the GIs' performance. The next day was worse. The two Marine divisions continued to move forward on the flanks while the army division dug in, deepening the U. Holland Smith took a long look at his situation map and blew his top. He told Admirals Turner and Spruance: "Ralph Smith has shown that he lacks aggressive spirit, and his division is slowing down our advance. He should be relieved."[35]

Manchester further reported that after Ralph Smith's departure, the spirit of the 27th "momentarily rose and the army moved in step with the Marines." He also supported the Marine version of the later Japanese *banzai* charge on 7 July in which two army battalions "were immediately overwhelmed, cut off, and carved into bewildered pockets," the situation being remedied only by Marine artillerymen.

Clearly, the myths concerning the relief of Gen. Ralph Smith are still alive and potent forty years after the event. It is time for them to be put to rest and a detailed account of the Saipan affair substituted in their place. All the documentary material relating to the Central Pacific previously classified is now available, and Gen. Ralph Smith has agreed to break his long silence and for the first time publicly discuss the events preceding his relief. The following chapters attempt to present an objective picture of the rivalry between the Marine and Army commanders that culminated in Gen. Ralph Smith's relief on Saipan on D day + 9.

2 | THE MARINES' SMITH

HOLLAND MCTYEIRE SMITH REPRESENTED A number of strains in twentieth-century America. Born at Hatchechabbee in Russell County, Alabama on 20 April 1882, only seventeen years after the Civil War, he was a child of the middle class whose parents had reluctantly accepted the verdict of the war between the states. His rural childhood, according to his own account, was as happy as it was parochial.[1] Most of his early years were spent in Seale, the county seat, a very small community that served the needs of the surrounding farms. His father, Charles V. Smith, a native of Georgia, had attended Alabama Polytechnic at Auburn for a time, then taught school. Eventually he read for the law and was admitted to the bar. During Holland Smith's youth, his father was one of the most prominent men in the county, eventually becoming President of the Alabama Railway Commission. His mother, Cornelia McTyeire, a native of Alabama and a good churchwoman, exercised great influence over the young man. His education until he was sixteen years old was at a one-room schoolhouse in Seale, and then he was sent off to the college at Auburn where his father had studied. He appears to have had an undistinguished academic career during his three years there. He was more of an athlete, and, in contrast to his later years, recalled that he did not like the uniforms all undergraduates had to wear nor the military drill they had to perform. He graduated in 1901.

Probably because of his father's standing in Alabama politics, Holland Smith was offered an opportunity by his congressman to take the examination for the U.S. Naval Academy. He did not do so largely because of his parents' concerted opposition. They did not wish their son to serve in any northern-dominated military force. Instead, Smith dutifully followed his father's wishes and attended law school at Auburn for two years. He did not like it and barely managed to graduate in 1903. He joined his father's law firm, and if his reminiscences can be believed, he must have been one of the worst lawyers in the state, losing every case he tried. He must have thought many times about the lost opportunity of attending the Naval Academy. Perhaps he had grown tired of an unsatisfying career and of laboring in the shadow of his father when, against his father's wishes, he travelled to Washington to see his congressman about getting an Army commission. Smith was told that there were no Army vacancies at that time, but that the Marines had openings. The man who would become one of the most vociferous defenders of the Corps had to admit he had never heard of the Marines. Despite such ignorance, he was ready to take a chance if it would get him away from life as a rural lawyer in Alabama. He enrolled in a school that prepared candidates to take military tests, and, in February 1905, he passed the examinations. He was commissioned a Marine 2nd Lieutenant on 28 March 1905.

The Corps he joined was, depending on one's viewpoint, either an elite group or a small detachment of Naval police that drew to it some of the worst elements in society. It was small, with an authorized strength of only 275 officers and 8000 enlisted men. Its major function during much of the nineteenth century had been to provide additional support for naval ships, most of the larger ones having a complement of Marines on board. This primary role had been expanded from time to time when the nation needed small, well-disciplined units for specialized tasks or to participate in the major wars. In the Mexican and Civil Wars, the Marines were used in much the same way as Army troops. Later, in World Wars I and II, the Corps would be greatly expanded and would again be utilized as infantry in conjunction with Army units. Their use as specialized troops would be exploited repeatedly in a number of different locations in Central America and the Caribbean as Presidents Taft, Wilson, Harding, and Coolidge tried to uphold the Roosevelt corollary to the Monroe Doctrine.

During his career of over forty years in the Marine Corps, Holland M. Smith would participate in all of the different tasks assigned to the Corps. His first years of service followed a course not unlike those of junior officers in any of the branches of the small military forces of the United States. He spent two and one-half years in the Philippines, travelled to China and Japan, served at Mare Island and Annapolis and briefly in Nicaragua in 1909–10, was among those mobilized in the following year to counter the revolution in Mexico, and then spent fifteen months on board the U.S.S. *Galveston*. In June 1916, he was a part of the 4th Regiment sent to Santo Domingo to help restore the deposed President of that republic to power. He was involved in the march to Santiago where, although prepared for the worst, the Marines found little resistance to their occupation. Smith was appointed Military Commander of Puerto Plata, one of the quiet areas of Santo Domingo. By all accounts he was a good administrator; there were no rebellions in his province during his tenure. It was quiet enough that his wife Ada, whom he had married in 1909, and their child lived with him. In July 1916, after eleven years in the Corps, he was promoted to Captain. Then in May 1917 he was ordered to the Marine Barracks in Philadelphia.

The dual crises in Mexico and Europe had led to a continuous expansion of the Corps to 15,000 in August 1916 and 31,000 in May 1917. Smith's 5th Regiment was the first to be mustered for war service. As the commander of a machine gun company, Smith and the first contingent of Marines sailed for France along with the Army's 1st Division in June 1917. The Marines were at first posted to Gondrecourt, south of Verdun, for further training. Many of them were sent back to St. Nazaire in August where they unloaded supplies for the next two months. H. M. Smith was promoted to Major and sent to the Army General Staff College at Langres for an intensive three-months' course. He was the first of only six Marines ever to complete this course. In February 1918 he joined the newly formed Marine Brigade, formed of the 5th and 6th Regiments, which was assigned to the Army's 2nd Division at a relatively quiet sector southeast of Verdun. For some months Smith was the Brigade Adjutant. When Army Maj. Gen. James Harbord assumed command of the Brigade, Smith became the Brigade liaison officer, responsible for overseeing all internal communications within the Brigade. As such he played "a vital though undramatic" role during the fighting at Belleau Wood. Shortly thereafter he was posted to the 1st Corps where he served as liaison officer on the general staff of Gen. Malin Craig. After the armistice he continued staff work as a member of the Third Army's general staff, where his duties mainly concerned issuing reports. Tired of such work and obviously eager to get home and resume his duties with Marine troops, H. M. managed to get orders for a return home, smoothed out all problems of transit, and boarded the battleship U.S.S. *Georgia* for Norfolk. His joy at being back with his "own people," rather than the Army was exemplified by his pulling off his spurs and heaving them over the side of the ship.

There are a number of things which should be noted about this thirty-seven-year-old Marine major. The most obvious is the transparent pride he took in being a Marine. Smith was more than proud to be a member of the Corps. Quite possibly, he had already acquired that almost mystical attachment to the Corps that would be so noticeable later in his career. He had also been made aware by the Navy on many occasions that the Marines were considered a lower form of life, one only to be tolerated, not treated as equals, and certainly not listened to. Smith's memoirs indicate how deeply he felt these slurs, particularly as opposed to the differential way the Navy treated Marines in such mundane matters as the sale of tobacco and candy, and mess fees. Smith had vowed as early as his Nicaraguan service that if he ever had a chance to rectify these wrongs, he would do so immediately.

Smith had very little actual combat experience. He had come under fire in Nicaragua, Santo Domingo, and France, but had not commanded Marines in any desperate fighting.

Even at Belleau Wood he had held a staff position. He had proved himself a good administrator and staff man, but no matter how he may have wished it, he was not a "fighting" Marine. Without pressing the issue, this may have been a factor in his actions much later in World War II. Conceivably, those factors that would make H. M. Smith such a vociferous defender of the Corps and would earn him the sobriquet "Howlin' Mad" were already present when he returned to peacetime duty in 1919.

The next two decades of H. M. Smith's career brought him into closer contact with senior Naval officers with decidedly different ideas about amphibious warfare and the way Marines should be utilized in any future war. As early as 1920, as one of the two Marine officers attending the Naval War College, Smith ran head-on into the conservative defensive-minded strategy of the Navy. Smith was not exaggerating when he claimed that almost all the senior officers there from Adm. Sims, the commandant, downward could see no need to restudy the problem of landing troops on a hostile shore. He wrote:

Under the old Navy doctrine, a landing was a simple and haphazard affair, involving no planning and very little preparation. Assault forces were stowed in boats 5000 yards off the beach and given a pat on the back with the hope that all would go well. Warships threw a few shells into the beach and that was all.[2]

Thus began a continuing debate between, on the one hand, the Navy and, on the other, Smith and other farsighted Marine officers who wanted to upgrade the methodology of amphibious warfare. He carried on the debate as a member of the War Plans Division in the Office of Naval Operations and on the Joint Army Navy Planning Committee. He noted of this period in his career:

But I was a bad guy. I always have been a bad guy in interservice arguments and I often am amazed that I lasted so long in the Marine Corps.[3]

Once again he was in trouble when he attended the Field Officers Course at the Marine Corps School at Quantico. His insistance on the value of morale, of offensive warfare, and on learning from the immediate experiences in France did not make him popular. Despite having been responsible for all the communications plans for the entire 1st Corps in France, he almost flunked the communications portion of the course because of the textbook solutions required at the school.

Some of the ideas of Smith and other like-minded officers with regard to amphibious operations were slowly and reluctantly adopted by the Navy. For example Smith was made responsible for leasing two small islands near Puerto Rico in order to provide for more ambitious landing operations. The new commandant, Maj. Gen. John Russell, and his Naval superiors created the Fleet Marine Force in 1933. These 3000 officers and men became a part of the regular organization of the United States Fleet. The following year saw the Marine Corps adopting the *Tentative Landing Operations Manual*, which would be copied by the Navy in 1938, and was adopted almost verbatim by the Army three years later.[4]

However, there was still much to disturb Colonel Smith in 1937 when he became an assistant to Maj. Gen. Thomas Holcomb, who had just succeeded Russell as Commandant. He had witnessed many amphibious exercises, particularly those off Oahu, and was appalled that the Navy could not see the need for specialized landing craft. All landings by the Marines were made in standard ship's boats that were not designed for either heavy surf or coral reefs. The boats could hold only a few troops; there were not enough boats to land enough men at one time to gain a foothold on a beach. Smith concluded that, despite the powerful presence of the Navy, the assault forces in these exercises would be wiped out by the defenders. Smith's commitment to improved landing craft led him to a central role in the behind the scenes struggle with the Navy. When, in the spring of 1940, he commanded the 1st Marine Brigade in landing exercises, he noted that, despite the adoption of ramp boats by other countries, there was not a single one available for the Marines. Ship's boats were definitely unsuitable. The argument continued until late 1941 when the Navy reluctantly accepted the Higgins boat, a prototype of which had been available in 1927.[5] This fight over suitable landing craft may have been H. M. Smith's ultimate contribution to victory; the early ramp-style boats became the prototype for a whole series of landing craft used in every theater of action during World War II.

Much to Smith's chagrin, the Navy exercised a detrimental control over the development of the Marine Corps through the office of the Navy Budget Officer who had to pass on all Marine requests. Smith disputed the competency of any naval officer to have the final determination of equipment for the Corps. This was simply another example of relegating the Marines to a secondary role. He made clear at every opportunity his displeasure at the Navy's unwarranted assumption of such authority. One must keep in mind that these clashes did not take place within an impersonal bureaucracy. Smith obviously made a number of enemies during the 1930s while upholding what he saw as the logic of his position.

One of those men with whom Smith clashed was flinty Rear Adm. Ernest J. King, the future Chief of Naval Operations. This was during Fleet Exercise number 7 (FLEX–7) in the spring of 1941. King was in command of the operation and Smith was a Brigadier General in charge of the landing forces. They quarreled over a number of items; chief among them was the choice of the landing beaches. During these same exercises, Secretary of the Navy Frank Knox criticized the appearance of the Marines. Smith had to explain to him, probably with less than his usual humility, that they were involved in training under near combat conditions. Because of his differences with Admiral King, Smith was certain that his service in the Marine Corps would be terminated.[6] King, however hardheaded and tough, valued competence, and it was obvious to him that H. M. Smith was an excellent administrator and training officer. Soon after the exercises were concluded, Smith was promoted to Major General and was given charge of the large scale training operations at New River, North Carolina. The Army's 1st Division was placed temporarily under his command and, in conjunction with the 1st Marine Division, the division conducted exercises during August 1941.

When war came, H. M. Smith fully expected to get one of the senior combat commands. However, he was passed over.

The newly formed 1st Marine Division, the first Marine unit to go overseas, commanded by an old friend, Major General Vandegrift, was rushed unceremoniously into the first great major offensive action of the war at Guadalcanal. In September 1942, Vandegrift's West Coast counterpart, Maj. Gen. C. B. Vogel, was sent to the South Pacific to take charge of the 1st Amphibious Corps, and Smith replaced him as commander of the Second Joint Training Force. Although Smith resented not getting a combat command, he had reason to be proud of his training command record. He was involved in the training of all the new Marine divisions as well as the amphibious training of the Army's 7th, 77th, 81st, and 96th Infantry Divisions. His retention as commander of one of the major stateside training units can be viewed as a compliment to his success, rather than as a conspiracy of his enemies. However, H. M. Smith did not see it that way. He became convinced that he had enemies in high places who were set on thwarting him in his desire to have a combat command. Such a suspicion was reinforced by the near-comic opera details of the medical examination he was required to take upon reaching his sixtieth birthday while still at Quantico. He found out that he had been diagnosed as having a severe case of diabetes. He rushed to Washington to confirm the details and met Secretary Knox, who assured him that, despite the adverse medical report, the Navy would not force him to retire. On Smith's return to Quantico, he had three additional blood sugar tests done, all indicating that he did not have diabetes. Eventually the Navy informed Smith that the error was due to a technician's mistake. This was a perfectly logical explanation, but Smith did not fully believe it. He was still convinced that someone was out to get him.[7]

As senior training officer, Smith went along as an observer when the Army's 7th Division landed at Attu in May 1943, but he brooded that the war was passing him by. He had no way of knowing, but his wishes for a command closer to the fighting were about to be granted. Despite warnings against trying to mix the volatile personalities of H. M. Smith and Rear Adm. Richmond Kelly Turner, his naval expert on amphibious landings, Admiral Nimitz had decided to bring H. M. Smith to the Central Pacific. Nimitz did not make this choice unaided. There is some evidence that he did not want Smith, but had been convinced by the arguments of both Vice Adm. Raymond Spruance, Commander of the 5th Fleet, and by Turner, to be the new commander of the about-to-be-formed V Amphibious Corps. Spruance noted much later his attitude toward bringing "Howlin' Mad" and "Terrible Turner" together. He wrote: "They were both strong and determined characters but I had confidence that they would work things out between them, which they did."[8] After the Attu invasion, Nimitz invited Smith to accompany him on a tour of the South Pacific areas. Smith had thought he was being introduced to the area prior to taking command of Marine operations there. However, Admiral Halsey had selected another commander. As H. M. Smith related the event, on the way back to Hawaii he was in a most depressed mood, believing that he would never be given a combat command, when Admiral Nimitz informed him that he was to come out in the fall to take command of all the Marines in the Central Pacific.[9]

In August 1943, H. M. Smith once more took advantage of his position as senior Training Officer to go to Adak, which was Army headquarters, for the attack on Kiska. These units had received their amphibious training at Ft. Ord under the direction of Smith's Joint Training Force and were now planning to drive the Japanese from their base in the Aleutians. Smith went to Adak with a part of his staff to supervise the continued training of the troops under Arctic conditions and to observe how they functioned under attack. The commander of the Task Force was Vice Adm. Thomas Kincaid, and the Army commander was Lt. Gen. Simon B. Buckner. Maj. Gen. Corlett commanded the 7th Division, which would make the attack. All of this was for naught, however, since the Japanese quietly slipped away; all the Americans found at Kiska was abandoned equipment. This futile exercise at Kiska was not to be H. M.'s last observation of an attack as an observer. He would be forced to consent to a similar role half a world away when the 2nd Marine Division and the 165th Regiment of the Army's 27th Division assaulted the Gilbert Islands.

On 5 September 1943, the Clipper arrived in Honolulu, bringing Maj. Gen. Holland M. Smith to his new command, one which a few months before he would not have believed was within his reach. Ironically, he was met by his superior, Rear Adm. Kelly Turner, whose shortness of temper was legendary in the Navy. Turner was just as certain of the correctness of his views about the Navy as was H. M. Smith about the Marines, and he was also convinced that his method of conducting operations was the correct one. Turner was not one to shirk the responsibility of command, and at that time he considered it the duty of a Task Force commander to control the actions of the ground personnel assigned to him.[10] As Spruance wrote, the two senior commanders worked "things out between them," but he failed to note that the compromise was on Turner's terms. It took some time before Turner was willing to change his attitudes and allow Smith to make most of the key decisions regarding such matters as the loading of ships, the number and type of assault vehicles, and the many smaller details relating to an amphibious assault. Thus, H. M. Smith's role in the taking of the Gilbert Islands of Tarawa and Makin was not major.

H. M. Smith brought to his new command in Hawaii certain skills. He had proved himself a fine administrator, a good planner, and capable of functioning very well in a series of staff positions and as the officer in charge of the two largest amphibious training centers in the United States. He was correctly considered an expert in this type of training. Further, Smith was basically a simple, straightforward individual whose personal integrity was beyond question. When he believed himself correct, Smith was not afraid to speak out, no matter whom he was addressing. He had an explosive temper, and when aroused was likely to say things he would later regret. The nickname "Howlin' Mad," used by friends and enemies alike, attests to this characteristic. For over twenty years he had fought the Navy "brass" on large and small issues. He chafed at the constraints placed on the Corps and would continue to work to free up Marine commanders from the dead hands of battleship admirals. He had a near-mystical allegiance to the Corps and this, combined with his protective attitude, made him take exception to anything, no matter how small, which tended to reflect poorly on Marines. That in many of his battles with the Navy he was correct is not the point to consider. Past experience with senior naval officials had convinced him that, despite the war, they still thought of the Marines as secondary baggage. He had not had much to do with the Army after World War I, but he was sharply critical of their training methods and their officers. On the basis of little evidence, he suspected their fighting qualities. H. M. Smith was also a man given to introspection; imagined personal slights were easily converted in his mind to slights against the Corps. While difficult to prove, it seems clear that Smith could play favorites and also harbor grudges long past the time when they should have been forgotten.

H. M. Smith came into a highly confusing command situation in the Central Pacific area. His arrival added a further complication. Admiral Nimitz was the overall commander of all forces in the Northern, Central, and South Pacific areas. This appeared to make considerable sense, since areas held by the Japanese could be reached only by ship. The primary task in the war's early days was to blunt Japanese offensive operations that could threaten the vital supply lines to the South and Southwest Pacific theaters. Once the United States took the offensive, the role of Naval commanders became a serious subject of debate. Where should their direct authority end? Some of the senior naval officers, including Kelly Turner, believed they should retain control even after a bridgehead had been secured. This was disputed by every Marine officer who had the responsibility of clearing a given island objective of the enemy. The quarrel remained a Navy affair as long as only Marines and the Navy were involved. But what if Army troops were to be used? The Army commander in the Central Pacific was Lt. Gen. Robert C. Richardson, whose headquarters was responsible administratively for all Army personnel in that theater. How far did his authority extend? The obvious answer, and the one adopted by the Navy, was that it extended only up to the embarcation of Army troops. After that, the Task Force commander assumed responsibility. This potential confusion of command did not exist in the Southwest Pacific, where Gen. Douglas MacArthur held supreme authority. Naval, Air Force, and in some cases Marine personnel were under the direction of an Army general, whose primary area of expertise was maneuvering large bodies of troops on land.

In his theater, there was no question of where the lines of authority led.

Personalities exacerbated interservice rivalry. Much as they may seem so in retrospect, most senior commanders were not *prima donnas*. Each seemed convinced that his ideas were correct and that if everyone recognized that salient fact, then the war would be shortened considerably. General Richardson may have chafed while serving under Nimitz, but he did not dispute Nimitz's role in the strategic planning for the reconquest of the Central Pacific. What disturbed him most was the choice of Marine units to bear the brunt of the conquest of the designated islands and the concomitant possibility that Army troops would fall under Marine command. He made no secret of his conviction that Marine generals had not been trained to command units larger than divisional size. In this conviction, he was supported by the Army high command, including General Marshall. Thus the announcement that H. M. Smith would be the commander of the newly authorized V Amphibious Corps, although not designed to be so, was nonetheless a rebuff by the Navy. Since Nimitz planned to use more Marines in the capture of Japanese positions in the Central Pacific, it seemed to him only logical that Corps command, when needed, should fall to a Marine. Even before H. M. Smith arrived in Oahu, the decision to appoint him was being seriously questioned. Nimitz's decision permanently placed General Richardson in a secondary role in the Central Pacific command.

H. M. Smith's problems in Hawaii were at first not with the Army, but with his old nemesis—the Navy. Problems began almost immediately after his arrival when he found that the quarters assigned him, a senior major general, were in a section normally assigned to Navy captains or even more junior officers. He protested immediately and was shortly reassigned to better quarters in the admiral's section. The explanation for this apparent slight was that it was the fault of the billeting officer. Smith never accepted that as the true reason. It appeared to him that this was merely another example of the Navy treating Marines differently from their own. In this instance, Smith may have won this small skirmish for himself and the Corps, but he may have also lost by it—quite likely, much of the antipathy that developed between himself and Admiral Nimitz is traceable to this minor occurrence.[11]

H. M. Smith and Admiral Turner were soon at loggerheads over the problem of command. As noted, Turner believed in retaining control over troops as long as possible, even after a beachhead had been established. Smith wanted the troop commander to assume control as soon as was practical. There was more to this than just a simple disagreement on tactics. Smith saw himself as the lone protector of the Corps. He told his aide:

Nobody will fight the goddamned Navy but me. They don't know how or they haven't got the guts. They are all looking out for themselves. I have to do it all myself or the Navy will run over us . . .[12]

Kelly Turner and Smith would later work well together, and after the war, each tended to minimize their differences. But to Smith in September 1943, those differences were very real. Captain Charles J. Moore, Spruance's Chief of Staff, recalled:

Holland Smith particularly complained about Kelly Turner. . . . He loved to complain. He loved to talk and he loved to complain and he would come and sit on my desk and growl about Turner. "All I want to do is to kill some Japs. Just give me a rifle. I don't want to be a commanding general. Just give me a rifle. I'll go out there and shoot some Japs. I want to fight the Japs."[13]

This is hardly the reaction of a senior officer even if confronted with a superior who was just as truculent as he. This brief quote indicates two other characteristics of H. M. Smith. He loved to talk, not always being careful of what he said, and he wanted to present himself as a tough-as-nails fighting Marine.

The general planning for GALVANIC, code name for the seizure of footholds in the Gilbert Islands, had been underway for a considerable time before H. M. Smith arrived in Hawaii. But most of the detailed planning was done after 5 September. As commander of V Amphibious Corps, Smith played an important role in this phase of the operation, but in his memoirs,

Coral and Brass, he stated that his Corps staff did most of the work. This was not correct. Planning went on concurrently at all levels, and the Divisional plans when complete were checked and approved at Corps level and then finally by Admiral Nimitz's headquarters. H. M. Smith was only partially responsible for a major change in the general plan, which originally had the Army's 27th Division attacking the phosphate-rich island of Nauru simultaneous with the 2nd Marine Division's assault on Tarawa. It was much more of a joint decision than Smith indicated in his book. Admiral Spruance did not like the idea of conducting these two operations located almost 400 miles apart. He was worried about the widespread deployment of Naval forces if the Japanese chose to attack. Not too many on CINCPAC staff considered his objection seriously, until he had H. M. Smith write a letter on 24 September stating his objections to the Nauru operation and suggesting Makin as the target instead. Spruance presented this to one of the bi-monthly CINCPAC-COMINCH conferences. Admiral King reluctantly agreed to the change and Makin became the target for the 27th Division.[14]

After fighting Turner to a draw over the question of command, H. M. Smith had yet another disappointment in store. In October, the operations order for GALVANIC was issued and H. M.'s name and those of his staff were omitted. It was obvious that someone senior to him had deliberately decided that his presence was not needed either at Tarawa or Makin. He went charging over to Spruance only to find that the Admiral knew nothing about the omission and insisted that H. M. Smith go along. Smith suspected Turner, but he too denied prior knowledge of the full contents of the order. Turner even protested to Nimitz the plan that would have left H. M. Smith behind in Hawaii while the men he had helped train were sent into combat. Smith eventually found out that Vice Adm. Charles McMorris, who had succeeded Spruance as Nimitz's chief of staff, was the man responsible for the calculated omission.[15]

In *Coral and Brass,* H. M. Smith describes this late-developing situation in some detail. He omits only one key fact. Although it was agreed that he should go along on the operation, it was only as an observer. The Navy's decision stood.

There was to be an overall commander for the operation, Admiral Spruance, Commander of the 5th Fleet. Kelly Turner was Commander of Task Force 54 in charge of the landing operations. He had decided earlier when Nauru had been the target to remain with the northern force; in case the Japanese fleet attacked, he would be in a better intercept position. Rear Adm. Harry Hill was named Landing Force Commander for the Tarawa operations. The designated land force commanders were Maj. Gen. Julian Smith of the 2nd Marine Division at Tarawa and Maj. Gen. Ralph Smith commanding the 165th RCT of the Army's 27th Division at Makin. The line of command went from the two admirals directly to the divisional commanders. H. M. Smith officially had no responsibility in the Gilbert operations, except that delegated to him by Admiral Turner. Even Edmund Love in his detailed history of the 27th Division was confused by H. M. Smith's presence on Makin when he wrote: "In command of all landing forces on both islands was Major General Holland M. Smith, U.S.M.C."[16] H. M. Smith was taken along by Kelly Turner because of his protests and was used by him as an advisor. As Gen. Ralph Smith has confirmed, "Turner commanded everything." Thus, contrary to many accounts of the GALVANIC operation, H. M. Smith was not the Corps Commander. He had no direct responsibility whatever. He was ordered on board the Admiral's flagship, the battleship *Pennsylvania,* and was kept on a tight leash throughout the entire operation. Although the 2nd Marine Division was to be involved in a desperate struggle at Tarawa, H. M. Smith was not allowed to intervene in any fashion with the course of the fighting there. Instead, he was used by Turner as a liaison man to the 165th RCT on Makin.[17]

It is very important in analyzing later developments between the two Smiths to keep this in mind—H. M. Smith had no official command in the Gilbert Islands. This action by the Navy obviously hurt him deeply. Taken with all the other real and imagined slights he and the Corps had suffered from the Navy, it may explain in part his bellicose attitude toward Gen. Ralph Smith and the Army troops at Makin. There are few other logical reasons for his behavior toward the Army in general and Ralph Smith in particular. He and the Corps had been slighted and there was nothing he could do but accept the situation. Angry as he was, he struck out at the only people he could attack without too much fear of retribution—Gen. Ralph Smith and his untried troops of the Army's 27th Division.

3 | THE ARMY'S SMITH

RALPH CORBETT SMITH WAS AS MUCH A PROD-
uct of the Midwest as his future antagonist, Holland M. Smith,
was of the old South. His ancestry claimed a *Mayflower* settler
and a host of farmers, doctors, and teachers in New England.
His great-grandfather, a teacher, abandoned Massachusetts for
western Illinois in the early 1830s, and his son, a minister,
moved to southern Nebraska where he homesteaded a farm.[1]
There was a strong Presbyterian strain in both the Corbett and
Smith families, as well as a commitment to education. Ralph
Smith's grandfather graduated in 1858 from Westminster College in Fulton, Missouri and attended Princeton Theological
Seminary, and his father, Carl, attended Peekskill Military
Academy in the 1880s. After marrying May Corbett, Carl and
his wife moved to Omaha, where the future general was born
in 1893.

Ralph Smith spent the first fifteen years of his life here in the
largest city in Nebraska. His father's health failed in 1909 and
the family moved to a more healthy area near Fort Collins,
Colorado. The family finances were bad enough that Ralph
could not immediately complete high school, but instead attended Colorado State College, taking a practical course in
agriculture while working a farm. Despite the difficulties, he
did return to high school and graduated in 1912, and was then

employed to teach in a country school for a year. His education from this time onward was determined by the economic needs of the family. By 1916, he had completed two years of college, taught school, and successfully managed a 160-acre irrigated farm.

Ralph Smith's introduction to the military came when he joined the Colorado National Guard just before it was called to active duty in 1916 because of the crisis between the United States and Mexico. His unit spent the summer in Golden, Colorado, where he learned of a chance to gain a commission in the Regular Army. This was possible because the National Defense Act of 1916 more than doubled the size of the Army. Smith was one of two men from his National Guard unit to pass the examinations and was commissioned a 2nd Lieutenant on 30 November 1916. The possibility of war with Mexico passed and Smith was mustered out of the service. Returning to college, he had completed all but twenty units for his Bachelor's degree when he was recalled to active duty in January 1917. Later he would complete the necessary course work and receive his degree, but only after service in France. It is obvious from Smith's later career that he was drawn to intellectual pursuits, and that, as with so many of his contemporaries, he was prevented from pursuing more advanced degrees by his economic condition. However, fate had caught up with him—in the Army, he found a chance for a satisfying career in an organization that valued his keen mind and dedication.

Most of the newly commissioned 2nd Lieutenants from Texas, New Mexico, and Colorado were ordered to join the 16th Regiment, which had only recently been a part of General Pershing's punitive expedition into Mexico. The 16th was a part of the newly formed 1st Division, which was scheduled to be the first of the American units sent overseas to show the French that they could count on immediate assistance from the United States. After an uneventful train journey from El Paso, the 16th Regiment embarked for France on 12 June 1917. In retrospect, it is ironic that H. M. Smith should have been a part of the large convoy bringing the first large contingent of American troops to St. Nazaire, and would also be posted in the same area near Verdun.

The 1st Division was stationed at Gondrecourt, south of Verdun, where it underwent the rigorous training that had not been possible in the United States. Ralph Smith's first experience under fire came when his battalion was ordered into the trenches north of Luneville on a training exercise in October 1917. A German attack on the unit next to his produced the first American casualties in the "Great War." A most fortuitous event occurred during this training period. Col. John L. Hines, a friend of General Pershing who had been his adjutant during the Mexican campaign, took over the regiment. He was very impressed with Smith's work in command of an automatic rifle platoon and asked him to join his staff to help work out the details for training the entire regiment. In January 1918, the brigade was ordered into the trenches in the Rambecourt-Beaumont area, where it spent a relatively quiet two months. After a brief respite and further training, the 1st Division was ordered to the western section of the line to help stem the great German spring offensive of 1918, where it launched the first major American offensive at Cantigny. Colonel Hines was promoted to Brigadier General and given command of the brigade. Smith went along as a member of the brigade staff. As such, he participated in the offensive south of Soissons on 18 July. After this severe action, Hines was again promoted and assumed command of the 4th Division. Once again, Smith was taken along to serve on the divisional staff and was promoted to Major. The 4th Division was ordered into the line in September and took part in the Meuse-Argonne campaign, the greatest American offensive of the war. On 8 October 1918, Ralph Smith was wounded in the wrists and thigh. These were not life-threatening wounds, but serious enough for him to spend the rest of the war in a hospital at Neuf-Chateau.

A very distant cousin of Ralph Smith's had earlier moved to France before the war, and shortly after the armistice, Smith spent a couple of months on convalescent leave in the south of France, a visit that enabled him to improve his knowledge of French. His ability to speak French fluently would play a most important role in his future career. Soon after rejoining General Hines, who now commanded a corps in Germany, Smith took a course of study at the Sorbonne covering a variety of fields relating to French culture. Completing this in July 1919, he returned to occupation duty as adjutant of the 2nd Brigade. In the fall of the year, the 2nd Brigade returned to the United States and Smith was temporarily stationed at Camp Merritt on Long Island. After the 1st Division was demobilized, a cadre of 1st Division officers and non-commissioned officers was sent to Camp Taylor in Louisville, Kentucky. By this time, Ralph Smith had reverted from his wartime rank of Major to his permanent rank of Captain. He had believed he would be posted to ROTC duty at his old school at Ft. Collins, when he was assigned unexpectedly to West Point as an instructor in French. Gen. Douglas MacArthur, then Superintendent, wanted a number of non-Academy graduates on the staff. Smith was probably selected as an instructor because of the courses he had taken at the Sorbonne.

This teaching assignment, unexpected as it was, set the tone for much of Ralph Smith's career between the wars. The workload was not onerous, and the necessity of teaching four sections of French forced him to keep up his own French. During the summer of 1921, he was sent to Paris for a further concentrated course in French and took advantage of the posting to take a long trip through Central Europe and the Balkans. In the spring of 1923, he was ordered to Ft. Slocum, where the 18th Infantry was posted for a brief tour, before receiving orders to take the course at the Infantry School at Ft. Benning. Smith's standing in the course can be judged by his selection as an instructor at the school. There he would remain until 1927, while a number of officers, including Dwight Eisenhower, passed through the school. From Ft. Benning, Smith was sent to Ft. Leavenworth to the Command and General Staff School, which he completed in 1928. From there he was posted to the 30th Infantry at the Presidio in San Francisco, first as a battalion commander and later as the regimental executive officer. Here he would finally regain his wartime rank of Major. After two years on the West Coast, he was once again ordered to Ft. Leavenworth as a member in the G–2 section teaching Military History and Military Intelligence. This duty was briefly interrupted by orders to Oregon to aid in establishing Civilian Conservation Corps camps. After his successful short tour, he returned to Ft. Leavenworth where until 1934 he was again a teacher, this time of senior officers who like himself were destined for high command.

Ralph Smith, as one of the most promising young officers, continued his education as a student at the War College for a year. In 1935 he was selected for the much sought-after assignment to the prestigious *l'Ecole de Guerre* in Paris. France was viewed as the premier power in Europe and, as befitting that reputation, its military schools were regarded as the world's finest. The *Ecole de Guerre* stood at the apex of that system. Each year about 120 French officers were selected to attend and 20 places were reserved for foreign officers. Students selected for the school had already shown outstanding leadership and intellectual ability. One of Ralph Smith's classmates at the *Ecole* was another Smith who would also have a brilliant career in the Pacific and later Korea. This was the future Marine general, Oliver P. Smith.

Each class at the *Ecole* was divided into sections of twenty officers, generally with four foreign officers. Prior to the beginning of the course, Ralph Smith was assigned to French army units to become familiar with French tactics and methodology. He spent one month with an artillery regiment near the Pyrenees whose headquarters was near Valence, the home of his wife, Madeleine, whom he had married in 1924. The second month was with an alpine infantry regiment on maneuvers in the high Savoy mountains. The subsequent months of the first year were spent dealing with problems of command, particularly at the divisional level. The problems addressed were very much like those dealt with at the Command and General Staff School at Ft. Leavenworth. There was no instruction during the summer of 1936, and Major Smith and his wife travelled extensively throughout Germany and Central Europe. This vacation and observation journey also took them to Berlin and the Olympic games.

The second year's course was basically a reiteration of the problems and solutions given the first year, only with a concentration on operations at the corps level. At the conclusion of the second year, Smith wrote for the War Department a long, detailed report on the *Ecole,* stressing the tactical as well as theoretical aspects of the instruction. He was not aware of it then, but that report was widely circulated among senior officers and later he received a number of compliments for its thoroughness. The report would be of great importance to his career. It confirmed its author as one well-suited to high command, and helped secure his appointment to the War Department General Staff. Before this happened, he was assigned to Ft. Sill to take charge of the full wartime strength demonstration battalion of the 29th Infantry stationed permanently at the Artillery School.

In the summer of 1938, General McCabe, the Army's G–2, asked for Ralph Smith's assignment to his staff. At that time the War Department General Staff was a very select group of only eighty-eight officers. Each was a graduate of the War College and was designated to a set position by name to replace an officer who had been reassigned. Ralph Smith relieved Robert Eichelberger, later commander of the Eighth Army, who was leaving after four years to take command of the 30th Infantry Regiment. Smith joined an elite group headed by George Marshall, the newly appointed Chief of Staff whom Ralph Smith had first known in France when he was S–3 of the 16th Infantry and Marshall was G–3 of the 1st Division. Dwight Eisenhower soon became chief of the War Plans Division and Smith's old friend, Albert Wedemeyer, was in his section. Omar Bradley was in the G–1 section. Walter Bedell Smith, then a major, was at first Assistant Secretary of the General Staff, and then later became Secretary during Ralph Smith's tour.[2] Charles Willoughby, later MacArthur's Intelligence Chief, was recruited by Ralph Smith to head one of the projects being pursued by the Plans and Training Section. Ralph Smith's immediate superior was General Sherman Miles, who used him as his executive officer. Later, in the Plans and Training Section Smith was made responsible for Military Intelligence reserve activity.

At this crucial period in the nation's history, Ralph Smith was deeply involved in the army's transition from a small, somnolent organization to a much larger and better equipped, although still inadequate, force. More than most, the members of the intelligence sections could appreciate the inferiority of American arms when compared to the *Wehrmacht,* which had made the startling conquests of Poland, Denmark, Norway, the Low Countries, and France. After the war in Europe began, there was a considerable expansion of intelligence activities, in which Ralph Smith played an important part. In the course of his duties, he came to know Frank Mason, former head of NBC, who, as a dollar-a-year advisor to the government, played a key role in coordinating intelligence efforts with his friend, the Secretary of the Navy Frank Knox. Smith also had close contacts with John McCloy, who served as an advisor to Secretary of War Stimson, William "Wild Bill" Donovan, former commander of the 69th Regiment and later head of the O.S.S., and many officials in the FBI. All of these acquaintances were made because of the obvious need to upgrade, expand, and modernize the intelligence services in the face of the danger to American security in Europe and the Pacific.

In the summer of 1941 Ralph Smith was promoted to Colonel. Since he was coming to the end of his tour on the General Staff, Smith was looking forward to a posting where he would once again command troops. In late November, in preparation for the new command, Smith was selected as one of a group of young colonels from various duty stations in Washington, D.C. to take a refresher course at Ft. Benning, then commanded by Brig. Gen. Omar Bradley. On 6 December 1941, he took the train from Washington to Atlanta and arrived the next day. After being assigned quarters, he went to the officers' club for lunch, and it was there that he heard of the attack on Pearl Harbor. Soon afterward, he received a call from General Bradley notifying him that he was needed in Washington immediately. Bradley provided a car, and Smith left for Atlanta and caught a civilian plane back to Washington where he resumed his duties in the now frenzied atmosphere of the capital of an ill-prepared nation abruptly at war on two fronts. In early 1942, his superior, Sherman Miles, was transferred to Boston to take command of a corps. Soon afterward Smith was promoted to Brigadier General and at the conclusion of his General Staff appointment was named Assistant Divisional Commander of the newly formed 76th (Liberty) Division at Ft. Meade, Maryland.

During General Smith's twenty-five-year Army career before World War II, he held a number of different positions in both combat and peacetime, and without fail he excelled in each of them. Even before the conclusion of the First World War, Smith's potential talent had been recognized, and he was given the first of a series of increasingly important responsibilities. Although he commanded troops in the interwar period, he had spent most of his time attending advanced military schools, teaching at West Point, Ft. Leavenworth, and Ft. Benning, and had spent four intensely demanding years as a member of the General Staff. Thus, like so many marked for senior command during this period, he had been involved mainly with the theoretical operations of various units of an army through the level of corps. Another point, ironic in retrospect, is that he was one of the few genuine European experts in the army. He had spent considerable time in France, including two years at the *Ecole,* had made a thorough study of European armies, and had taught, over and over, the strategy and tactics of the First World War. He had either served in regions where much of the next European war would be fought, visited those areas, or walked over the ground of the battlefields of northern France. By comparison, most of his contemporaries who would become commanders in Europe were profoundly ignorant of that continent. If modern war were rational, then Smith's knowledge combined with his proven military skills would have been utilized. The necessities of providing commanders for the rapidly expanding army precluded such a logical selective process, however, and Ralph Smith would be given command of a division in the Central Pacific theater, while men less knowledgeable would later be assigned to duty in Europe. Because of the size of the operations in Europe, promotions came more rapidly. Although Ralph Smith denied that his assignment had any effect on his career, it is quite conceivable that he, like many of his associates in Europe, could have aspired to Corps command. His contemporaries, Charles Corlett and Joe Collins, who were transferred from the Pacific, did indeed become Corps commanders under Eisenhower. Perhaps even more important, had his European expertise been recognized, he would have been operating in a theater not dominated by the Navy and Marine Corps and would have avoided the later, much publicized conflict with H. M. Smith.

Since personalities play such a large role later in the Saipan controversy, it would be well to inquire into that of Ralph Smith. His Marine antagonist's personality has been very well summed up by the nickname "Howlin' Mad," not always affectionately applied. Ralph Smith had no such appellation attached to him. As with most division commanders, he was called "The Old Man," although he was younger than many of his staff, being only 49 when he took command of the 27th Division. Those who served with him in the Pacific are unanimous in their description of a man who seldom raised his voice yet was very decisive. Tall and handsome, Gen. Ralph Smith commanded attention by his presence and obvious self-assurance. Without making him a paragon of virtue, it is obvious that he did not yell at his subordinates nor, under the strain of decision-making, curse them or his superiors. Col. Henry Ross, the G–3 of the Division on Makin who was also on Ralph Smith's staff on Saipan, was asked whether the general was prone to lose his temper. He replied:

Oh, hell, no. I have never, never seen him angry. I have seen him disturbed, but I never heard the level of his voice go up any more than in normal conversation. As a matter of fact, I don't recall the Old Man ever saying even a "God damn."[3]

Such calm self-possession, although in most cases a virtue, was probably a handicap in dealing with such a loud, quick-tempered colleague as H. M. Smith. Most other senior officers would not have permitted H. M. Smith the latitude exercised on Makin. Perhaps if Ralph Smith had been more like H. M., there would have been a showdown there that could have prevented the later, more serious clash of personalities. As will be shown, Ralph Smith's natural courtesy toward an older and more senior officer was combined with his assurance that H. M. Smith's rantings and posturings were not harming the operation. As he said much later, he "just considered the source and let it go at that."[4]

Gen. Ralph Smith demanded much of himself and expected the same from his officers and men. That he did not always get the response he expected is inherent in any large organization, particularly one such as a National Guard division in World War II. However, Ralph Smith refused to dismiss subordinates without evidence that they had indeed failed to meet his standards. Later, this would be used by his detractors to try to make a case that he was weak.[5] Far from being weak, Smith simply could not be sure of the combat effectiveness of his senior commanders until they had been in combat, and he did not prejudge them. In 1942, Ralph Smith was one example of how fortunate the nation was in the Army officers who had endured the interwar period. One of the finest historians of World War II, Brig. Gen. S. L. A. Marshall, left a record of his first impressions of Ralph Smith that sums up a number of similar statements by others. Marshall recalled:

On first meeting Ralph Smith, I felt it was the beginning of a lifelong friendship and that we would always understand one another, with no small questions being asked. Ralph is rangy in build and breezy in nature. His extreme consideration for all other mortals would keep him from being rated among the great captains; he is a somewhat rarer specimen, a generous Christian gentleman.[6]

During the spring and early summer of 1942, Smith and the other senior officers of the newly formed "Liberty" Division were busy trying to accommodate the steady flow of recruits from the reception centers. These arrived at Ft. Meade in groups of one to two thousand and they had to be assigned to units within the three regiments, accommodated in temporary barracks, and provided with basic training. During the late summer, Smith, on a visit to Ft. Belvoir, came down with a very bad case of influenza and was hospitalized for ten days. Following his release, he was given a month's convalescent leave which he spent with his family in Tucson. While there he was notified by Ground Forces Command that he was to be promoted to Major General and given command of a division. That division, the 27th, was at that time providing for the defense of the outer islands of Hawaii. On 20 November 1942, Ralph Smith assumed command of the division which he would lead until relieved by H. M. Smith on Saipan on 24 June 1944.

The 27th Division was a New York National Guard division, elements of which had a very proud history dating back to the Revolutionary War.[7] Perhaps the most famous was the 69th Infantry Regiment, which had first gained fame during the Civil War. It was a part of the division at the time the 27th was reactivated on 20 July 1917 for service during World War I. The 69th was soon thereafter detached from the 27th and gained its greatest distinction as the "Fighting 69th" as a part of the 42nd Rainbow Division. In 1940, it would be reattached to the 27th with a change of its regimental number to the 165th Infantry. The four Infantry Regiments, the 105th, 106th, 107th, and 108th, of the 27th under the command of Maj. Gen. John O'Ryan, fought with distinction as a part of the 2nd Corps in breaking the Hindenburg Line in early October 1918. At the conclusion of the war, the 27th returned to National Guard status, still commanded by General O'Ryan. In 1922, O'Ryan relinquished the 27th to Maj. Gen. Charles Berry, formerly commander of the 105th Infantry. Then, in 1926, a former Regular Army officer who had commanded the 69th in the border troubles with Mexico took over the division. This was Maj. Gen. William Haskell, who retained that position until 1941.

In the wake of the Nazi triumphs in Europe, the Congress of the United States in 1940 most reluctantly accepted the President's proposal to increase the size of the relatively impotent armed forces. This was to be accomplished in two ways. A peacetime draft, the first in the nation's history, was begun, and certain selected National Guard units were federalized in order to absorb these new draftees whose term of service was supposed to be only one year. The 27th was one of the infantry divisions mobilized. The Presidential Order was signed on 15 October 1940 and the understrength unit was assigned to the 2nd Corps area of the 1st Army commanded by Lt. Gen. Hugh Drum. The division's base was Ft. McClellan, Alabama. Later it was shifted to the 2nd Army commanded by Lt. Gen. Ben Lear. By January 1941, the 27th, still a square division, had been brought to full strength. In many ways, it had already been profoundly changed by the influx of new recruits and a host of dependency discharges that removed many key personnel. Units were also shifted about. The 107th Regiment was transferred out in 1940 to become a Coast Artillery unit. The 106th was also redesignated a Field Artillery unit, although the numerical designation was retained. The 10th New York Infantry took the 106th's number. The 165th also rejoined the 27th at this time.[8] Like all the recently activated units, the 27th suffered during 1941 from foul-ups and a chronic shortage of equipment, many of which could not have been avoided, given the speed of the army's expansion. Nevertheless, during the maneuvers in Tennessee in May and June and later in Louisiana in August–September, the 27th acquitted itself well.

H. M. Smith in *Coral and Brass* would later paint the 27th in 1943 as a "silk stocking" unit with low morale and suspect patriotism. He did this in part by abstracting a report made in *Life* magazine in 1940 about the actions of some members of the 27th who were disgruntled with army life and wanted to go home.[9] Like so much of H. M. Smith's asides in his book, this section left the reader with a wrong impression of the unit. First, the report dealt with events in 1940, three years before H. M. Smith's association with the division. It must also be remembered how generally unpopular the draft bill was in 1940; only a few weeks before Pearl Harbor, the decision to extend the term of the draftees' service to 30 months passed the House of Representatives by the margin of a single vote. The nation's temper was considerably different before 7 December than after the Japanese sneak attack. In his book, H. M. Smith also left the impression that soldiers of the 27th Division were the only ones in 1941 who were members of the O.H.I.O. club (Over the Hill in October). The fact is that this type of protest against continued service was started at Camp Dix by another federalized National Guard division. During the early winter there, the men had encountered a series of unfortunate experiences, chief among them being no heat in their barracks. Ultimately, steam locomotives were brought in to help alleviate this problem. Some of the men, echoing the sentiment of a popular song, "Goodbye Dear, I'll Be Back in a Year," publicized their fond hopes of being out of the service in October 1941.[10] Some men of the 27th were also vocal enough on this subject to be quoted in an article in *Life*.[11] The unit Ralph Smith took over in November 1942 was hardly the same as that of 1940. The changes were not only in the generalized outlook toward the world held in common with the rest of the American public, but of major personnel and structural changes to the division as well.

During the last few months of 1941, all men over twenty-eight years of age who so wished were discharged. This brought the size of the division down to only slightly more than thirteen thousand men at the time of Pearl Harbor. There had also been a change in command. Elderly General Haskell was replaced by Brig. Gen. McT. Pennell, another older, regular officer who had previously been in charge of the artillery brigade. He commanded the 27th during its hasty move from Alabama to California, which was begun seven days after Pearl Harbor. Units of the 27th were then scattered all over California to help the regular army troops and the 40th National Guard Division protect vital installations. During this interim, 7,852 enlisted men and 196 officers were assigned to bring the division once again up to strength.[12] When the immediate invasion scare had passed, the 27th was then concentrated at Ft. Ord. There General Pennell was notified that the 27th was to be sent to aid in the defense of Hawaii. From 28 February until 1 April 1942, units of the 27th Division were convoyed from San Francisco to the islands. The 27th thus had the distinction of being the first combat division to leave the continental United States after Pearl Harbor.

In those months before the battle of Midway, all military personnel in Hawaii had one primary mission—the defense of the islands against a possible Japanese invasion. As soon as it landed, the 27th Division was given the responsibility of guarding the outer islands while the 24th, 25th, and later 40th Divisions were posted to Oahu. This meant that the division was broken up into manageable defense units posted throughout the Hawaiian Islands. The 165th, for example, was sent to Kauai in early March 1942 and soon after was placed temporarily under the command of the 40th Division.[13] While the success of the United States fleet at Midway took much of the pressure off the defenders, they still continued to guard the beaches, airfields, and important installations in the same manner as before the victory. The daily duties and responsibilities soon became routine and boring. With the division so scattered, it was nearly impossible to give the troops meaningful training. Further structural changes were in the offing; in July, General Pennell received orders to triangularize the division. Subsequently, the 108th was transferred to the 40th Division, leaving the 105th, 106th, and 165th as component regiments of the division.[14]

After nine months in the outer islands, the 27th Division was pulled back to Oahu in preparation for transfer to the South Pacific to back up the hard-pressed 1st Marine Division on Guadalcanal. Hardly had the shift been completed and vital training programs instituted when there was a change in plans. Instead of the 27th, the 25th Division of Maj. Gen. "Lightning Joe" Collins was designated for Guadalcanal. To bring the 25th up to strength, over 3500 men were transferred from the 27th.[15] This was a major disappointment for the officers and men of the division, many of whom had been in service for over two years. Instead of a combat assignment, they went back to stationary guard duty. Bernard Ryan, a company commander who had transferred into the 165th, recalled:

The bad thing was that we were put back on the beaches and even worse the Air Force was the big thing there [Oahu]—the Navy was still recovering—an Air Force general appeared to be in charge of most things. The Air Force was first priority—they didn't even guard their airfields. We guarded Hickam Field, guarded Kauhoku, an airstrip opposite Kanohe Point. It was discouraging trying to train men who had been up all night. But the most disillusioning thing was that the war was getting further away.[16]

The 27th Division had undergone a number of major changes within a few months, which would have had an unsettling effect upon the units even had they not been separated for such a long period. Commenting upon the morale and training of the division just before the Makin invasion, James Mahoney, who commanded a battalion on Makin and Saipan, commented:

I think its training was good and I think the units were very good. I do think there was one thing that hurt us. We spent one hell of a long time on the beach in defensive positions—setting up wire, manning gun positions and like duties. I think this probably took the edge off.[17]

From the reports of officers involved with direct troop command, the 27th had apparently lost its edge even before Ralph Smith assumed command of the division. There was also a feeling among many of the officers that Brig. Gen. Ogden Ross, a longtime member of the 27th, should have been given command of the division. There was little the new commanding general could do immediately to ease the boredom of the continued garrison duty, or to counter those officers who believed that Ross should command. What he could do was to intensify training wherever possible and show himself to the junior officers and men of the division. Unlike Haskell and Pennell, he made a practice of getting to know his men. Long before the Gilbert Islands operation, he established himself as the most popular commander the division ever had. His staff and troop commanders, down to the level of the company, had come to like him and respect his ability.[18] Two interconnected questions raised by H. M. Smith in *Coral and Brass* need, however, to be examined. Were the senior officers of the division competent to hold their commands, and was Gen. Ralph Smith too softhearted to weed out those not up to the high standards needed for combat commanders?

There is some truth to H. M. Smith's accusations concerning the nature of command in the 27th Division which was, after all, a National Guard unit. A common feature of most such divisions was the clannishness of the senior officers. At worst, some of the National Guard units during World War II were at first commanded by political appointees who knew very little about leading large numbers of men into combat. In most cases, the major fault of the officers of such a division rested on their familiarity with one another. They had come from the same communities and served together for years in units which, during the interwar period, were noted more for social functions than for hard-nosed combat training. This had been true of the 27th, and even after all the personnel and structural changes after 1940, most of the senior officers of the division were those who had been with the unit when it was federalized. H. M. Smith, in retrospect, could accuse Ralph

Smith of being softhearted for not replacing his regimental commanders, Colonels Gardiner Conroy of the 165th, Leonard Bishop of the 105th, and Russell Ayers of the 106th, and then proceeding downward throughout the division, sweeping out the supposed deadwood. But this is not only judgment after the fact, but also presumes that those men alluded to by H. M. Smith in *Coral and Brass* were indeed inadequate to their tasks. A further presumption is that there is some way a commander can recognize in a rear echelon, noncombat area those officers who will be excellent combat leaders and those who will not. Even the Marines, who were fortunate in having a high percentage of professionals in the upper echelons of command, had no infallible way of determining this. Ralph Smith did not, and although he was aware of rumors about certain officers, he made it very clear to his staff at the beginning of his tenure that he would not countenance any such generalized accusations. He was interested only in specific details of nonperformance.[19] Each of the members of his staff and the senior regimental officers performed their duties very well while the division was in Hawaii. Any faults in these officers could only show up in the stress of combat.

Another tacit assumption of H. M. Smith and many other senior Marine commanders must also be considered. This is that all infantry units should behave like Marines and if they fell short of Marine standards, then they have failed. This idea runs counter to the Marines' own proud boast that they were different. They were elite troops whose specialty was amphibious warfare. No Army unit in the Pacific, however distinguished its past record, could match the Marine divisions in their specialty. Much has been made of the difference in tactics of the Marine Corps and Army units in the attack. The differences were real and would play a role in the disagreements over joint operations on Saipan, Peleliu, and Okinawa. The most substantial difference lay, however, in the recruitment practices of the two services. The Marine units were made up mostly of volunteers, young men who for whatever reason saw in the Corps not only a way of serving their country, but of expressing their manhood. Once in the Corps, their training emphasized the offensive nature of their units, and they joined their officers in believing they were the best. One reason why they were elite units was not only the training, but their age. There were only a few of the "Old Breed" in the Corps by 1943. Most were volunteers who were only eighteen or nineteen years old.

All Army units, on the other hand, were composed largely of draftees. Even with National Guard units such as the 27th, a large number of the enlisted personnel who had been in the division in 1940 had been discharged to be replaced by draftees. There are no reliable statistics on the average age of an Army rifleman, but there is no doubt that he was considerably older than his Marine counterpart. There was no way an ordinary Army division could compete with a Marine unit in stamina, dash, and elan, particularly if that comparison was in the Marines' specialty of seizing and exploiting a beachhead. This must be borne in mind when considering the later charges made by H. M. Smith and other Marines levelled at Army units.

Another factor which distinguished even the best Army units from their Marine counterparts was the differential tactics pursued by their commanders. The various Marine units in the Pacific were primarily shock troops. They seized the beaches, drove immediately inland, generally against fanatical and determined resistance, and took their objective, but sustained very heavy losses. The Army units, even though they were trained in amphibious warfare, tended to be more cautious. This was not a fundamental flaw, nor did it indicate a lack of bravery. Army commanders had been taught at every level to utilize to the fullest the supporting arms and to avoid, if possible, direct frontal attacks upon enemy strong points. Col. James Mahoney put this difference very succinctly:

The Marines were gung-ho. They would go straight ahead—to hell with the obstacles, whereas we would try to figure out some tactic to get around it. I never saw the Marines do that. I admire the Marines—their courage, their daring, and dash—but there was a fundamental difference in our approach.[20]

Thus, long before H. M. Smith became directly involved with Army units placed under his command, there was already discord in any cooperative venture with the Marine Corps.

These differences were not insurmountable if the Corps or Army commander understood them and sympathetically tried to draw on the strengths of both services. A Roy Geiger or Pedro del Valle would have been able to do so. Unfortunately for all units concerned, however, with the reconquest of the Pacific, during one of the pivotal campaigns utilizing Marine and Army units, the overall commander could not. Instead, H. M. Smith by training and temperament could not rationally evaluate the minor problems which arose because of his command of Army troops. By the time of operation GALVANIC, Ralph Smith and his staff had corrected many of the problems connected to the built-up boredom that had afflicted the 27th Division during its beach-watching days. With new leadership, more specialized training, and the certainty of finally moving out of Hawaii, the 27th had become a good division, a fact, despite its detractors, which was later proved on Makin, Eniwetok, Saipan, and Okinawa.

4 | Makin

THE JAPANESE TIDE, WHICH HAD SEEMED SO UN-
stoppable during the first six months of the war, had been
halted by the end of 1942. The naval battles of the Coral Sea
and Midway had been very costly in men and materiel, and
any plans that Admiral Yamamoto might have had for the
eventual conquest of the Hawaiian Islands were permanently
shelved. General MacArthur in the Southwest Pacific theater,
using green American and Australian troops, had halted the
Japanese short of Port Moresby and then forced them onto the
defensive along the north coast of New Guinea. The 1st
Marine Division had been thrown into an obscure island in the
Solomons to protect the long allied supply line to Australia.
Although the battle for Guadalcanal would be continued by
Army troops until February 1943, the issue had been decided
against the Japanese some months before. Admiral Halsey had
committed the bulk of the naval vessels under his command to
the protection of the Marines and Army forces on Guadalcanal, which resulted in a series of naval engagements that, in
retrospect, were as important as the land battles. The Japanese
had lost the initiative in the vast Pacific arena scarcely a year
after their devastating attack on Pearl Harbor. From this time
onward, they would stand on the defensive, attempting to
guard their far-flung empire, which stretched from India to the
eastern frontier of their mandated Pacific islands.

Although in retrospect it is obvious that the first phase in the Pacific War had ended, such was not evident to military planners of the time. The Japanese might have been on the defensive, but they still had local superiority in men and equipment. The great naval and air bastions of Rabaul, Koror, and Truk were relatively untouched. Their navy, despite having sustained heavy losses, was still a most formidable entity. Admiral Yamamoto and, after his death, Admiral Koga still commanded a potent mix of battleships, cruisers, and aircraft carriers which operated on interior lines to support the Japanese garrisons on the many islands in the Gilberts, Marshalls, Marianas and Caroline chains. The question on the minds of all concerned in planning, up to the level of the Combined Chiefs of Staff, was where and how to penetrate the heart of Japan's Pacific empire, always keeping in mind that the demands of the Pacific theater could not be allowed to hamper the Allied buildup in Europe.

The decision to invade the Gilbert Islands was arrived at by complex maneuverings that appear to have ignored several salient strategic realities. One reason for the decision was the simmering feud between the Navy and the Army concerning responsibility for the defeat of Japan. General MacArthur in the Southwest Pacific proposed a series of attacks aimed toward securing northern New Guinea, capturing Rabaul, and ultimately reconquering the Philippines. He wanted the Navy in both areas of the Pacific to play a secondary role. One of the earliest heroes of the Pacific War, General MacArthur had powerful support for his ideas within the administration, as well as in the media, where the powerful Hearst newspaper chain was agitating for a single Pacific command with MacArthur in charge. The Navy and particularly the Chief of Naval Operations, Admiral King, disputed MacArthur's strategy, holding that the shortest and easiest route to Japan lay across the Central Pacific where, because of the vast distances, the Navy would have the premier role. Thus the question of selection of targets for 1943 was only partially dictated by military considerations. The Navy in the Central Pacific had stood on the defensive after Pearl Harbor. Except for a few nuisance raids, little had been accomplished offensively. It was imperative to begin offensive operations in the Central Pacific, or

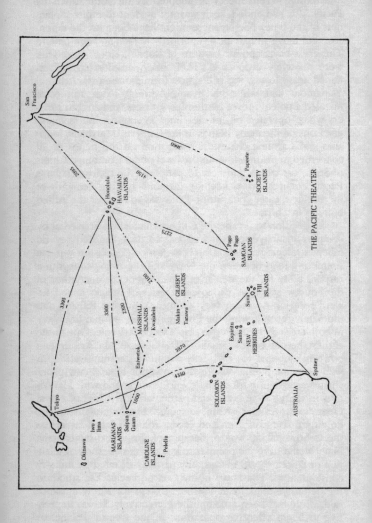

THE PACIFIC THEATER

MacArthur's plans might be adopted by the Joint Chiefs. In May 1943, the Joint Chiefs decided to limit MacArthur, who wanted five more infantry divisions and more air groups to begin carrying out his plans for New Guinea and New Britain. Instead, the Joint Chiefs sanctioned attacks on Bougainville, New Georgia, Woodlark Island, and a continuation of the New Guinea campaign. These attacks would not entail the buildup of forces MacArthur had asked for. At this juncture, the Navy in the Central Pacific area obviously had to do something more than stand on the defensive; Admiral Nimitz and his staff proposed beginning the conquest of Japan's empire by seizing the Marshall Islands.[1]

The invasion of the Marshalls, set for 15 November, was tentatively accepted at Admiral Nimitz's headquarters in June. From a strategic viewpoint, this decision made sense. The islands, particularly Kwajalein, would provide good harbor and air facilities within the Japanese defense perimeter thousands of miles closer to Truk than the Allied advanced bases in the Ellice Islands. Tactically, however, the plan made little sense. As Admiral Spruance and others were quick to point out, the proposed simultaneous invasion of five of the islands would stretch the as yet untested capability of the amphibious forces. The invasion fleet would be within range of Japanese land-based air power, including that from the presumed fortress island of Truk. Finally, the intelligence reports available for the Marshalls were scanty. The Marshall plans were ultimately put off for execution in the spring of 1944. The capture of the Gilberts was substituted, even though neither Tarawa nor Makin would provide major anchorages for the fleet or good air bases.[2]

Much has been written since World War II about this decision, with a general consensus that Tarawa in particular never proved worth its cost in men and materiel. It is hard to escape the conclusion ' at the Navy planners, pushed by their superiors to come up with suitable offensive targets, chose the Gilberts not only to head off MacArthur, but also because they believed the operations would not be difficult. The invasions could be justified as a training ground for the Army and Marine units who had not yet participated in amphibious operations. The Gilberts were on the very edge of the Japanese

Pacific empire and something was known of their defenses—at least more than was known of the Marshall group of islands. It was believed certainly to be within the still-limited capabilities of the United States Central Pacific forces to seize the key positions in the Gilberts. The Navy planners had less information on Tarawa than on Makin, the other island eventually selected as a target. Air photos and reports by submarines constituted the bulk of information about Tarawa. Makin would be another story, since a portion of the 2nd Marine Raider Battalion commanded by Lt. Col. Evans Carlson had raided the island on 17 August 1942, destroyed equipment and installations, and killed 86 Japanese.[3] The raid gave naval planners more information about the Gilberts; it ultimately was self-defeating since it also alerted the Japanese to the Gilberts' vulnerability. In the year following Carlson's raid, the Japanese had strengthened their defenses in the Gilberts, particularly at Tarawa. So when Julian Smith's 2nd Marine Division struck Betio, they found a fortress atoll defended by Japanese army and Imperial marine personnel who believed themselves superior to any invading force. Makin had been secondary in Japanese defensive planning after Carlson's raid. Only a few hundred Korean laborers and Japanese regular naval troops had been sent there to replace those lost in August 1942. Installations had been rebuilt and some basic defensive fortifications constructed. However, the Navy, Marine, and Army planners were correct. Makin would be much easier to take than Tarawa.

The plan to capture Makin was something of an afterthought. The original target designated for the Army's 27th Division by Nimitz's headquarters on 27 July was the island of Nauru. The target was not changed to Makin until 24 September. Most of the summer was spent by the 27th Division's staff making plans to invade the phosphate-rich ex-British possession lying approximately 380 miles west of Tarawa in the direction of Truk. Admiral Spruance later made it very clear that he was never too happy about the selection of Nauru. Contrary to what H. M. Smith later wrote, it was not necessary to convince Spruance and Turner "after much argument" to change the target.[4] It was a joint venture between the Navy and Marine commanders to substitute Makin for Nauru. Other reasons for this change concerned the low foreshore of Nauru and the 100-foot-high cliffs immediately behind it from which the Japanese would be able to cover every inch of the beach. Also, the large circling reef at Nauru would make it difficult for the Navy to provide adequate close support. Spruance obviously agreed with H. M. Smith on these points and also pointed to a further problem—that of the necessity to separate the Tarawa and Nauru support fleets by many hundreds of miles. Nimitz and King were finally convinced and Makin was substituted.[5]

The dates involved for the planning of operation GALVANIC must be considered very carefully. H. M. Smith claims that his V Amphibious Corps headquarters did most of the planning for the two operations. That could not have been possible since planning by the 2nd Marine Division, located in New Zealand for the invasion, had been in progress during the summer of 1943. H. M. Smith did not arrive in Hawaii until 5 September and the decision to substitute Makin for Nauru was not fully confirmed until 24 September. Planning for the various invasions was undertaken at different levels concurrently, and finally approved only after consultation in Hawaii with Smith's Corps organization and Nimitz's headquarters.[6] The staff of the 27th Division had only a little over a month to plan for the capture of Makin. Ralph Smith was informed that, instead of employing the entire division as had been contemplated at Nauru, only the 165th RCT, reinforced, would be used at Makin.

Almost all who have written of the Tarawa and Makin invasions have assumed that since H. M. Smith had operational control of V Amphibious Corps on Hawaii, he continued to exercise a similar function in the Gilberts. In a recent book, the author goes into great detail tracing the line of command from Spruance downward and concludes by stating, "When everybody got on the ground, Holland Smith would take over command of the land forces from Turner."[7] This was not true. The command of all amphibious forces was retained by Admiral Turner and exercised at Tarawa through Admiral Hill. When the troops landed they passed directly to divisional control. On Tarawa this was Maj. Gen. Julian Smith, and at Makin Maj. Gen. Ralph Smith commanded.[8] H. M. Smith was a supernumerary during the Gilberts operation. He had discovered at the last minute that he was not even scheduled to accompany the troops and had forced himself on Turner, who kept him far away from Tarawa and his beloved Marines during that desperate fight. Turner used H. M. Smith as a deputy monitoring the fighting on Makin, a lowly role that infuriated H. M. Smith. He could not strike at Turner and the Navy who were responsible for his situation, but he could make life miserable for the Army commander and troops, which he, *a priori,* had already decided were not up to his standards.

The training of the 27th Division during the summer and fall of 1943 appears in retrospect to be as thorough as could be expected. Col. Henry Ross, then a Major, was one of the men selected earlier for training by the Marine Corps at Camp Elliot in San Diego, while H. M. Smith was still in command of amphibious training on the West Coast. The selected Army officers were given a two-month intensive training course. Meanwhile, the Navy had selected a site and constructed training facilities for all units passing through Hawaii. After his return, Ross was a member of the training staff, and each unit, battalion by battalion, was run through the school. Many of the troops had to be taught how to swim. After the basic instruction, they were forced to swim with combat gear, and to climb down 30- and 50-foot walls using cargo nets. Later the Navy provided LCVPs, LCVMs, and LCMs so that they could practice climbing into the boats as well as offloading men and supplies at the various beaches. At the same time the battalion staffs were put through course work, using models and cutouts, in how the various ships were to be loaded. The decisions had been made earlier to experiment with pallet loading of much of the heavier, bulkier equipment. The staffs also were instructed in the various Navy rules concerning men and equipment on naval vessels. Each unit was subjected to rigorous small unit training in jungle maneuvering and intensified weapons training. These were combined with the large-scale battalion and regimental exercises, including night operations. It is hard to disagree with Colonel Ross, who supervised much of this training, that if the training methods and procedures of the 27th were faulty, it was the fault of the Marines, whose training methods and doctrines were utilized in Hawaii.[9]

Obviously Gen. H. M. Smith did not share the opinion of the Army personnel assigned the task of amphibious training. Even before the Makin operation he had shown in a number of ways that he was concerned about the 27th Division and was capable of losing his temper over what appeared to him as slackness even before he had the facts. Bernard Ryan, then a lieutenant, recalled such an instance during practice landings on Kauai when his company was using amtracs for the first time. These were early models with a scoop-like device in front that would break in any but the lightest tide as the craft came toward shore. The amtracs would then dig in and dump everyone out. In this instance the problem was compounded because the drivers had lost their way and landed their company at the wrong place. Another company commander went off to tell Battalion Headquarters their location and Ryan remained on the beach. Ryan later remembered:

At about that time Howlin' Mad Smith's entourage came breezing up the same road and stopped. I reported to him. He began eating me out for standing there instead of running up the hill. I tried to explain to him what happened and we had people out finding the right way to go and to tell them what happened to our group. At that first meeting, he had certain expressions for the Army. He said the Army sits on its ass and are afraid to move, got a bunch of dumb lieutenants and sundry other things he told me about.[10]

This instance is not necessarily conclusive proof of H. M. Smith's habit of not being bothered with ascertaining facts before shouting at someone. However, there developed a major difference with Ralph Smith and the 27th Division at this same time over practice landing procedures. H. M. Smith made a brief but damning comment about this in *Coral and Brass*. He wrote, "In Hawaii, I had to pressure the Twenty-seventh to get the division into a dress rehearsal for the Makin operation. One of Ralph Smith's objections was that his equipment might be damaged."[11] If this statement is to be believed, one must imagine that Ralph Smith was the worst type of *prima donna,* one who on the eve of an amphibious operation didn't want to give his troops the necessary training because of an overweening concern with equipment. The truth is slightly more complex.

There was no disagreement on the necessity of training. As already noted, land, shipboard, and amphibious training had gone on all summer under instructors who had been trained in Marine Corps schools in California. The quarrel H. M. Smith refers to concerns off-loading all the equipment on the last of the practice landings before Makin. The 27th was further advanced at this stage than most units in palletizing its supplies, and they had already combat-loaded the ships designated to take the 165th to Makin. H. M. Smith wanted a full-scale landing practice with all men and materiel unloaded on the selected beach at Maui. Ralph Smith and his staff protested that this was unnecessary and that, if done, the pallets and their equipment could be damaged. Even if this did not happen, it would be a major problem getting the equipment back on the ships in the proper order in time to meet the sailing deadline. The suggestion was made to Corps Headquarters that only a small amount of equipment be unloaded. Eventually a compromise was worked out whereby only a percentage of the equipment would be unloaded, but the token amount had to reflect an approximate across the board debarkation of all types.[12] With this agreement, the last practice of amphibious operation took place without serious incident.

It will serve little purpose to try in a short space to give a detailed account of the Makin operation. This has already been done adequately by the official publications.[13] It is necessary, however, in order to show the beginnings of the myths concerning Ralph Smith and the 27th Division, to give a general overview of the invasion and subsequent fighting on Makin. The division planners had relatively good information about the island from the Marines, New Zealanders who had been on the island before the war, and Private Freddie Narruhn of the 1st Fiji Infantry, a native of Butaritari, the largest island and main objective, who would also accompany the troops. Two important pieces of information were lacking—the strength of the Japanese garrison and accurate, detailed hydrological charts of the island. Many authors who read H. M. Smith's account have assumed that the exact number of Japanese were known. This was not true, nor would it be in most of the islands seized later in the war. American intelligence services simply did not have that kind of detailed information. It was suspected that, even with reinforcements, the Japanese garrison would be outnumbered by the 165th, but not by the amount given by H. M. Smith. While there were about 6500 men in Ralph Smith's 165th RCT in the operation, this number included all the noncombat support people as well. The three assault battalions numbered only about 3000 riflemen. Planning estimates for the attack were based on the Japanese having 800 troops on Butaritari manning prepared defenses of unknown quantity and depth.[14] The lack of up-to-date charts would later cause some difficulties at both Red Beaches and Yellow Beach and interfered with the smooth landing of many of the assault troops. The most recent information about the atoll had been secured by the submarine *Nautilus* which had cruised offshore, taking pictures through its periscope, and by air photos taken at various times after July.[15]

The maps and photos revealed Butaritari Island as a ribbon-like, low-lying island approximately twelve miles long and averaging only about 500 yards wide throughout most of its length. The axis of Butaritari was in a southwesterly to north-easterly direction, open to the sea on the south and protected by a lagoon formed by coral reefs on the north. At the extreme southwest part, the island widened to form a larger mass which, when viewed from above, appeared not unlike the apex of a crutch. An adjacent island to the northeast, Kuma, which the Japanese had not fortified, could be reached at low tide by means of a coral ridge connecting the two islands.

Butaritari was a flat island with many shallow ponds and marshy areas. Before the war the major export had been copra; in places the coconut palms were so thick it appeared as if they had been planted in groves. Each tree was a potential hiding place for snipers, who caused the attacking forces more trouble than any of the better-organized Japanese defense areas. The secondary vegetation was quite heavy and, combined with the other natural obstacles, would channel the 165th's attack. The major food source for the 1500 or so villagers was the *bobai* (taro) plant, which was grown in deep pits. There were a hundred such pits, and their locations were unknown

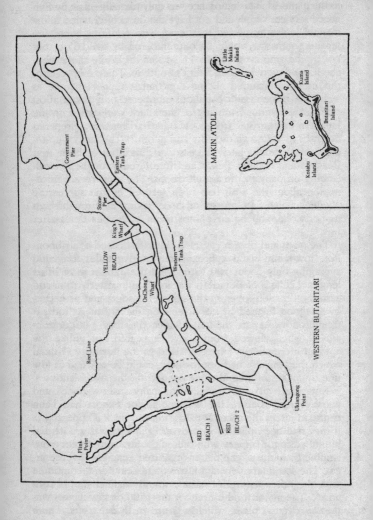

to the planners. This ignorance was only partially offset by Pvt. Freddie Narruhn. A native of Makin, he helped identify the location of some of the *bobai* pits as well as supplementing more general information about the island's buildings.[16] As with so many of the Pacific islands to be recaptured by American forces, the terrain proved as much of a handicap as Japanese resistance.

The main road on Butaritari was unpaved and ran almost the entire length of the island paralleling the lagoon shore. Where it crossed marshlands it became a causeway, often surrounded by heavy vegetation. In the central part of the island there was another unsurfaced road along the southern, seaward side, connected by dirt roads and trails to the main road. This central portion of the island was where the main buildings were located and where the Japanese were expected to put up the heaviest resistance, as they had during Carlson's raid the previous year. The dominating features of this region were the three piers jutting out into the lagoon. The westernmost was called On Chong's Wharf, extended out only about 400 feet, and was unuseable at low tide. Approximately 1000 yards northeast was King's Wharf, which was about 1000 feet long and could be used at both low and high tides. At the end of King's Wharf the Japanese had built seaplane ramps. Proceeding northeast one then encountered the Stone Pier about a mile from King's Wharf. Near the Stone Pier were a concrete church, hospital and radio station. The Japanese had created a clearing in the undergrowth running across the island approximately 3000 yards from the southwestern end of the island. Here they had constructed tank traps and blockhouses. This was called the Western Tank Barrier and was duplicated about two miles northeast by a second line, the Eastern Tank Barrier.[17]

The tactical plan developed by the planners of the 27th Division was simple—bringing to bear on any strong point overwhelming superiority in numbers and firepower.[18] Preliminary bombardment by B–24 Liberators from the 7th Air Force base at Nanomea began a week prior to the landing and continued up to D day. The Northern Attack Force directly commanded by Admiral Turner on the battleship *Pennsylvania* comprised four battleships, four cruisers, ten destroyers, and nine aircraft carriers. The planes from these small carriers took over from the heavy bombers of the 7th on the morning of the invasion and struck at specific and general targets in coordination with firing from Turner's support ships. That naval bombardment began at 0620 on 20 November. By the time the close support was no longer needed, the fleet had expended almost 2000 rounds of 14″ and 1645 rounds of 8″ shells.[19] This was early in the assault on Japanese-held islands, when such furious, concentrated bombardment for a short period was believed to be more effective than it actually proved. Tarawa and later experiences at Saipan and Peleliu modified the Navy's opinion of what offshore shell fire could actually accomplish. But at Makin and also Tarawa, there was no doubt that the naval bombardment had some effect on the Japanese defenses, and planes from the carriers controlled the air.

The landings were to be made at two separate locations. The 1st and 3rd Battalions were to land at 0830 on the southwestern extremity on Red Beaches 1 and 2. They were to be led in by specially trained, heavily armed shock troops in LVT Alligators. There were 19 Marines from V Amphibious Corps and a reinforced platoon from the 2nd Battalion. Their job was to quickly secure the flank of the Red Beaches. They would be followed in by seven waves of troops at both beaches. Each wave consisted of approximately 200 men in LCVPs accompanied by LCMs bringing in light tanks. Two hours after the initial landings, the 2nd Battalion would begin its assault on Yellow Beach located between On Chong's and King's Wharves. By this time, it was assumed the troops that had landed on the Red Beaches would have reached the first phase line. The Japanese in the western part of the island would thus be caught between the two battalions from the Red Beaches and the 2nd Battalion advancing from the lagoon side of the island. Although the Japanese resistance was light, the conditions of the beaches prevented the orderly landing that had been planned. Red Beach 1 proved to be an area unsuitable for landings. Many of the landing craft were broached on the coral, some were forced to put to sea again, and even those that crossed the reef could not reach the very narrow, usable part of the beach. Colonel Mahoney, who assumed control of the 1st Battalion in the late afternoon of D day, recalled:

There were some errors in the hydrographic information so the end result was the boats didn't quite make it to shore for the most part. The first wave or two got in all right with little or no opposition and the others kind of stacked up behind them because there was no other place to go—too much coral and rock.[20]

Despite such problems, the two western battalions advanced rapidly inland, meeting only sporadic enemy fire mostly from snipers. By early afternoon they had advanced over 1000 yards eastward, having been halted at midmorning so they would not walk into the Navy's covering fire for the 2nd Battalion landing on Yellow Beach. Special detachments had captured Flink Point to the north and Ukiangong Point to the south. The twelve 105s of the 105th Field Artillery Battalion were also in position and ready to fire by early afternoon. Each of the battalions and regiment had command posts established and operating, and the advance command station for Division was established near one of the road junctions, approximately 50 yards inland from Red Beach 2.

The landing of the 2nd Battalion on Yellow Beach also ran into problems. They, too, were paced by 120 men in Alligators from the 105th RCT who were specially trained in amphibious landings. As at the Red Beaches, their job was to seal the flanks of the landing area. All seemed to be going according to plan until the landing craft approached the beach, when it was discovered that the tide was going out and the boats were stranded a considerable distance from shore. Bernard Ryan, then a company commander, recalled the problems caused by the faulty hydrological information:

Instead of landing on the beach, we landed up to our necks in water. My company, E Company, and the company to the left probably lost half their equipment. We didn't lose a lot of men, but half of those we lost were from the hulks on each side of the beach . . . If everyone had had Amtracs we would have been just like the Marines at Tarawa and rolled right up on the beach.

. . . Things like flame throwers, satchel charges, radios, anything that water could affect was damaged.[21]

The Navy called off the advance to the beach after the 3rd wave, until the resistance from the hulks and a large bunker about 100 yards inland had been eliminated. For over an hour naval ships and planes concentrated their fire on the hulks and central zone. Some of the shells intended for the Japanese fell among the troops of the Second Battalion, causing some casualties.

The major problems were either overcome or ignored by 1300 hours and the rest of the 2nd Battalion began to land. Later, the three companies of the battalion drove south and east in order to cut off the Japanese from each other on either side of the central zone. Against increasing resistance, the battalion by the end of the day had secured most of that sector. Company E swinging to the left was to drive northeastward to the road junction adjacent to King's Wharf. However, they ran into a major trench and bunker system. Bernard Ryan, who during the day was the senior officer on the eastern flank, remembers:

It was a huge position that went almost all the way across the island and it had firing positions all over. During the day we figured out what to do if we had something to blow up the ends while neutralizing the top. We asked for artillery but it was too close for either artillery or mortars and they wouldn't give us either. We had our own 61s, but they didn't do any good—just bounced off of it. Late in the day when the engineers finally came in we had the place surrounded but you couldn't get past because if you did you got shot in the back. As soon as we could get the engineers up we covered them and they went up and blew the thing to pieces. The Japs streamed out the back; there must have been a hundred guys in there.[22]

Soon afterward the order came down from Division to halt the advance, dig in, and wait for daylight.

To the southwest the advance had continued after the pause to allow the 2nd Battalion to land on Yellow Beach. Because of the narrowness of the island, the 1st Battalion pinched out the 3rd, which then went into reserve. Little concerted opposition was encountered from the Japanese, although some did take advantage of the gullies, trees, and *bobai* pits. The 1st Battalion, expecting to encounter heavy opposition and hampered by the terrain, moved slowly and cautiously to the West Tank Barrier. In so doing they isolated a number of Japanese west of that barrier. By midafternoon, they had made a linkage with the 2nd Battalion on the ocean side of the island before they, too, were halted for the night.

In the afternoon a few hundred yards west of the West Tank Barrier near a bend in the main road, the Regimental Commander, Col. Gardiner Conroy, was killed. Because this incident would later become a part of H. M. Smith's charges against the 27th Division, it would be well to go into it in some detail. The events surrounding his death are well established because of the number of observers. The group, led by the regiment's second in command, G. W. Kelley, included Col. S. L. A. Marshall, the historian, and Col. James Roosevelt, on detached duty with the Army because of his previous experience as Executive Officer to Carlson in the Marine raid of the previous year. Basically, the Japanese had established a defensive position keyed by a machine gun in the area south of the coast road and by 1500 their fire had halted the advance of Company C. Colonel Kelley and party were stopped by 2nd Lt. Daniel Nunnery, who advanced to reconnoiter the area from the vicinity of a large palm tree. Nunnery was killed and an enlisted man accompanying him was wounded. At about that time Colonel Conroy, the Regimental Commander, came forward and concluded that the advance was being held up by only a single sniper. Nevertheless, he was persuaded by Kelley to go back and bring up light tanks in case the Japanese position was held by more men than Conroy had imagined. In the meantime, Kelley had gone forward to the palm tree and Catholic Chaplain Meaney rushed up to give assistance to the wounded enlisted man.

S. L. A. Marshall recalled this sequence of events:

Meaney charged forward to give that soldier the last rites. Japanese bullets riddled his left arm and chest and but for the fact that an identity disc deflected one round, he would have died. Two or three other rankers were cut down, and with that the whole movement became paralyzed or "pinned down" as the saying goes.

Colonel Kelley was hugging earth. Next to him were Lt. Col. Jimmy Roosevelt and Col. Clark 'Nick' Ruffner, later a four star general and army commander. All three of these men have displayed high courage under fire, but for the moment they were spellbound by the situation.

Col. G. J. Conroy, the regimental commander, convinced that the flank was being held in check by a solitary sniper, came forward on the run. Ruffner and Roosevelt tried to shout him down. He wouldn't listen. Getting close to Meaney, he was hit by a hail of bullets. Ruffner and Roosevelt started to crawl toward his body. Kelley yelled at them, "Don't do it! He's dead!"[23]

Thus, just before 1600 hours, the regiment lost its commander; Colonel Kelley assumed command, while James Mahoney took his place as commanding officer of the 1st Battalion. It was decided that the tanks could not be used for fear of firing into friendly positions. Kelley then ordered a platoon to attack the machine gun position. They had to retire after launching grenades in its direction because of another machine gun firing into the area. However, they did manage to find Father Meaney and bring him back for needed first aid. Because of darkness no further attempts were made to take the strongpoint, which was overrun the following day.[24]

Although the fate of the Japanese on the island had been sealed by the close of the first day, the defenders had no intention of giving up. They attempted to infiltrate the American lines on subsequent nights. The first night this caused a rash of unnecessary firing by Army riflemen. But, contrary to H. M. Smith's later charges, one of the Marines attached to the 27th told Ryan that that was the way it had been on Guadalcanal the first few nights. He said, "Don't worry. It will get better."[25]

The second day of fighting revealed even more than the first about the 165th RCT's approach toward ending Japanese resistance. It would be a cautious, go-slow, policy. Whenever a unit would be held up at a particular location, it would call in tanks, artillery, or in some cases aircraft to help clear the way. Gen. Ralph Smith and his staff did not want to rush the conquest and take heavier casualties than necessary by doing so. Nevertheless, by the end of the day, the troops of the 27th stood a few yards west of the Stone Pier. They controlled King's Wharf and, except for a few snipers, had fairly cleared the central and western portions of the island.

On the third day, the 3rd Battalion, commanded by Lt. Col. Joseph Hart, moved up to take the brunt of the attack on the East Tank Barrier. Two reinforced platoons of Company A under Capt. Lawrence O'Brien were transported by Alligator three miles beyond the barrier in order to seal off the escape route for the Japanese. After setting up, they killed or captured forty-five Japanese without themselves suffering any casualties. The sanctuary of Kuma Island was also denied the Japanese by another water-borne operation, which transported a special detail of men from Company M of the 105th Infantry to the southwestern tip of that island. By the evening of D day + 3, Admiral Turner had announced the capture of Makin "though with minor resistance remaining" and congratulated Gen. Ralph Smith and the 27th on their success.[26] The hardest fighting was yet to come; beginning at dusk of the evening of the 22nd, the Japanese, many of whom were drunk, struck at the perimeter lines of the 3rd Battalion. During the sporadic but hard fighting of this *"Sake* Night," the 27th suffered three dead and twenty-five wounded. In the morning, fifty-one dead Japanese were counted in front of the American positions. This was the last major concentrated effort of the Japanese on Butaritari. At 1030 the next day, tanks and infantrymen from Companies I and K reached the eastern tip of the island. Gen. Ralph Smith then sent a message to Admiral Turner, "Makin taken, recommend command pass to commander garrison force." On the afternoon of the previous day, he had been instructed to prepare most of the 165th's troops for reembarcation beginning at dawn on D day + 4. Actually, the 2nd Battalion had begun to leave Yellow Beach at 1400 on the previous day. Except for sporadic isolated sniper fire in the following days, the fighting at Makin was over.[27]

To an unprejudiced observer, it would appear that the invasion and capture of Makin was an unqualified success. An untried regiment had overcome its natural jitters and had achieved its objective with minimal cost. Officers and men had learned a great deal about amphibious operations, maintaining a supply system, and fighting the enemy in swampy jungle terrain. The cost in lives had not been extreme: 58 killed in action, 150 wounded in action, of whom 8 later died, and 35 injured but not in combat. By contrast, over 400 Japanese had been killed, and, by the time the island was declared secure, 104 prisoners had been taken, only three of whom were Japanese, the others being Korean laborers.[28]

In the light of the foregoing, why did Gen. H. M. Smith leave the impression then and later that the 27th and its commanding general had not done a good job? Furthermore, why did Admiral Turner, despite his congratulations to Ralph Smith on D day + 3, say about the Army units "Frankly, they were jittery before they started and they stayed that way."[29]

While it is much easier to understand the attitude of Admiral Turner, one could suspect that his negative judgments were arrived at after he had received H. M. Smith's reports. Admiral Turner wanted to end the fighting on Makin as soon as possible. Much later Ralph Smith indicated that he understood and appreciated Turner's position when he commented:

The viewpoint of the landing troops, the Army and Marines, is directly opposite of what the Navy wants because the Navy is in its most critical phase when it can't maneuver around—while they have to unload and get the stuff ashore . . .

I fully recognized that the Navy was running the risk of what happened to the *Liscombe Bay,* but, on the other hand, the Army troops and Marines were exposing their bodies.[30]

The *Liscombe Bay* was an escort carrier which was torpedoed by a Japanese submarine early in the morning of D day + 5. Explosions and fires caused the ship to sink within 20 minutes. The air group commander and captain of the ship and 643 men died when the ship went down.[31] It seems illogical for anyone to blame this heavy loss on the 27th Division since it happened after most of the division had left the island, but it is possible to construct a case that, if Makin had been secured on D day + 2, then possibly the *Liscombe Bay* would have been somewhere else. However specious this argument, it could explain in part why Admiral Turner was prepared to accept H. M. Smith's reports on the inadequacy of the 27th Division and its commander, Ralph Smith.

There is still another set of circumstances to consider. The 2nd Marine Division had been projected into a bloody killing match at Tarawa. Despite the Marines having overwhelming superiority in air and sea power, the Japanese from their well-prepared defenses exacted a terrible toll from the attackers. For a brief period, whether the Marines could hold on was in doubt. In the end, the Marines took the island with a loss of 997 killed and missing and 2124 wounded. In addition, the Navy suffered thirty killed in action and fifty-nine wounded.[32] H. M. Smith was a Marine, the senior marine general present in the Gilberts. He had wanted to be at Tarawa, but was prevented from being there because of orders from Admiral Turner. Whether he would have been an asset or liability at Tarawa is not the point. He wanted to be there; he obviously received the messages from Tarawa with a heavy heart and resented deeply the task of keeping an eye on the 165th assigned to him by Turner. Even a less pugnacious, suspicious, and bad-tempered officer might not have been psychologically prepared to accurately evaluate what he saw at Makin. With the passage of time and the invidious comparisons made by some newspapers about the comparative loss of life at Makin and Tarawa, H. M. Smith became even more convinced of the correctness of his views. These he later set down in the *Saturday Evening Post* articles and *Coral and Brass*.

The major points from H. M. Smith's account in *Coral and Brass* to consider are the accusations that the 27th was not moving fast enough and should have secured the island more quickly, the reports of indiscriminate firing by men of the 27th, the death and burial of Colonel Conroy, and finally his own general behavior, particularly toward Gen. Ralph Smith. Although this work is not intended to be simply a literary counterpoint to Smith and Finch's book, it is necessary to quote their statements at length and then test them against other evidence.

In his memoirs, H. M. Smith was blunt in comparing the Marines' quick advances to the slowness of the 165th RCT. He wrote:

At Makin, however, the Army troops were infuriatingly slow. Butaritari, the objective island, should have been secured by dusk on D–day. Any Marine regiment would have done it in that time. At Eniwetok, the 22nd Marine Regiment captured Engebi, a far stronger island than Makin, in seven hours, but on the morning of the second day the end of the Makin operation was not even in sight.[33]

He continued by reporting:

Only a brief examination of the situation ashore sufficed to show there was little opposition. I stressed to Ralph Smith the importance of cleaning up the island as soon as possible, and early on the morning of the third day I called for a report. I received one saying that there was still heavy fighting at the northern end of the island, which delayed final capture. This seemed highly improbable, so I took a jeep and drove to the scene of the reported action.[34]

According to H. M. Smith, nothing was happening. "It was quiet as Wall Street on Sunday." He concluded, presumably to Ralph Smith, "Sometimes a General has to go up front and let the troops see him . . . That's the only way he can make them realize there is nothing ahead of them."[35] He then in part betrays the reason for his anger by noting, "I was furious with Ralph Smith. I was anxious to go to Tarawa and here he was fiddling around with an operation that should have been ended long before in my opinion."[36]

All this seems logical if one is unaware of some of the basic facts of the situation. Ralph Smith had come ashore at about 1830 on D day. He did not transfer his entire headquarters from shipboard because of communications problems, but he immediately went forward toward the front lines to discover for himself how the situation was developing. He found that despite all the problems of the landings, almost all the day's objectives had been achieved. H. M. Smith did not come ashore until the afternoon of D day + 1 when he established himself next to Ralph Smith's headquarters. As already noted, by this time the 165th had captured all the island except those areas northeast of the East Tank Barrier. The end of the fighting was well in sight by the time H. M. Smith arrived. He should not have been surprised at the movement of the 165th. They had met all their objectives on time when H. M. Smith arrived, and he had approved of the phase lines on these plans while in Hawaii. Whether the Marines could have done better is nothing but conjecture. To imagine that any unit landing at Yellow Beach could have reached the northeast end of the island in the scant time between 1300, when the later waves of the 2nd Battalion were allowed to proceed, and dark is to present a situation without obstacles, bunkers, or Japanese. To simply traverse the eight miles through the typical terrain of Butaritari with a regular pack and no opposition would have taken any rifleman at least four of the seven hours that H. M. Simth believed necessary for the island's capture. This calculation, among other things, of course, discounts snipers.

The snipers were everywhere. They strapped themselves to the tops of coconut trees and waited for their best opportunity to kill or maim advancing Americans. Some painted their faces green and had caches of water and food in the trees. These men were normally supported by two or three riflemen on the ground. Although they did not cause heavy casualties, they did slow down the advance. 1st Sgt. Pasquale Fusco reported:

We could not spot them even with glasses and it made our advance very slow. When we moved forward it was as a skirmish line, with each man being covered as he rushed from cover to cover. That meant that every man spent a large part of his time on the ground. While prone, we carefully studied the trees and the ground. If one of our men began to fire rapidly into a tree or ground location, we knew that he had spotted a sniper, and those who could see the tree took up the fire. When we saw no enemy, we fired occasional shots into trees that looked likely.[37]

The danger from snipers continued even after the island had been declared secured. Col. Henry Ross recalled his own experience with a later sniper:

Joe Hart's battalion was to remain behind as garrison. Hart and I had been friends for many years. I came originally from the 165th and so when I was about ready to board ship I told Keg [Colonel

Stebbins], "I think I'll run up and say goodbye to Joe." So I ran up with the Jeep—he was halfway down the island when I ran into him so he said I'll go with you. I want to say goodbye to Ralph. So we got back into our Jeep and hightailed it down this dirt road. All of a sudden out of a tree came a couple of rounds; we hit the deck. One of the drivers thought he saw where this was coming from and he emptied a clip up there—he got the Jap. I had ridden up and down that road at least six times during the past 40 odd hours and so did a lot of other people and that guy was tied up in that tree and why he just selected that particular time to do it I don't know.[38]

There was continuing opposition on the northern end of the island on the morning of D day + 3, as Ralph Smith informed H. M. Smith. It is difficult after many years to recall conversations accurately, but it is doubtful whether Ralph Smith used the term "heavy fighting" since a few hours later Admiral Turner, on his advice, declared the operations concluded except for some "minor resistance," and at 1400 on D day + 3, the 2nd Battalion began to load onto the boats preparatory to leaving Makin.[39] As for H. M. Smith's journey to the front line where he found it completely quiet, Ralph Smith reports that H. M. Smith never got near the front line that day, but moved into areas already secured. That was the reason he found it to be so quiet.[40] If this is correct, then his didactic statement to Ralph Smith concerning going forward and showing the troops who you were means little. In any case, Ralph Smith had gone forward to the front areas even before H. M. Smith arrived on the beach.

In *Coral and Brass,* H. M. Smith makes a great point of indiscriminate firing by the green Army troops. He reports how he experienced "one of the worst nights I ever spent in the Pacific at the Command Post ashore on Makin."[41] This must have been the night of 21–22 November. The cause of his discomfort was supposedly the trigger-happy Army sentries putting a few rounds through the command post tent and clipping coconuts from a nearby tree. After he "implored the sentries to stop shooting at shadows," he went back to his cot, presumably to close out a restless night. Col. Henry Ross was a witness to this affair, and recalled what happened somewhat differently than H. M. Smith:

. . . there were a lot of disturbing things going on and of course it was all blamed on our men. I'm not too sure it always was. I know that at least in two instances the Japs were running about yelling in fairly good English. They were trying to find out where the positions were because they wanted to penetrate them. But this particular night the disturbance got to Gen. Howlin' Mad Smith. I don't know whether it disturbed his sleep or not and he just got rip-roaring mad. He was about 20–25 feet away from me. He started raking Ralph Smith to "Quiet this Goddamned noise; stop the shooting." He acted to me, well, we are supposed to be officers and gentlemen and I don't believe he was.[42]

H. M. Smith relates in more detail another instance of how he had to admonish green Army troops for not controlling their fears and firing indiscriminately. He relates what purports to be the accurate account of this encounter with "trigger-happy Army troops." He wrote:

I was driving along the beach where hundreds of troops were unloading supplies. A company came through, firing indiscriminately right and left and forcing the unloading party to take cover in the belief it was enemy fire. Jumping from my jeep, I located the lieutenant in command and asked what he was firing at.

"I'm trying to clean out snipers in this area," he replied.

"Can't you see there aren't any Japs around here?" I shouted. "Our men are working all over the area and you come shooting at treetops when any damn fool can see there aren't any Japs up there. Why, the enemy is thousands of yards up front."

"I was given orders to clean out this area," the lieutenant persisted. "And I think there still may be Japs around here. I'm shooting at everything so we won't be taking any chances."

This did make me howling mad. "If I hear one more shot from your men in this area I'll take your damn weapons and all your ammunition away from you," I said, revealing my identity. I was wearing my utility suit, without insignia. The shooting stopped and unloading was resumed.[43]

It should be noted that no one who has written of the 27th has ever tried to present them at Makin as skilled, combat-hardened troops. They were not. There were a number of cases, particularly during the first two nights, when units as well as individuals fired at shadows. They were jumpy; the night noises did not help, nor did the Japanese practice of yelling English phrases and infiltrating. Gen. Ralph Smith, when asked about this, replied:

Of course it's true. This was the first action of the 27th Division and all the troops were keyed up. They don't know what's going on and they piss in their pants. That's the kind of thing which always happens.[44]

This comment rings more true than H. M. Smith's bombastic statements. Marines as well as Army troops their first time in combat tend to be tense.

There appear to have been at least two incidents involving H. M. Smith and Army personnel whom he accused of undisciplined, unwarranted firing. It is difficult to determine which H. M. Smith was referring to in his story in *Coral and Brass.* The first incident involved S/Sgt. Emanuel De Fabees. According to a report by his company commander, Charles Coates, Jr., he had on orders sent two anti-sniper patrols east of the West Tank Trap. Sergeant De Fabees and 2nd Lt. Merrit Pequeen, who were in command of the two patrols, had been given specific instructions to maintain good fire discipline because of the possibility of friendly troops in the area. According to Captain Coates' statement, he was informed that the patrols had gone about 200 yards when firing broke out to their rear. Almost immediately the sergeant was "stopped by an individual who identified himself as Maj. Gen. [Holland M.] Smith." General Smith, upon learning the name and rank of De Fabees, then "thoroughly berated S/Sgt. De Fabees in very profane language and ended by stating that if the promiscuous firing continued he [General Smith] would take the rifles away from the platoon." The General did not accept the reply that the platoon had not fired a shot, that the shots had come from the vicinity of a graves detail to the rear. Lieutenant Pequeen joined the group, reported to H. M. Smith, and also denied firing, but was similarly dressed down, the General repeating his threat to take away the patrols' rifles. Captain Coates' report on the incident concluded by stating that soon after completion of the patrol, two snipers were killed "within 200 yards of the spot where General Smith was encountered."[45]

Captain Coates assumed that this was the incident reported by Sherrod in his *Time* article and most readers of *Coral and Brass* have believed that Lieutenant Pequeen was the young lieutenant referred to. There is, however, new evidence that a similar incident took place involving another junior officer. Bernard Ryan, then commanding Company E of the 2nd Battalion, recalls an encounter with H. M. Smith on his last day before leaving Makin. His company, which had been the lead unit in the drive eastward, was evacuating an area and being replaced by Company A, commanded by Capt. Lawrence O'Brien. Before departing, some of his men had sprayed the surrounding trees with rifle fire. Ryan maintains that he learned this from the Marines who were attached to the 165th for the Makin operations. They told him that they learned on Guadalcanal that bullets are cheaper than men—and when they went into or left an area where there might be snipers they always fired into the trees just to make sure there were no Japanese there. Ryan continued his story:

This was what we were doing because we were leaving the area. Some lieutenant, I don't know who he was—he wasn't in my company and I talked to O'Brien and he wasn't in his company—was just standing there. There were a lot of people around—a lot of people in small spaces on that little island—and H. M. began eating this lieutenant out for what the men were doing and the lieutenant looked like he was going to cry. He didn't know what it was all about and he was trying to tell him he didn't have anything to do with it. Smith had reporters with him and he was toting his tommy gun and was wearing his knives and in a loud voice told everyone what he thought of the army. O'Brien had walked up to me and we were behind Smith's group and he said, "Did you report to him?" and I told him, "No, he hasn't acknowledged me and I haven't been able to get in front of him." So when H. M. got into his jeep O'Brien reported to him and I asked him when he came back, "What did you say to him?" He said words to the effect that he told him he [General Smith] shouldn't come out here like this without finding the person in charge to find out what's happening. H. M. just told his driver to take off and he left.[46]

There might be some excuse for H. M. Smith's later intemperate criticism of the 27th for its inactivity—such as his memory of imagined past wrongs and his anxiety about the Tarawa battle. What appears to be unwarranted criticism of certain junior officers of the 27th for unnecessary firing might even be excused in part because he was passing through areas with which he was unfamiliar and made certain incorrect assumptions which he continued to report as fact long after. However, there is no excuse for his statements on the aftermath of the death of Colonel Conroy. The only conceivable purpose in writing what he did could only be to blacken the character of the officers and men of the 165th RCT. H. M. Smith and his ghostwriter Finch wrote:

Speaking as a Marine, faithful to service tradition, I was greatly disturbed by a certain incident at Makin. On D-day, Col. Gardiner Conroy, commanding officer of the 165th Regiment, exposed himself while making a reconnaissance and was killed by a Japanese sniper. With him at the time was Lt. Col. James Roosevelt, son of the President, who was a Marine observer attached to the Army. Two days later, I was shocked to find the gallant Colonel's body still lying where it had fallen. No attempt had been made by either his officers or his men to recover the body and give it a Christian burial.

The body lay a few yards from the main road traversed by troops, jeeps and trucks, in full sight of hundreds of men and only a short distance from the beach. It was inconceivable to me that soldiers of a regiment, whose loyalty is centered on the man directly in command, their Colonel, could permit his body to lie unrecovered for two days. There was no danger involved in recovering it and even if there had been, such negligence was inexcusable. To me this callous disregard of a soldier's common duty to his commanding officer was an ominous commentary on the morale of the regiment. I ordered Ralph Smith to recover the body immediately and bury it. In that order I used emphatic language.[47]

This story is simply untrue. The body of Colonel Conroy was removed as soon as the pocket of Japanese resistance was wiped out and it could be done so safely. Gen. Ralph Smith, normally mild in his criticisms, bridled when questioned about this incident. He stated, "That's as much of a lie as you can possibly imagine and that's been established in the official history by Love."[48] Ralph Smith's reaction is confirmed by a number of other sources. Col. James Roosevelt, with Colonel Conroy when he was killed, stated, "To the best of my recollection Colonel Conroy's body was not only retrieved but taken back to the beachhead."[49] The most concise compilation of statements refuting H. M. Smith's story was contained in a long letter to the editor of *America* by John Lynch in reply to a previously favorable review of *Coral and Brass.* Lynch quotes a number of men who were involved. Father Lafayette Yarwood, the Catholic Chaplain on Makin, stated, "I know definitely that the burial [of Colonel Conroy] took place at 1500 hours on 21 November 1943. The statement of H. M. Smith is absolutely counter to the facts." Capt. Ernest Flemig reported, "Colonel Conroy's body was moved from where it fell, by parties unknown to me, at about 0800, 21 November 1943 . . . I personally viewed Colonel Conroy's body under a blanket at the Regimental Aid Station at about 0900 hours, 21 November 1943." In the same communication, Lynch quoted the 165th Regimental Journal for the date and time of the burial ceremony and Gen. Ralph Smith, who wrote, "Father Yarwood officiated at the burial which took place about 3:30 on 21 November . . . I took Gen. Holland Smith to this ceremony."[50]

This episode shows more clearly than any other how flawed H. M. Smith's reporting about Makin was. Some attempt has already been made to explain H. M. Smith's motives for some of his bizarre actions on Makin. However, there can be only partial explanations for his reasons. One thing is quite clear—he did not like the Army and by some shift of thinking he came to blame Gen. Ralph Smith for his various misfortunes, instead of blaming himself or the naval commanders responsi-

ble for his predicament. Ralph Smith epitomized for him all
that was wrong with the Army; he took every advantage of his
situation to badger the Army commander. H. M. Smith did
this with full knowledge that while he had held no official
command at Makin, other than that allowed him by Admiral
Turner, he still would be the commander of the V Amphibious
Corps when they returned to Hawaii. Thus he would technically be Ralph Smith's superior later. His position on Makin as
Turner's eyes meant that Ralph Smith and his subordinates
had to treat him with the courtesy reserved for a commanding
general. Col. James Mahoney, in charge of the 1st Battalion on
Makin, recalled an incident he witnessed in which H. M.
Smith yelled at Ralph Smith about what he considered the
165th's slowness of movement. Mahoney said:

There was no great need to be in a rush. Nobody ever indicated
to us that we weren't on schedule. And after the 2nd Battalion got
in we pushed on up the island and cleaned them up. I was in the
command post and heard a little of this, I saw Howlin' Mad rais-
ing hell, saying move, move, since he wanted to detach four battalions of the regiment to support the Marines over at Beito and
he was very explicit about this. That's why he wanted all this
mopped up, but I wasn't greatly impressed—I hadn't lost any ma-
jor-generals so I didn't hang around there [the command post].[51]

The most damning picture of H. M. Smith and his actions,
and particularly his attitude toward Ralph Smith, comes from
S. L. A. Marshall, for whom Makin was the first area where he
could test his experimental method of combat reporting. Marshall recalled this incident of D day + 1:

The fight was still going on, though the citadel had been stormed
and taken and our troops were advancing beyond it. Gen. Ralph
Smith had come ashore and had set up his command post in a tent
halfway between Red Beach 1 and Yellow Beach, where the
Corps commander, Maj. Gen. Holland M. Smith of the Marines,
continued to harass him.
  We three sat there together batting at mosquitoes while Holland Smith nagged at Ralph. Suddenly there was a crackling of
rifle fire, close in and on three sides. An excited assistant S-3 came

running our way, shouting, "Snipers! They've got us surrounded!"

Ralph Smith picked up his field phone and told the regiment to have a couple of rifle companies prepare to sweep our way from either direction.

Holland Smith picked up his carbine and stalked into the bush. He was gone for about five minutes, and then returned rubbing his hands. "Well, I took care of those bastards."

It was about as ridiculous a grandstand play as I have ever seen by a general officer, which is saying a lot. The sniping continued for about twenty minutes following his boast.

Then he turned on Ralph Smith. "Get your troops going: there's not another Goddamned Jap left on this island."

Ralph Smith said, "General that plain isn't so."

Right then I decided I would take a very special interest in Holland M. Smith. He was clearly a bully, something of a sadist and, I guessed, tactically a chowderhead.[52]

It is important to note in concluding this brief report on the Makin operation that it was, indeed, a minor affair. If Tarawa was a mistake, then Makin also could be considered a superfluous operation, but the 165th RCT performed its assigned tasks adequately. It took all its objectives on time as planned and with minimal casualties. It entered the operation as a green unit commanded by untested officers. The regiment did not emerge from the battle a premier fighting unit nor is there any claim made that its officer corps after Makin became like the Phoenix rising from the ashes, reborn as outstanding military captains. Equally true, however, is that they and their units should not have been viewed as inferior. Gen. Holland M. Smith of the Marine Corps, in spite of the evidence, left Makin convinced that the 165th and by extension all of the 27th Division was a bad unit and that the senior officers, particularly Gen. Ralph Smith, were unfit. This attitude, which he carried with him into the Saipan campaign, meant that he was continually on the alert for what he would consider Army foulups. What he would forgive in a Marine unit would be magnified out of proportion if the offenders were Army personnel of the 27th Division.

5 | INTERLUDE: THE MARSHALLS

TRANSFER OF COMMAND TO COL. CLESEN TEN-
ney, the designated garrison commander at Makin, was made
at 0800 on 24 November. By that time the 2nd Battalion of
the 165th had already been reembarked, followed by the 1st
Battalion on the 25th. The 3rd Battalion, along with a field
artillery battery, a tank platoon, six batteries of coast artillery
and other specialized units, remained behind to provide services and protection for the engineers, who had begun immediately to construct a thousand-foot-long airstrip. The main
elements of the Northern Task Force had arrived on Oahu by
2 December. The officers and men of the regiment without
doubt viewed their first action under fire as satisfactory. The
objective had been taken according to schedule with minimal
casualties despite mediocre intelligence reports, logistical foul-
ups, and the difficulty of getting adequate artillery support.
Most did not suspect that Admiral Turner, who never came on
shore and who depended largely upon H. M. Smith's reports,
considered their performance substandard. News of Turner's
displeasure would be the first of a number of negative reports
based upon hearsay or *a priori* evidence that would plague the
27th Division in all its actions in the Pacific.

It is well established that H. M. Smith was dissatisfied with
the 165th RCT in general and the Divisional Commander,

Ralph Smith, in particular. His opinions, which he apparently was not hesitant in voicing, soon became general knowledge. However, he never held an overall critique of the Makin operation with Ralph Smith or his staff. Neither Admiral Turner nor any senior member of his naval staff offered to point out to the division its specific weaknesses relative to its actions in the Gilberts.[1] Ralph Smith reported to General Richardson in person and all the pertinent information concerning the campaign was made available to his headquarters. One author whose later works on the Pacific War smack of fiction has Ralph Smith, stinging under the criticisms of his Marine counterpart, complaining to his mentor about "the indelicacies heaped upon him by a goddam Marine."[2] Ralph Smith denies that this conversation ever occurred. Although not numbering H. M. Smith among his closest friends, he got on well with him when they met on official duty or social occasions. One member of H. M. Smith's staff even recalls seeing the two Smiths exchanging tales and laughing. If there was rancor in their relationship in late 1943, it was mainly from H. M. Smith, who, in private conversations, would give his candid opinion of Army operations. There is no evidence Ralph Smith had any reason to imagine the depth of H. M. Smith's negative feelings toward him.[3] He had been made very aware by H. M. Smith's actions on Makin that the Marine was not satisfied with the 165th's performance. But to Ralph Smith, that was in the past and he considered such opinions to be groundless. To him, his regiment had performed well.

The behind the scenes struggle for dominance between the Army, Navy, and Marine Corps would ultimately affect Ralph Smith and the 27th, although they were largely innocent bystanders in what transpired in Hawaii. General Richardson had never been content with his own largely supportive role in the command structure of the Central Pacific Theater. In addition to his personal desire to advance himself, he felt genuine concern that the Army was being shunted aside in favor of Navy and Marine command. He had voiced his objections toward Marine generals commanding large bodies of troops to Admiral Nimitz before the Gilberts operation. Perhaps spurred on by the activities of H. M. Smith on Makin, he returned to the attack on 27 December by constructing a memorandum "For Eyes of Admiral Nimitz Alone." In this he alleged that Marine senior officers in general and H. M. Smith in particular were not capable of exercising Corps command. He charged that since the Marine Corps had never had Divisions, let alone Corps, it had only a few officers trained for Corps staff duty. This was the reason why V Amphibious Corps staff was inexperienced and untrained. He also criticized the overlapping duties of Admiral Turner and H. M. Smith's command, and closed by aiming a few barbs at H. M. Smith's own performance in the Gilberts operation. His recommendation was that there be a role reversal—that Smith's Corps be restricted to administrative duties and actual tactical command and any future operations be reserved for the Army.[4]

Richardson was not alone in these opinions. They were held by most senior Army officers, including General Marshall, who doubted the ability of Marines to handle the problems of Corps command.[5] However justified Richardson's critique was, his suggestions had little chance of being adopted. They would have required a complete reorientation of the command structure. Even if Nimitz was exasperated with H. M. Smith from time to time, the long history of Marine subordination to the Navy meant there would be no substitution of Army senior commanders for Marines. Aside from their obvious expertise at amphibious warfare and the excellence of Marine troops, the Navy dominated the Corps in a manner not likely to be duplicated by the Army. Richardson's suggestions were circulated to Admiral King and General Vandegrift and received scathing rebuttals from both. There was never any doubt that H. M. Smith would retain his position as head of V Corps, which was then involved in planning the complex invasion of the Marshall Islands. Richardson's memo, despite the "Eyes Only" note, had become common knowledge to the senior officers of all services and served only to exacerbate relations between the services. H. M. Smith, who bore by implication the bulk of Richardson's remarks, reacted predictably. He was hurt and defensive of the Corps and transferred his displeasure not just to Richardson, but to "the Army."

Nimitz's staff had been planning the Marshalls' capture since June 1943, when Nimitz had been directed by the Joint

Chiefs of Staff to prepare plans for invading these atolls and islands, which stretched over 10° of latitude. The Marshalls comprised 32 coral atolls and over 800 reefs, the most important being Wotje, Maleolap, Majuro, and Kwajalein, the largest. Code named FLINTLOCK, the initial tentative plans were completed by September and passed on to Corps. The first Corps plan, calling for landings on Wotje and Maleolap on 1 January 1944 and Kwajalein the next day, was completed by mid–November. On 7 December at a staff meeting Admiral Nimitz, much to the consternation of H. M. Smith, Spruance, and Turner, suggested bypassing the outer islands of Wotje and Maleolap and going directly toward the main objectives of Kwajalein and Roi-Namur. Despite all arguments, Nimitz decided to target Kwajalein as the next objective with the modification that Majuro be seized first in order to protect the lines of communication. D day was set as 17 January.[6]

Ralph Smith's 27th Division staff was not involved in any way in the planning for this first phase of the Marshalls campaign. The 106th RCT, which had been available for use since the Nauru invasion had been cancelled, was removed from Ralph Smith's command and assigned to V Corps for the operation. All activities of the detached units of the 27th would thenceforth be coordinated with the 106th's commander, Col. Russell Ayers. The units designated to make the main attacks were the 4th Marine Division, which was targeted to seize Roi-Namur, and the Army 7th Infantry Division, which was to take Kwajalein. The entire 106th RCT was at first scheduled to attack Majuro, but intelligence sources cast doubt on the existence of a large concentration of Japanese troops there. H. M. Smith decided on 26 December to use only the 2nd Battalion, reinforced with a reconnaissance company and a defense unit in the Majuro invasion. The rest of the 106th was to remain with the 22nd Marines as a floating reserve.

The date for the first Marshalls operation was changed a number of times; finally 31 January was selected. There is no reason here to go into detail on what has been described as the most nearly perfect operation of the Pacific War. The preparatory naval and air bombardment of all the targeted islands was much more thorough than during the Gilberts operation. The 4th Marine Division, despite localized heavy opposition, secured the twin islands of Roi and Namur by D + 3. Their casualties were 313 killed in action and 502 wounded. The official Japanese losses were placed at 3563. Meanwhile the Army's 7th Division, commanded by Maj. Gen. Charles Corlett, was inflicting even heavier losses on the enemy at Kwajalein. This was largely because the division landed some of its 105 and 155 mm. howitzers on neighboring islands and their plunging fire did more damage to the defenders of Kwajalein than had the heavy naval bombardment. Such use of artillery had previously been suggested to the Marines during the planning for the Gilberts operation but had been rejected. Despite its proven effectiveness, the early off-loading of artillery on other islands would be refused by Admiral Hill later at Eniwetok. That the Marines and Army had learned from the disaster at Tarawa is shown by the comparative casualty figures. On Kwajalein the 7th Division had only 173 killed and 793 wounded while eliminating 4823 Japanese. Thus, for a total of less than 1800 casualties, the U.S. forces in the Marshalls had disposed of almost 8400 Japanese. At Tarawa the Marines had taken 3300 casualties to eliminate 4690 of the enemy.

The role of the 106th RCT during the battle was minimal. Two battalions remained in floating reserve; only the 2nd Battalion was used for the landings at Majuro. Despite fears to the contrary, there was no resistance at this very important atoll. The main islands were attacked by naval bombardment and airstrikes, but the forward elements of the 106th discovered by talking to natives that there were few, if any, Japanese there. The most dangerous part of this operation concerned the breakdown in communications between the troops on land and Admiral Hill's support group. Before this could be remedied, Navy planes strafed the Army troops on Darrit Island. The Majuro operation was a very real exercise in amphibious landing and assault procedures for the 2nd Battalion.

This phase of the Marshalls operation was in all probability the high point of H. M. Smith's career as commander of V Corps. Despite a few foul-ups at the beginning of the Engebi assault, the operations had gone smoothly. Afterward, there were no embarrassing questions as at Tarawa and later Saipan. It appeared that H. M. Smith in his first overall Corps command had silenced his critics. Even Richardson had to admit that all elements had functioned well. However, even here the differences between Army and Marine tactics apparent in the Gilberts caused H. M. Smith to fume at the imagined slowness of the 7th Division, one of the acknowledged better Army divisions in the entire Pacific theater. The rush and bypass tactics the Marines used were in sharp contrast to the more methodical advance of the Army, and this angered H. M. Smith. Although Kwajalein was secured on D + 4, he believed the island could have been taken earlier. While praising the Marines for their "vigor and elan," he reported to the commandant of the Corps that "the slow progress [of the Army on Kwajalein] has tried my soul."[7]

H. M. Smith and General Corlett had been associated during the Kiska invasion. Although their professional contacts were proper, neither apparently cared much for the other. Corlett was much more forceful than Ralph Smith in dealing with his irascible Corps commander. The following story recalled by S. L. A. Marshall illustrates their relationship, as well as showing that H. M. Smith, even during the Kwajalein operation, was still attacking Ralph Smith. Marshall wrote:

Corlett sent for me next morning. He had a story that he wished to make of record. He had taken seriously what I had told him about Holland Smith. Two days later General Smith had called him to talk over the operation. He quickly began ridiculing Ralph Smith. Corlett arose and said: "Don't you dare ever talk about me that way," and Holland Smith stomped out.

When shortly afterward Holland Smith was promoted to Lieutenant General, the marine returned to the attack. "Corlett, you were insubordinate to me the other day."

Corlett arose. "I'll say the same thing again." and repeated what he had said. Again, Holland Smith turned on his heel. Then, when the order came out, Corlett learned that Holland Smith was on the command ship, *Rocky Mount,* with the admiral, whereas he, Corlett, had been put on another transport. On the advice of his staff, Corlett had made a sticking point of it; either he would go on the *Rocky Mount,* or he would ask to be relieved. He got his way.

Then, two days before we reached Kwajalein, Smith came to

him and asked when Corlett proposed to go ashore. Corlett said he didn't know, then asked: "Why is it important?" Smith said he would go ashore at the same time. Corlett said: "I don't want you ashore until the fighting is done. This is my battle. You may put some staff officers ashore as observers. If I find they have tried to issue any orders, I'll have them arrested."

To his surprise, Smith gave him no argument.

On the morning the battle ended, Smith came ashore on Kwajalein. Immediately, he called a press conference. Corlett came up behind him to hear Smith telling the newsmen that the infantrymen had done a poor job on Kwajalein compared to the fight of the marines at Roi-Namur. That was too much for Corlett. He broke in to inform the correspondents that the corps commander didn't know anything about either battle since he had been kept aboard ship the whole time.[8]

Whatever had triggered it, deep-seated rancor against Ralph Smith still agitated H. M. Smith at Kwajalein, thousands of miles from where most of the 27th Division was training in Hawaii.

By D + 6, all islands in the Kwajalein group had been secured and on 6 February, most of the Army and Marine units were embarked to return to Pearl Harbor. One unit which did not was 2/106, which stayed behind as garrison for Majuro. The rest of the 27th had begun more serious exercises preparatory to the next step in the neutralization of Japanese power in the Central Pacific. This was to be Kusaie and Eniwetok, located over 300 miles northwest of Roi but still in the Marshall group of islands. Initial general plans formulated in Nimitz's headquarters called for the 2nd Marine Division to seize Eniwetok on 19 March 1944, and the 27th Division to invade Kusaie ten days later. The target date for these invasions was subsequently moved up to 1 May—until in mid-January Admiral Spruance suggested an immediate seizure of Eniwetok. He was prompted in this decision by the relative ease of movement of his 5th Fleet in the Central Pacific, combined with intelligence reports indicating that Eniwetok atoll was lightly held. Further study by V Corps staff indicated the feasibility of Spruance's idea. Admiral Hill flew to Pearl Harbor from Kwajalein on 3 February and in the next few days the detailed plans for invading Eniwetok were firmed up.

The Eniwetok plan, code named CATCHPOLE, was the most impromptu of all Pacific invasions. The assault forces were assembled in just seven days. The Army historians who later wrote the detailed story of the campaign noted:

While the expedition against Eniwetok was not exactly makeshift, it was, by previous standards, thrown together hurriedly without the meticulous preparation that characterized most large scale amphibious operations.[9]

Although not as large as the Kwajalein-Roi-Namur assault group, the invasion force was still formidable, comprising the 22nd Marines, only recently transferred from Samoa, and the Army's 106th RCT less the 2nd Battalion and a number of support units. The overall commander was Admiral Hill; the Landing Force Commander was Marine Brig. Gen. Thomas E. Watson, in charge of a newly formed organization called Tactical Group 1. Once again Ralph Smith had nothing substantive to do with this invasion, since the 106th had been detached from the 27th Division on 23 December. Unit planning for Eniwetok fell to Col. Russell Ayers and his regimental staff. H. M. Smith, although in charge of Corps planning for the invasion, had decided not to accompany Admiral Hill on the Eniwetok assault.

At first Corps had scheduled the assault for 12 February, but this was much too optimistic and D day was rescheduled for 17 February. Japanese main line naval and air units were to be attacked by Rear Adm. Marc Mitscher's powerful fleet, which would neutralize Truk, the so-called Gibraltar of the Pacific. On the 15th the invasion ships left the shelter of the recently conquered Kwajalein lagoon for Eniwetok. Eniwetok atoll contained thirty islands in a rough circle approximately seventy miles in diameter. The main islands were Engebi in the north, Parry in the east, and Eniwetok Island, the southernmost of the group. Intelligence knowledge of the atoll was scanty; air photos were still being taken during the latter stages of the Kwajalein operation and some updated photos were even dropped to the command ship while the convoy for Eniwetok was on its way. There had been no time for close-in inspection of the landing beaches. This particular lack would prove very serious when the 106th attempted to land on Eniwetok Island. The number of Japanese troops available also was not known. Earlier in the year it was believed that there were only 700 men present, with the largest number on Engebi, the site of the airstrip. Later it was confirmed that the Japanese 1st Amphibious Brigade had arrived in January, but its size was only estimated. The planners were not aware that the Japanese commander had sited his headquarters on Parry and had 1115 men with him. Eniwetok was believed to be the lightest held of any of the major islands—one reason why it was given the lowest priority in terms of tons of naval fire support. Ultimately there would be 1,180 tons expended on Engebi, 944 on Parry, but only 204 on Eniwetok.

The allocation of fire support was an error based on the assumption that Eniwetok Island would be a walk-over. Planning for the three operations also reflected this attitude. The initial plan called for the two battalions of the 106th to land in columns, with one battalion of the 22nd Marines in reserve. One of the battalions was to be withdrawn after only two hours and sent to support the 22nd Marines' attack on Parry. Information later obtained from natives and Japanese prisoners placed the number of Japanese on Eniwetok at between 500 and 1000 men. Fortunately Admiral Hill was concerned enough about this new information to order a modification in the plans and, on the 17th, he postponed the Parry attack. Ayers and his staff were given only a few hours to make this radical change for the proposed attack on 18 February.[10]

Despite how the invasion of Eniwetok had been planned and initial foul-ups in the first landings, ultimately all went well. On the 17th, the Corps Reconnaissance Company and a portion of the Marine Tank Battalion seized three small islands near Engebi. The scheme that had worked so well at Kwajalein was repeated. Artillery was then landed on these islands to support the 22nd Marines' attack the next morning. Engebi Island was flat with natural cover for the defenders only in one small section of the island. There were no large fortifications; the fixed defenses were mainly trenches and spider holes, which had been shattered by naval and artillery bombardments. When the two assault battalions of the Marines hit the beaches, they found little resistance. Within six hours, the island was declared secure. Later H. M. Smith, in his book, ignored the complete differences in terrain and natural and fixed positions, using the Engebi operation to contrast the slowness of movement of the 165th on Makin.[11] If one ignored salient differences, Engebi appeared to prove H. M. Smith's and Watson's arguments for rapid forward movement by infantry. Nevertheless, Engebi's capture cost the Marines 85 killed and 521 wounded. The total number of Japanese killed was placed at 1276, with 16 prisoners taken.

On 18 February the 106th had its baptism of fire. Four destroyers provided direct covering fire and at 0810 carrier planes swept in on strafing runs. Six LSTs discharged seventeen LVTs at 0730 and proceeded to circle around until the LCMs with the two platoons of medium tanks arrived after a choppy twenty-five-mile trip from the north. Admiral Hill postponed H hour until 0915, when the assault on the lagoon side of Eniwetok Island would begin.

Eniwetok Island from the air resembles the fuselage of a modern Boeing 747, with the widest part of the island in the southwest. The plan for its capture was deceptively simple. The 1st Battalion would land on Yellow Beach 2 and the 3rd Battalion would land to their left on Yellow Beach 1. The 3rd Battalion of the 22nd Marines would remain in reserve. Company A of the 1st Battalion would, after landing, pivot to the right and on its left flank the remaining two companies, with B in the lead, would drive south to cut the island in half. The 3rd Battalion, after landing, was to duplicate these maneuvers to the east and, after reaching the southern part of the island, was to hold the line and block reinforcements from reaching the main force elements of the Japanese, who were expected to be in front of the 1st Battalion. In view of later criticism, it is important to note that the mission of Lt. Col. Harold Mizony's 3rd Battalion was always to be a backup to the major thrust and he was at first not informed that he was expected to drive ahead to the eastern part of the island as quickly as possible.

From the very beginning, the hastily drawn, simple plan went awry. The Japanese were not stupid; they expected the assault in roughly the area of the landings and they had con-

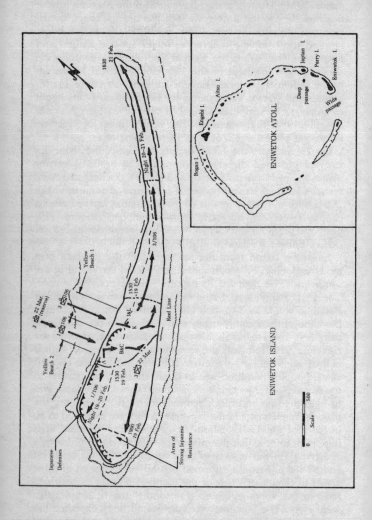

centrated much of their beach defenses in well-concealed positions, particularly in front of Yellow 2. The maps and aerial photos used by Tactical Group 1 showed the major terrain features, but apparently no one in higher level command had noticed that there was a small, steep bluff line between eight and ten feet high paralleling the landing beaches. Thus, instead of the LVTs charging directly inland as fast as they could go as they had on Engebi, the drivers found their way inland blocked. While some struggled to surmount the bluff, others backed down to the beach, crowding the limited landing areas. The coxswains of many craft landed troops in the wrong places and a number of landing craft took hits from the Japanese. In one encounter three boats were caught by enfilade fire; twenty men were killed and eighteen wounded out of a complement of fifty-three men from Company C. One of the LVTs sunk contained Lt. Col. Winslow Cornett commanding the 1st Battalion. Although he was picked up, he did not land until the next day. Many other key personnel of both battalions would also not make it ashore until after some of the hardest fighting was over.

Out of this confusion emerged some superlative efforts by junior officers and enlisted men that saved the operation. Among these were 2nd Lt. Ralph Hiles and PFC William Hollowiak who, after leading a group inland, were caught within a Japanese strong point of a spider-like network of radiating trenches concealed by vegetation. Using grenades and rifle fire, the two men killed approximately twenty of the enemy and neutralized a portion of the position so that Company K of the 3rd Battalion, which had been stalled, could pass through toward the ocean. Elsewhere the story was much the same. Company A turning west encountered thick underbrush and a series of dugouts and trenches. Not until tanks and LVT(A)s came up was that portion of the line straightened. The hardest fighting, however, was in front of Company B, which had the task of securing the left flank of the westward advance. Here an unlikely hero emerged. 1st Lt. Artie Klein, a professional enlisted man who had been forced to accept a commission, was weapons platoon commander of B Company. Landing in a trailing wave, he quickly took charge of the green, scattered troops along the beach. He reformed platoons and companies from one end of the beach to the other and led them in counterattacks against the major Japanese positions. Klein had become the *de facto* commander of the 1st Battalion. He was instrumental in stopping the first major counterattack launched by over 300 Japanese just after noon along the front of the 1st Battalion. Klein is singled out from the rest of the junior officers and men not only because of his heroic actions, which might well have saved the 1st Battalion from a very bad beating, but because of the way his actions were later recognized. Called Omak, the One Man Army, by *Yank* magazine, he was recognized by the historian of the 27th Division as the bravest man he had ever met and the most important man on Eniwetok that first day. Artie Klein received only the Bronze Star for his exploits, despite the fact that Colonel Cornett later collected fifty-two affidavits from the men who had served under Klein and subsequently recommended Klein for the Medal of Honor.[12] By contrast, two senior commanders later received Navy Crosses, the second highest Navy decoration, for their actions. One of these, the award to Col. Russell Ayers, would later have an important bearing on Ralph Smith's freedom of action in commanding the 27th Division on Saipan.

At 1245 Colonel Ayers, under prodding from General Watson, realized the task of clearing the western part of the island was too much for one battalion, and committed his reserve, the 3rd Battalion, 22nd Marines. They were to pass through the Army lines and take up positions on the left flank. At the same time the 3rd Battalion of the 106th, which had adopted a holding posture on the east, was ordered to advance. By 1830 the Marines had reached the southwest part of the island. Ayers ordered the attack continued through the night. This was a questionable order, although in keeping with the pressure placed on him by his superior, General Watson. In the darkness, it was not possible for the 1st Battalion to remain tied into the Marines on the left flank; a gap of approximately 100 yards developed between the units. The next morning a major Japanese counterattack struck at that gap. The Marines suffered eight dead and an equal number wounded in repulsing the Japanese.[13] This incident confirmed many Marines in their belief that Army units were no good and their officers could not be trusted. Elements of the 1st Battalion of the

106th and the 22nd Marines had broken all enemy resistance in the west by nightfall of the 20th. The next morning the Marines and tanks were reembarked to take part in the assault on Parry Island. The 1st Battalion continued mopping up operations in the west and on the 22nd took over this same task from the 3rd Battalion in the east.

On D day the 3rd Battalion had encountered the same near-chaotic conditions on Yellow Beach 1 as had the 1st Battalion to the west. Mention has already been made of the actions of Lieutenant Hill and Private Hollowiak of Company K in countering Japanese strong points in the heavy underbrush. Once the battalion had reached the ocean side of the island, at this point about 300 yards wide, it established a holding position until shortly after noon, when Colonel Mizony received orders to advance eastward. This movement began about 1530. Progress was very slow, since the troops encountered a dense belt of bush paralleling the coast, covering in some areas half the island's width. Many of the bushes were actually small trees ten to twelve feet high. The Japanese had concealed themselves well in this undergrowth so the riflemen had to advance slowly, clearing out each yard of ground. The undergrowth was resistant even to tanks, which would run over the bushes only to have them pop back into place. Nor could artillery or naval gunfire help much. There could be no sudden rush to secure the eastern part of the island quickly because the untested infantry had learned the lesson that "you cannot by-pass Japs. If you go by and leave them behind you, they'll get out of their holes and kill you."[14] Mizony purposely slowed his right flank company so that it maintained contact with its counterpart working slowly through the bush. The battalion had reached the narrow point of the island by the evening of D day. Despite continuing the attack during the nights, the 3rd Battalion did not reach the eastern tip until midafternoon of 21 February; in spite of slackening Japanese resistance, the troops still had to search through the tangled growth for the enemy. The following day the 3rd Battalion embarked to act as the floating reserve for the attack on Parry Island. The two and one-half day operation on Eniwetok Island resulted in light casualties. Only ninety-six Army men were killed, more than one-third of these during the fight on the beaches. There were also 311 wounded. By contrast, except for 23 prisoners, the entire Japanese garrison of almost 900 troops were killed.[15]

The Eniwetok operation was completed by the assault on Parry Island by the 22nd Marines. Initial plans had called for that attack simultaneous with the 106th's landing on Eniwetok. This was yet another example of the over-optimistic views of the planners based on inadequate information. Navy guns and aircraft worked over Parry more thoroughly than they had Eniwetok, and there was no significant barrier to the landing of the LVTs followed by the medium tanks. Despite the normal mix-up on the beach and some Japanese resistance, the Marines could push rapidly inland. They found the defenses on Parry basically the same as on Engebi and Eniwetok, except for the dense bush found on the latter island. Close cooperation with destroyers smashed the enemy artillery and the Marine tank-infantry teams made short work of most of the enemy defenses. By the evening of D day, the island was declared secure, although small groups of Japanese made hopeless attacks on Marine positions during the night. The island was mopped up by tanks and infantry on 23 February. On the same day, the 3rd Battalion of the 106th relieved the 22nd Marines as the garrison force. With the exception of a few Japanese and Korean prisoners, all the Japanese on Parry Island were killed.

In the two months following the capture of Eniwetok, the 22nd Marines and some Army troops from the 11th Regiment took control of several small islands that, at worst, were lightly defended by the Japanese. With the 111th's capture of Ujelang Atoll 140 miles southwest of Eniwetok on 22 April, the conquest of the Marshall Islands was considered completed. Wotje, Mille, Jaliut, and Maleolap were simply ignored, their garrisons left to die on the vine. Majuro became a major U.S. fleet anchorage, as did Eniwetok and Kwajalein which served as staging bases for the Marianas campaign. In addition, an airstrip was constructed on Majuro and used for harassing raids on the Japanese garrisons of the bypassed atolls. Larger airstrips were built on Roi and Kwajalein and the Japanese field on Engebi was lengthened and improved. Heavy bombers based in the Marshalls effectively neutralized Japanese air and naval power at Truk. Ultimately, Japanese central command headquarters were forced to move to Koror in the Western Caroline Islands. The stage had been set for the next step in American dominance in the Central Pacific, the conquest of the Marianas. The Marianas invasion and its naval actions would later be seen as the crucial battles of the war in that theater; the Japanese would never recover from their defeats there. For the purposes of this study, the Saipan operation represented the climax of the already major differences between the Army and Marine Corps.

Those differences, although not critical to the success at Eniwetok, contributed to the growing antipathy between the Marine Corps and Army. General Watson had reacted to the alleged slowness of the Army units in advancing inland from the beach with predictable ire. Without adequate information about why the Army units were pinned down on the increasingly congested beach, he had ordered Colonel Ayers at 1004 on D day to "push your attack" and a few minutes later to "move troops forward and inland, clear beaches. Advance."[16] While Watson, sitting with Admiral Hill back on the command ship, might be faulted for excessive zeal given his limited knowledge of the beach's conditions, one can understand his annoyance with Ayers' handling of the situation. Admiral Hill later recalled:

As a regimental commander, Colonel Ayers did not impress me as a fighting leader or an inspiring one. In the above instance [moving inland], it was General Watson who had to order him to tell his troops to advance. Furthermore, Colonel Ayers showed no desire to go ashore and take command of his troops, and was finally ordered by General Watson to do so.[17]

At the conclusion of the Eniwetok operation, General Watson filed his report and, again ignoring the problems, showed his displeasure with the 106th by stressing its failure to move quickly inland. He then added a comment on their failure to realize the capabilities of and use of naval gunfire and close support aviation—a comment which was certainly uncalled for. It is questionable whether any Army unit commanders, with the possible exception of Ayers, could have influenced

Admiral Hill to give more air or naval support for an operation which was firmly believed to be a pushover, and which had received only about one quarter of the scheduled support given to the Marines on Engebi and Parry. However one might argue with General Watson's reasons, the fact remains that he was very displeased with the performance of the 106th. H. M. Smith's attitude toward the Army got a further boost by Watson's reports. H. M. Smith wrote to the Commandant of the Corps, expressing his jubilation over the Marines' performance:

Oh! Boy!—it is a grand feeling to see our grand old Marine Corps delivering the goods. . . . After the war the Marines will be further recognized as the best fighting men in the world.

Eniwetok opened many eyes . . . when two Army battalions were held up [a battalion of Marines] went through these like grass through a goose.[18]

While neither poetic nor accurate, Smith's words are a good mirror to his view of his Corps as compared to units of the 27th Division.

A relatively minor situation developed after Eniwetok that should be considered because of its later effect upon command relations at Saipan. This concerned General Watson's recommendation that the Navy Cross be awarded to Col. John Walker, commanding the 22nd Marines. Colonel Ayers was not included in the original list of persons to be awarded a decoration. Admiral Hill called this omission to Watson's attention, pointing out that this might cause a further deterioration in interservice relations. Watson was adamant. Hill noted:

He [Watson] didn't think Colonel Ayers deserved any meritorious award. I advised Turner of this problem as I was sure that interservice relations would be very severely strained if no awards were recommended. At his suggestion, I talked again to Watson who, although demurring very vociferously, decided to recommend Ayers for some lesser award than the Navy's highest.[19]

The decision was passed on to higher headquarters. Watson was subsequently given a direct order to recommend Ayers for

a Navy Cross. It is not certain at what level this order origi-
nated. Hill believed that H. M. Smith backed up Watson but
lost the argument, presumably to Spruance and Turner. On
the other hand, the historian of the 27th Division and a number of officers on the divisional staff believed that H. M. Smith
concurred in the decision, believing Ayers to be a better commander than Ralph Smith. Certainly Ayers looked the part of
the handsome, dashing leader of men. One of his associates
later recalled:

Russell Ayers was the kind of commander who walked around
with a swagger stick and changed his uniform 3 or 4 times a day—
the British Colonel.[20]

In the sometimes confusing war of words between the Marines and Army in the aftermath of Saipan, there was little
agreement between Edmund Love, the Army historian, and
the apologists for H. M. Smith's actions. There was, however,
one point of consensus: Love agreed with Watson's assessment
of Ayers. He considered Ayers confused by his responsibilities. Love stated:

Just before we went to Saipan—a few days before—there was a
big ceremony at Scofield Barracks. Holland M. Smith, himself,
personally came out to Scofield and awarded Russell Ayers the
Navy Cross for his actions at Eniwetok. Now this was the most
absolutely foolish miscarriage of justice that I have ever seen because there is no question in my mind that he never got off the
command ship at Eniwetok, never knew what went on in that
battle, and he had no control of the troops. He was a lost soul and
then for H. M. Smith to come up there and give him the second
highest award for his incompetent performance, what kind of spot
did that put Ralph Smith in?[21]

The explanation for Ralph Smith's position regarding Ayers
is simple—he had made a rule that he would not accept hearsay evidence against his senior officers. Ayers had performed
his noncombat duties well and, although Ralph Smith had reason to suspect Ayers' combat performance, he had never observed the 106th's commander's handling of troops in action.

Immediately after Eniwetok, he had changed an order issued by Ayers, which would have restricted the award of the Combat Infantryman's Badge to only 60 percent of the troops involved. The possibility of injustice in the awards, which would be detrimental to morale, was obvious to the commander of the 27th and he immediately countermanded Ayers' order.[22] This instance, although it might indicate a flaw in judgment, was no reason to reprimand, let alone dismiss, a regimental commander. If Ralph Smith were judicious in his self-imposed rule regarding the performance of his other officers, how much more should he have been with reference to Ayers? The award of the Navy Cross had made Colonel Ayers even more untouchable, until his incompetence could be demonstrated in a combat situation. H. M. Smith never gave Ralph Smith the time for such an evaluation. After Ayers was removed by General Jarman on Saipan, he defended himself by pointing out that the Navy had cited him previously as an outstanding battle leader.[23]

With the arrival in Hawaii of the bulk of the 106th Regiment from Eniwetok, Ralph Smith once again commanded a fully manned division. The 165th and 105th after Makin had been brought up to strength and had resumed the usual regular land and amphibious training. The divisional staff in this interim completed plans for and put into effect new schemes of loading and unloading supplies, which resulted in most of the support equipment for the 27th Division at Saipan being palletized. They studied the recent landings, both by the Marines and Army, trying to abstract lessons from them for the next task. This assignment was not known until the latter part of March, when it was learned that the 27th Division would once again act as a reserve force for the projected invasion of the key islands of the Marianas group. If committed to action either at Guam, Saipan, or Tinian, this would be the first action of the 27th acting as a division. For many of the officers and men it would also be their first action. The 105th had not been utilized previously, and the 2nd Battalion of the 106th at Majuro had had nothing more than a tense amphibious exercise. However ambiguous the 27th's ultimate target in the Marianas may have been, there was one certainty. The division would once again be a part of V Amphibious Corps commanded by H. M. Smith, a newly appointed Lieutenant General. The rank might have been new, but his prejudices against the Army and the 27th Division were of long duration.

6 | THE MARIANAS: PLANNING

ALL PREVIOUS OPERATIONS IN THE CENTRAL Pacific had been preliminary to attacking the Marianas. The importance of these islands had been recognized at the highest command level as early as the Quebec meeting of the Joint Chiefs of Staff in August 1943, when basic goals in the Pacific theater were set. Admiral King, who at that time favored the ultimate seizure of Formosa, was especially committed to the neutralization of Japanese power on the main islands of the Marianas. He viewed their capture as imperative; it would precipitate the most critical phase of the war in the Central Pacific, he believed, since Japan would probably commit the bulk of its remaining fleet units rather than lose the key islands of Saipan, Tinian, and Guam. Later, in the discussions of those who planned the strategy for the Pacific, King received the support of Air Force General Arnold, who saw these islands as bases from which the growing fleet of B–29s could strike at the very heart of Japan only 1300 miles distant from Saipan.

At the Cairo meeting in November 1943, the Joint Chiefs approved the Marianas operation targeted for 1 October 1944. The basic time frame for Central Pacific operations was given to Admiral Nimitz's headquarters in mid-December, and the earliest general plan was issued on 27 December with the scheduled date moved forward to 15 November 1944.

There were many modifications to this general plan in the following months, due to the unparalleled success of the fleet units in negating Japanese naval and air forces in the Central Pacific, especially those at the major Japanese bastion of Truk. The relatively easy capture of the Marshalls was also a spur in advancing the time for operations against the Marianas. A Joint Chiefs of Staff order on 12 March 1944 directed all Pacific Fleet transports and cargo vessels not then in use transferred to Nimitz's command. The next day Nimitz cancelled all planning for the Truk invasion and a week later issued the first CINCPOA joint staff study for the Marianas operation, code name FORAGER. This outlined the seizure of the three main islands located 1200 miles from the nearest U.S. base. Planners would have to muster troops from a number of locations and transport them from 4,000–7,000 miles under the protection of the 5th Fleet, which for this operation would number over 800 ships.[1]

Despite any reservations General Richardson and the Army might have had, the actual seizure of the Marianas was intrusted to V Amphibious Corps and its commander, H. M. Smith. Staff Corps planning began immediately after the first FORAGER study was issued and, as soon as possible, concurrent planning was begun by the various divisions involved in the operation. The initial plans called for a simultaneous invasion of Guam and Saipan. D day for Saipan was scheduled for 15 June, while Guam was to be assaulted three days later. Both invasion forces were to be under Admiral Spruance, commander of the 5th Fleet. There were a total of five major sub-commands, the major ones being the Northern Troops and Landing Force (NTLF) for Saipan and Tinian, and the Southern Troops and Landing Force for Guam. Since the Guam invasion has little to do with events under examination, it should be pointed out only that the optimistic view of the planners at Pearl Harbor could not be sustained and the invasion of Guam was postponed because of fierce Japanese resistance on Saipan. Both attack forces were to be commanded by Admiral Turner, who would also function in the joint role as commander of the NTLF. Admiral Hill was in charge of the Western Landing Group, which would make the landings on Saipan. H. M. Smith, who would be the commander of the troops once they had landed, was thus rather far down the scale of command.[2]

Two Marine divisions (reinforced) had been assigned to H. M. Smith for the Saipan operation. These were the 2nd Marine Division of Tarawa fame, now commanded by Major General Watson, and the 4th Marine Division led by Maj. Gen. Harry Schmidt. The 27th Infantry Division was to act as the floating reserve force for both southern and northern operations, being prepared to land on any of the targeted islands. The Army's 77th Division was to be in general reserve in Hawaii, but could not be expected to be available before D + 20, due to the scarcity of transport. The proposed Normandy invasion in Europe would absorb most of the available shipping. The planners for FORAGER could launch their attack only by conserving to the utmost the available shipping. It would take twenty days for those ships involved in the initial assault on Saipan to return to Oahu, pick up the 77th, and return. Thus, for all practical purposes, if things went bad in the Saipan assault, only the troops scheduled for the Guam invasion would be immediately available for relief. H. M. Smith formed two staffs—one, the "Blue Staff," was to coordinate planning for the Expeditionary Forces, while the "Red Staff" was only for the NTLF.[3]

By 1 May the basic operations plan 3–44 had been issued, calling for the Marine divisions on D day to land on the western beaches of Saipan. The 2nd Division was to land on Red and Green Beaches north of the town of Charan Kanoa, with the 6th and 8th Marines in the assault. At the same time the 4th Division was to land on Blue and Yellow Beaches south of the town, with the 23rd and 25th Marines in the assault. Once landed, the Marines were scheduled to push rapidly inland to an overly optimistically drawn 0–1 line. The 2nd Division then was to turn north and seize Mt. Tapotchau and Mt. Tipo Pole, while the 4th would drive straight across the waist of the island to seize Aslito airfield. Since the attack on the western beaches had to be made across a reef line, the main landings were to be by LVTs transported to Saipan on LSTs. The 2nd Division had two Marine amphibious tractor battalions and one Army battalion assigned to it, while the 4th Division had one Marine and two Army tractor battalions. A diversionary movement by the reserve regiments of both divisions, the 24th and 29th Marines, was to be made at Tanapag Harbor with the objective of freezing Japanese defenders there. H. M. Smith's Chief of Staff, Brig. Gen. Graves Erskine, came up with another plan, to have a battalion of the 2nd Division land on the night of the 14th at Purple Beach on the northern shore of Magicienne Bay. Once landed, it was to drive westward toward Mt. Tapotchau.[4]

The planners at all levels had little accurate information on any of the Marianas Islands until after the carrier strikes in late February. Corps planners continued to ask the Navy for full photo coverage of all the islands, a task which was only partially fulfilled. Late photos of Saipan were being delivered even as the attack forces were on the way. The slower LST groups did not get the updated materials before the landings. The handicaps faced by planners are thus obvious. They had to make assumptions on the basis of very scant and sometimes faulty terrain information. The Marine units made their landings on the basis of available data on 18 April. The Engineers had prepared a 1:62,500 scale map of Saipan and Tinian, but it was too small for any but the most general information about topography. A much clearer battle map was the 1:20,000, but this was based on incomplete photographic coverage made on 22–23 February and on Japanese charts captured during the Marshalls campaigns. It is well to remember in the context of Ralph Smith's relief later what a Marine historian had to say about the accuracy of this basic map. He wrote:

The contours shown on the map were actually 'logical' contours adapted from captured charts and partially revised from existing photographs. Once the map was in use, it was ascertained that these contours were not only inaccurate but they offered a misleading representation of the basic features of the island. As examples, sheer cliffs sometimes appeared as slopes and box canyons as ravines or draws . . .[5]

Thus anyone using this map could arrive at very questionable conclusions as to the nature of the terrain in which a unit was attacking. Some time after D day an excellent map of the island was captured, but this was not available until after the troops had already passed the Garapan-Mt. Tapotchau-Magicienne Bay line.

If the senior planners knew little of the features of Saipan, they knew even less of the numbers or quality of the Japanese defenders. Since the basic Corps plan was set in May, the estimate given at that time was crucial. On 9 May the intelligence estimate was that there were approximately 9,000–10,000 men on the island. On 24 May, this figure was revised to 15,000–18,000. Even if the latter figures were correct, however, the assaulting forces would still have a theoretical edge in numbers of men, but nowhere near the three–to–one bulge that most commanders of attacking forces would have liked. The D day estimate placing 22,702 Army and 6,960 Navy personnel on the island was much more accurate, but all the planning had been based on the lower estimated figures.[6] Thus, even with total American control of the air and mastery of the sea adjacent to Saipan, the Marine assault forces would ultimately face many more Japanese than expected.

The roles assigned to the two Marine divisions were straightforward. Their commanders, down to company level, knew what would be expected of them and could plan accordingly. This was not true of the 27th Division, which was to be in floating reserve and thus had to be prepared to be used on any one of the three target islands either as a reserve, or, in the case of Tinian, as the primary attack force. Many of the divisional officers did not believe they would be needed on Saipan, but would instead be used after the initial successful invasion there to assault Tinian. The speculation regarding Tinian proved correct—the division was notified just before leaving Pearl Harbor that, if all went well with the Marines on Saipan, the 27th would then invade Tinian.[7] But despite their conjectures, the divisional staff had to be prepared for any eventuality. The 165th and the untested 105th RCTs would be used first in any assault, because the 106th had been used in the Marshalls operation and the last elements of its 2nd Battalion did not return to Oahu and division control until 13 April. The 106th would be detached from the 27th during the Marianas operation and attached to the forces scheduled to invade Guam on 18 June. By 12 May, sixteen plans had been developed, twelve pertaining to the Saipan operation, two for

Tinian, and two for Guam. Ultimately, twenty-two different plans were drawn up to cover all conceivable uses for the division on any one of the three islands. The preferred plan for the division was for the 165th and 105th to land on Purple Beaches 1 and 2 in Magicienne Bay. There were also plans for landing on Red and Green Beaches behind the 2nd Marine Division and landing on Scarlet Beach on Tanapag Harbor.[8] The variety of divisional plans meant that the regiments and battalions had to have an equal number of plans. The uncertainty of the division's ultimate goal put a tremendous strain on Ralph Smith and his planners long before they embarked for Kwajalein on 1 June.

Training of all units assigned to V Corps for the Marianas operation began seriously during the second week of March and continued until the end of May. Emphasis was placed on individual and small unit training. There were day and night exercises as well as those stressing cooperation between tank and infantry teams, and naval and artillery support. Marine and Army units trained separately, but their training was basically the same. The 2nd Marine Division conducted amphibious maneuvers on Maui between 12 and 31 March and the 4th Marine Division duplicated these efforts from 13 to 26 April. On 17 May there was a full scale landing exercise with the two Marine divisions operating at Maalaea Bay, Maui. Two days later a similar exercise was conducted at Kahoolawe Island south of Maui, where the troops practiced under actual naval bombardment.[9] After Corps was satisfied with the actions of the Marine divisions, the 27th Division could hold similar exercises. The first drills on 20 May were mainly for coxswains and their crews to get the feel of unloading troops in the calm waters off Maui. The next day there was a major landing practice with the 165th and 105th RCTs in the assault and the 106th in reserve. Although limited by the lack of equipment on the beach, the exercise went off very well, and was particularly helpful to the Navy in practicing placing its ships for ship-and-shore movement and in cooperating with the Army in landing troops on the beach. On the 22nd, off Kahoolawe, the troops debarked in LCVPs while escort destroyers pounded the beach and planes made strafing runs. All senior officers who participated in the practice and critiques—both before

and after the 27th Division was returned to Hawaii on 24 May
—were satisfied that as much as possible had been done to
prepare the troops for actual combat. There were apparently
no serious criticisms from responsible officers on the performance of the Army troops.[10]

The slow-moving LST groups, loaded with the scheduled
first assault troops, artillery, and LVTs, were scheduled to
leave Pearl Harbor on 24 May, but a disaster forced a one-day
postponement. During loading operations an explosion blew
up one of the LSTs and the resulting fire engulfed five others.
Heroic efforts kept the fire from spreading farther, but the
damage had been done. None of the six LSTs could be sal-
vaged and all of the equipment and supplies on board were
destroyed. The 2nd Marine Division lost 95 men and the 4th
Division lost 112 men.[11] Replacements for the lost personnel
were soon made up from the Replacement Center. The valuable equipment lost was another matter. Oahu was searched
for guns, radios, ammunition, and other supplies to re-outfit
the damaged Marine units. Both General Richardson and the
Army recognized how gravely endangered the Marianas plans
were by this accident; they gave every assistance to the Marine
Corps. The LSTs departed for Saipan on 25 May. The one day
lost was regained in transit.

The officers and men of the 27th Division were all on board
the transports by the afternoon of 31 May. They left just before midnight for Kwajalein, enroute to their as yet undeter-
mined target. The troop convoy, under the command of Rear
Admiral Blandy, would refuel and take on supplies at Kwajalein and depart for Saipan on 11 June, arriving at the designated point northwest of the island on D + 1. Due to the
scarcity of ships, it was impossible to take a medium tank battalion. The division had to be satisfied with a medium tank
company and three light tank companies.[12] Gen. Ralph Smith
on 1 June informed the troops by loudspeaker of their destination and the general plans. Later, other small group briefings
filled in more details. The Navy and Army agreed to hold a
CPX each day regarding the various plans. This was later
changed to having only four; each CPX would be a problem-
solving event for the officers concerned. All information regarding the use of the 27th was passed on as soon as possible

to the officers.[13] By the time that Transport Divisions 7, 32, and 34 carrying the 27th arrived off Saipan on D + 1, there was little doubt in the minds of Ralph Smith and his staff that the division had been prepared for their coming ordeal as well as could be done. Yet no one knew what to expect from the Japanese defenders.

In order to understand what happened during the first few days in the invasion of Saipan, one must examine briefly the physical features of the island, the capabilities of Japanese forces present, and their plans to thwart the expected invasion. Saipan is not a large island. It is less than fifteen miles long and approximately seven miles at its widest, narrowing to three miles in the vicinity of Magicienne Bay. Its axis runs roughly in a southwest to northeast direction. Saipan's east coast does not have protective coral reefs except in places in Magicienne Bay, but the west coast is almost completely ringed by reefs. The east and northern sides of Saipan are noted for high cliffs, which in places present a sheer drop to the ocean. In most of these areas there is only a very narrow coastal plain. By contrast, the western coast is low-lying and has a broad coastal plain presenting only a few obstacles to movement inland. Aside from scattered hills, the major barrier to troops landing near Afetna Point was Lake Susupe and its swampy perimeter. The bulk of Saipan's population was concentrated in the west. The major towns were Charan Kanoa in the south located about midway between Agingan Point and Afetna Point, Garapan sited on the coast halfway up the island, and Tanapag set a few hundred yards inland from Tanapag Harbor. A narrow gauge railway connected all the western towns and almost circled the island. This was paralleled for the most part by the coastal road. There were few roads leading across the island. For the invading forces, the most important would be the two east–west roads that began south of Charan Kanoa and led to Chacha Village and Magicienne Bay.

Central Saipan's most dominant feature was the highlands blocking the way to the north. These highlands were anchored in the west by Mt. Tapotchau rising to over 1500 feet elevation and the smaller Mt. Tipo Pale and Hill 789. Approximately 1000 yards east of Tapotchau, across a relatively flat stretch of ground (later to be named Death Valley by the 27th

Division), was a long ridge line—Purple Heart Ridge—which ran roughly parallel to the coast. The terrain in these highlands was not even. There were a number of draws, and bluff lines intersecting the main ridges. Although the Japanese plans at first did not take full advantage of the natural defense of Saipan, it would be here, on the most rugged terrain of the island, and in the northern highland regions, that the Japanese would put up the strongest resistance. There were only a few routes northward through the Central Highlands and these could be covered very well by machine guns, mortars, and riflemen concealed on the high ground. In some places such as Death Valley, any troops attacking directly forward could be brought under fire from both flanks as well as from the front. East and west of the Central Highlands and beyond to the north the terrain was relatively smooth until the northern hills and ridges were reached. It was in these areas that the Japanese had planted sugar cane, the island's main crop. South of Magicienne Bay toward Nafutan Point the terrain once again became more difficult, with many irregular features which could aid the defenders. Most important, much of this region was covered by extremely rough, jungle-like growth, making advance difficult and dangerous.[14]

Until mid–1943, the Japanese had done little to improve the defenses of any of their island possessions in the Central Pacific. This was also true of Saipan, although the island was considered vital for the defense of the homeland. Tanapag Harbor provided good anchorage for the Navy and was the site of headquarters of the newly created Central Pacific Fleet commanded by Vice Adm. Chuichi Nagumo of Pearl Harbor fame. There were over six thousand naval personnel on the island. The major airfield, Aslito, was sited in the extreme southern part of Saipan. The Japanese had begun two other airstrips, one just north of Charan Kanoa and the other in the north near Marpi Point. Lack of materials had halted construction on these before 15 June. Lack of such vital materials as steel and concrete also hampered the belated efforts of the Japanese to build good permanent defenses for the island. Although the Japanese worked frantically in the two months before the invasion, they did not plan on completing the permanent defense network until November.

Despite the recognition of the importance of Saipan, neither the Japanese Navy nor Army commanders believed that an invasion was imminent. They believed the most logical target for an invasion by midyear would be the Palau group in the Western Caroline Islands. That is why so many transports sunk off Saipan had Koror as their original destination. The Japanese believed they would have time to complete the defenses. The best evidence for this belief is the large number of heavy weapons, searchlights, and antiaircraft guns that, still in depots, were later captured by the Marines.[15]

The Japanese had waited too long to begin fortifying and manning their island bases. By 1944 the U.S. Navy went almost unchallenged in the Central Pacific. Although the Japanese Navy was still very powerful, the High Command had not chosen to commit it to any major action. Japanese airpower was also present, but was nothing but a nuisance factor to the powerful U.S. fleets. The best example of the Japanese naval and air forces' powerlessness was the great strike at Truk in February 1944, which rendered this once safe haven impotent. Perhaps as important, although not as well known, was the veritable blockade established by American submarines across the vital north-south Japanese shipping lanes. By the spring of 1944, a major percentage of all Japanese ships bound for the Marianas, Marshalls, or Carolines were sunk by submarines. Even those which eventually did get through had been forced into circuitous routes. Supplies of men and materials took a very long time to reach the Central Pacific garrisons. The Army units on all Japanese-held islands were thus isolated and, because of lack of covering naval forces, were on their own.[16]

American naval and air superiority caused the senior Army officer in the Marianas, Lt. Gen. Hideyoshi Obata, in charge of the 31st Army, to sit out the battle for Saipan. He was at Koror in the Palaus on an inspection trip when the invasion began and could not get back to Saipan. This left the defense of the island to Lt. Gen. Yoshitsugu Saito, normally commander of the Northern Marianas Army group, and the reinforced 43rd Division. Although there were many Navy men involved in the fighting, it does not appear that Admiral Nagumo played much of a role. However, the Naval Guard

Force, the 55th *Keibitai,* was given the responsibility of defending Garapan and the territory immediately adjacent to the
town. Admiral Nagumo remained basically a passive observer
until the very end. The most important unit was the 43rd
Division, comprised of three infantry regiments—the 118th,
135th (less the 1st Battalion), and the 136th. The second most
important unit was the 47th Mixed Brigade, made up of three
infantry battalions. There was also a tank regiment, an infantry
battalion, an antiaircraft regiment, and two regiments of engineers that did not belong to either of the main army units.[17]

There were also many units trapped on Saipan that had originally been ordered to other islands in the Central Pacific. The
118th Regiment, for example, had arrived on 7 June, just one
week before the American invasion. It had been scheduled to
reinforce the garrison at Koror, but five of the seven ships in
the convoy had been sunk, which resulted in all of the unit's
heavy equipment and most of the individual arms being lost as
well as almost 50 percent of the 118th's personnel being
drowned. A Japanese intelligence officer, Maj. Kiyoshi Yoshida, who was captured later, claimed that of the more than
20,000 army troops on Saipan, only 15,000 had weapons.[18]

Given the problems of constructing an adequate defense
with minimal supplies and troops from a variety of units inade-
quately armed, General Saito decided that the best chance of
victory lay in defeating the invaders on the beaches. He dis-
tributed his available troops according to this premise. He and
his staff evaluated the hydrographic terrain information and
concluded that the American landings in all probability would
be on the north shore of Magicienne Bay, a very fortunate
decision for the Marines, who landed directly across the island
on the western shore adjacent to Charan Kanoa. Saipan was
divided into five defensive sectors. The area near Garapan
became the Navy's responsibility. In the Northern Sector,
Saito placed the 135th Infantry (less the 1st Battalion); the
136th Regiment (less the 3rd Battalion) guarded the Central
Sector; in the large Southern Sector were three independent
infantry battalions, an artillery regiment, and the antiaircraft
regiment. Saito had placed the 47th Mixed Brigade and the
9th Tank Regiment in the Eastern Sector, which was presumed
to be vital. He had also stationed most of the rest of his avail-

able troop strength as a general reserve between Chacha and Laulau villages just north of the Purple Beaches where the most elaborate of all the Japanese beach defenses had been constructed.[19] Fortunately, General Erskine's plan to land a Marine battalion on Purple Beach was cancelled at the last moment before the convoy left Pearl Harbor. Otherwise, the small unit would have been destroyed. The 27th Division had as one of its main plans a two regiment assault on Purple Beaches 1 and 2. Even though Saito's defensive preparations were badly damaged by naval and aerial bombardment, he still might have been able to carry out his threat of destroying the enemy on the beaches had the 27th landed where he expected. After D day, Saito pulled the bulk of the defenders of the Eastern Sector back into the Central Highlands—the area later designated to be directly assaulted by the 27th Division. General Saito and his staff recognized the importance of the natural defenses offered by the area from Mt. Tapotchau eastward to Purple Heart Ridge soon after the Marines had landed on 15 June. Saito's Command Post, which had originally been located in a schoolhouse in Charan Kanoa, was then moved to a cave in a small hill located approximately 500 yards northwest of Hill 500. On 19 June, with the situation worsening for the defenders, the CP was moved to a pit-like natural cave protected by rock slabs in the ridge directly above Chacha village. On 24 June, the general again moved to a large, elaborate cave located in a sheer cliff on the eastern side of Mt. Tapotchau.[20] This latter location placed him and his staff only a few hundred yards in front of the Army troops, who on 24 and 25 June were directly attacking one of the strongest natural defensive positions on Saipan.

Japanese optimism that there would be time to complete defensive preparations was shattered on 11 June when Vice Adm. Mitscher's powerful Task Force 58 began the preliminary bombardment of Guam, Rota, Tinian, and Saipan. Mitscher had one of the most powerful fleets ever assembled under his command: 8 large and 8 small carriers containing over 900 planes, 7 new fast battleships, 13 cruisers, and 58 destroyers. On the afternoon of 11 June, while still 200 miles east of the main Mariana group, he launched a fighter sweep of more than 200 planes which caught the Japanese completely by surprise and destroyed approximately 150 planes on the ground or in the air. This assured the attacking forces total air supremacy over Saipan four days before the landings even began. The softening up process by the guns of TF 58 continued the next day. The fast battleships fired for seven hours into the western coasts of Tinian and Saipan. Since this firing was at long range, the damage inflicted was likely not what the Navy expected. But on 14 June, the preparatory bombardment was taken over by Adm. Jesse Oldendorf's fire support ships, whose main punch were older battleships supplemented by cruisers and destroyers. Mine sweepers cleared the approaches and the big ships moved in closer to shore.[21] The bombardment and air attacks destroyed or rendered useless many of the prepared Japanese defenses and thus negated much of General Saito's plans to stop the invasion on the beaches. The pre-invasion pounding by ships surrounding the island continued for three and one-half days. Naval aircraft, unchallenged by Japanese planes, flew with impunity through the poorly aimed antiaircraft fire. While General Saito and his subordinate commanders were thus made aware that invasion was imminent, they still did not know where the landings would be made. They could only wait. They were nonetheless confident of victory, as was Admiral Toyoda, commander of the Combined Fleet in Tokyo, as he prepared to activate the Japanese Mobile Fleet and execute Operation A–Go to attack Spruance's Fifth Fleet in the Marianas area.

7 | SAIPAN: THE FIRST DAYS

ADMIRAL TURNER, ABOARD THE COMMAND SHIP *Rocky Mount,* gave the order at 0542 on 15 June to begin landing troops on the designated beaches at Saipan. The heaviest concentration of naval fire and air attacks on the island yet seen in the Pacific War had already been unleashed, and the close support forces of Admiral Oldendorf ringing Saipan in six separate sectors were beginning the immediate pre-landing bombardment. The day before, underwater demolition teams had operated under the protection of naval gunfire to locate and mark the best passages across the reefs and where it would be necessary to dynamite new ones for the LVTs. The LSTs containing these amtracs and the assault troops moved to the line of departure 4000 yards offshore of Saipan's western beaches. The Marines comprising the first waves, because of the lack of shipping, had been loaded aboard the crowded LSTs at Kwajalein and had spent six uncomfortable days in transit. Despite the known and unknown dangers of the coming amphibious landing, many probably welcomed any chance to get away from these pitching, overcrowded, prison-type vessels.

The plan called for the 2nd Marine Division to land on the Red and Green Beaches located at the north of Afetna Point and for the 4th Marine Division to land on the Blue and Yellow Beaches south of Charan Kanoa.[1] The initial assault was to be made by 48 troop-carrying LVTs for each division. These were accompanied by 18 LCV(A)s located on the flanks and in the center and by 24 LCI–G gunboats to give close-in support fire. Battleships, cruisers, and destroyers were only 1250 yards offshore, to deliver direct fire on the beaches and hill lines in the interior. The escort carriers had launched 72 planes which made repeated runs along the beaches, firing rockets and machine guns into any likely target. Despite all this, as with most plans for amphibious operations, the activity did not conform to theory. The first landing was made on Red Beach 2 at 0844 and within minutes the Marines were on every beach. But there were serious mistakes, particularly in the 2nd Division area where two battalions were landed too far north on the wrong beaches, causing dangerous congestion. The later scheduled waves were late in getting to shore, which meant that the Marines of the first wave, faced with very heavy Japanese resistance, were pinned down. The most serious flaw in the planning concerned the LVTs. It was believed that these could charge up from the beach and deposit the troops inland on the higher ground, facilitating a quick movement toward the 0–1 line which had been drawn on the maps roughly along the 100-foot contour lines. Although the LVTs were able in some places to penetrate inland for a few hundred yards, most were stopped on the beaches by the shore conditions and the very heavy Japanese artillery and mortar fire. This caused the Marines to leave many LVTs on the beaches, with some men having to wade ashore. They were forced into a desperate fight from the time the LVTs grounded.[2]

The major reason the plans so meticulously drawn up by Corps and the divisions did not work was the failure of the naval and air bombardment to silence the Japanese artillery. Despite the lessons of Tarawa, Kwajalein, and Eniwetok, the Navy and Marine Corps senior planners continued to believe that direct naval gunfire could destroy dispersed and well-concealed artillery, mortar, and machine-gun positions. It would be hard for an observer watching the battleships firing hundreds of rounds of 14″ and 16″ shells backed by cruisers and destroyers firing at point-blank range for days at a small land mass to believe that anyone could survive such a torrent of steel. Yet the Japanese did survive it. General Saito had moved some of his artillery to the reverse slopes of the hills, hid the rest in caves or valleys, and used excellent camouflage for them and his mortars and machine guns. Although expecting the main landings to be from Magicienne Bay, the Japanese commander had not neglected the western areas. There were pillboxes, interlacing trenches, mortar and machine gun positions facing the beaches. The Japanese had located these to cover specific areas and had them already zeroed in. Afetna Point to the north and Agingan Point on the south flank of the 4th Marine Division were particularly bothersome, since from there enfilading fire of all types could be brought to bear on the Marines.[3] Farther back along the hill lines, as far away as Magicienne Bay, the bulk of the Japanese 75mm and 105mm guns had survived the naval and air bombardment, and within minutes of the landings were pumping round after round into the Marines on the beaches. Even artillery sited on the north end of Tinian went into action against the southern beaches. Some naval vessels, including the battleship *Tennessee,* were hit by Japanese gunners on Saipan and Tinian. Naval support for the Marines on D day was also handicapped because many of the shore fire control parties' radios had either been lost or had become waterlogged and were useless. During the most crucial hours of the invasion, the Navy was thus reduced to firing its big guns blindly, without benefit of adjustment at real or imagined targets.[4]

The concentrated Japanese fire pinned down some of the Marines in the south on the beaches until after mid-morning. By 1000 the First Battalion of the 25th Marines had only advanced a few yards inland. The only effective close-in fire support the 4th Division received was from the Army's 708th Amphibious Tank Battalion. Two Japanese field pieces—on the high ground directly in front and their fixed defenses on Agingan Point—were the main reasons the extreme right of the Marines' line could not advance. It was easier for other units of the 25th on Yellow Beach, since some of the LVTs had carried the Marines over 500 yards inland. The division was hampered because of the lack of tank support. The fourteen tanks of one medium company were landed on the wrong beach and the other companies had sustained heavy losses. By

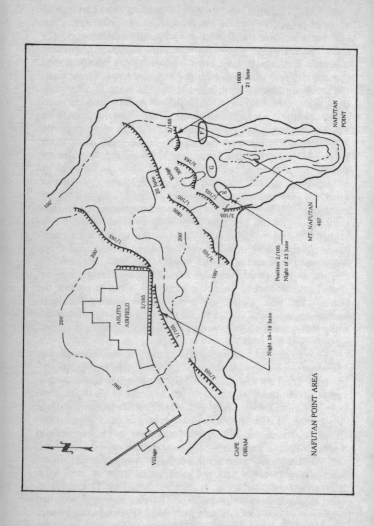

NAFUTAN POINT AREA

noon, however, the ten tanks of Company A had come to the assistance of the riflemen attacking Agingan Point. This Japanese redoubt fell to the 25th Marines by midafternoon.

The companies of the 3rd Battalion, 23rd Marines who landed on Blue Beaches met difficulties of a different kind. Those assaulting Charan Kanoa found little opposition in the town itself, but upon moving forward near the 0–1 line they were brought under accurate Japanese artillery fire that halted their advance. The 2nd Battalion of the 23rd, landing in the middle of Blue Beach 2, found, instead of the expected even gradient up from the beach, a vertical ridge five feet high or more. Once this difficulty had been surmounted, they ran into a swampy area which channeled all support vehicles onto the main Aslito Road. The regiment's reserve battalion was ordered in before midday for mopping up bypassed Japanese and providing security for the left flank of the engaged units. It too was put into the line later in the day.[5]

The situation confronting the 2nd Division immediately on landing was not much better than in the south. The initial mistake of landing the 2nd Battalion of the 8th Marines on the wrong beach would not be corrected until later in the day, when they moved to the correct one. The 6th Marines on the extreme left on Red Beach 2 could only push forward a few dozen yards to the coastal road. Here they met a counterattack from the north, combined with the accurate fire of a Japanese tank that had at first been believed to be abandoned. Exploding shells from LSTs hit by Japanese artillery posed a further hazard to the dug-in Marines. At 1000 the Regimental Commander committed his reserve battalion and later in the day, with the aid of tanks which had run the gauntlet of Japanese fire, the 6th Marines advanced about 800 yards toward the 0–1 line. Roughly the same progress was made by the 8th Marines, who found their way blocked by the swamps around Lake Susupe.[6]

By nightfall of D day all three regiments of the 4th Marine Division were ashore, as well as all their artillery, and more than half of the medium tanks were in operating condition. The 2nd Division had landed all but one regiment and had two of its five artillery battalions behind its narrow beachhead. As they settled in for the inevitable Japanese night attacks, the

Marines' situation was far from desperate, but it was hardly what Turner and H. M. Smith had planned. The Marines had reached the 0–1 line only on the flanks of the attack. Elsewhere they were only about halfway to this first day's objective. There was also a potentially dangerous gap approximately 200 yards wide between the flanks of the 2nd and 4th Divisions. The attackers had paid dearly for these advances. Although no accurate count was made at the time, it is estimated that the two divisions had taken over 2000 casualties.[7]

General Saito, still apparently not convinced that he was facing all the attacking forces, held back the bulk of his troops from attacking during the night of D day. In retrospect, it appears that had he made a concerted attack that evening with tanks and infantry directed toward the gap between the Marine divisions, he might have achieved his objective of "defeating the enemy" on the beaches. However, he did not do so, being content with uncoordinated counterattacks during the night. The most serious of these was against the left flank of the 6th Marines. The attack began at 0300 of 16 June and continued for almost two hours. The Marine lines were penetrated a number of times and there was close-in and hand-to-hand fighting in places. The Navy supported the defenders with star shells and direct fire; the line held and the Japanese survivors eventually retreated. The next morning a count revealed that over 700 Japanese had been killed in this fierce but abortive attack.

Although still far behind the optimistic forecasts made before the invasion, the position of the Marines on D + 1 had improved dramatically. Corps' plan for the second day was to have the 2nd Division act as the hinge point of a pivoting action, with the 4th Division making the greater penetration south and east. In carrying out this plan, the 8th Marines made their way to Afetna Point and captured it in a series of close-in fights with the Japanese. The capture of Afetna was especially crucial, since the mortars and machine guns located there had from the beginning laid down devastating enfilade fire on the northern Red and Green Beaches, as well as the boat passage through the reef. After clearing the Point, the 8th Marines pushed south to the pier at Charan Kanoa, the boundary between the two divisions. Thus, just before noon, the dangerous gap had been closed. Meanwhile, the 4th Division had begun its swing toward the east against heavy opposition. Japanese artillery was very effective in slowing down the Marines' advance. The Japanese gave ground grudgingly despite the air, tank, and artillery support for the Marines, which was far more effective than on the previous day. By midafternoon, the 3rd and 4th Battalions of the 10th Marines had landed their 105mm howitzers and, by dark, advance elements of General Harper's Corps artillery, the Army's 419th and 420th Field Artillery Groups, and 225th and 531st Field Artillery Battalions were in place. Despite the theoretical edge in guns, some of the units took a battering from the well-placed Japanese field pieces. One Marine Artillery Battalion suffered fifty-eight casualties during the early morning; one of its batteries was reduced to only two serviceable guns.[8] As more guns were brought into action and those not too severely damaged were repaired, a large part of their task all day long was counterbattery fire.

By the close of D + 1, it was obvious that the Marines were not going to be dislodged. Supplies of all types were moving onto the beaches and most of the artillery and tanks were in action. Although the 0–1 line had not been reached, the beachhead had been expanded to a depth of 2000 yards in places and the troublesome Japanese defenses at Afetna and Agingan Points had been taken. Advance elements of Corps Headquarters landed in the late afternoon and selected the Command Post in Charan Kanoa from which Corps would operate during the entire campaign. The plan was for H. M. Smith and the rest of the staff to transfer from the ships on the following day. The day's gains were costly; the Marines took 1500 casualties.[9]

General Saito, having lost his best opportunity to drive the Americans back into the sea, had finally decided on D + 1 that his troops in the west were facing the main opposition. He then planned a massive, combined infantry-tank attack directed at the lines of the 2nd Marine Division. Fortunately for the Marines, Saito's orders were confusing to his subordinates; there were no clearly defined objectives. He had initially planned to launch this attack at 1700 on 16 June when there would still be two hours of light. He also believed that the

Marines would be caught just digging in for the night. Here his intelligence was faulty, since the 2nd Division units had been in a holding position for most of the afternoon. The Japanese attack was not launched until 0300 the next morning. Even more fortunate for the Marines was the low state of Japanese expertise in infantry-tank-attacks and the fact that Japanese tanks were woefully inadequate by comparison even to American light tanks.

The attack began with 44 tanks advancing directly toward the 1st Battalion of the 6th Marines. Some of the infantry rode the tanks, while others followed behind. Many of the tanks were unbuttoned, the commanders standing in the turrets presumably to see better in the darkness. When alerted, the Marines requested illumination from the Navy, which responded with a continuous barrage of star shells. Then the 75mm pack howitzers and 37mm anti-tank weapons and bazookas attacked the advancing Japanese. Although a few tanks broached the lines before they were destroyed, most were knocked out before they reached the Marines. Because of the darkness and confusion, there was never an accurate count of the numbers of Japanese tanks knocked out. The estimates vary from twenty-four to thirty-one out of an original complement of forty-four. Saito's major counter-thrust had failed miserably.[10]

While the desperate fighting for the beaches was in progress, another problem of major proportions was confronting Admiral Spruance. Admiral Ozawa and the Mobile Fleet, comprising almost 90 percent of Japan's sea power, had left its base at Tawi-Tawi in the Sulu Sea on 13 June. As it made its way through the Philippine channel, it was shadowed by U. S. submarines. These fixes relayed to Spruance indicated that Ozawa might be in a position by the evening of the 17th to launch an attack against him. Due to the earlier air strikes, Japanese aircraft had made only a few runs at the spread out 5th Fleet and had inflicted only minor damage. It took little imagination to project what a large naval and air force could do to the transports and escort craft then engaged in one way or another in the Saipan operation. Spruance welcomed the opportunity to engage the main elements of the Japanese Navy, but he wanted to choose the area for that action. This meant that the 5th Fleet had to move rapidly toward the enemy, leaving the other, less powerful, fleet units to fend for themselves. The most vulnerable of these were commanded by Admiral Blandy, carrying the Army's 27th Infantry Division.

Spruance made his decisions during the night of D day, and on 16 June went on board the *Rocky Mount* to inform Turner and H. M. Smith. The most important decision was to commit the 27th Division immediately to the battle for Saipan and to postpone the proposed Guam invasion, originally set to begin the 18th. The troops initially planned for that assault would become the floating reserve for H. M. Smith's possible use on Saipan. Unloading of the ships would go on through 17 June, but, by then, all LSTs and transports not specifically needed would withdraw eastward while the escort carriers would continue to provide air cover.[11]

Spruance's orders were typically concise and logical. The postponement of the Guam attack, although opposed by Turner, would probably have been the proper decision even had the Japanese fleet not been approaching. The reports Spruance had received about the intensity of the fighting on the beaches indicated that the 27th Division could be profitably used to support the hard-pressed Marines. The threat from the Japanese merely made it necessary to commit the division earlier. In reporting the carrying out of Spruance's order, one of the foremost historians of the Pacific War has only this brief comment:

Shortly after noon Maj. Gen. Ralph C. Smith, USA, commanding the 27th Infantry Division whose transports were cruising well offshore, was ordered to prepare to land his 165th Regimental Combat Team. They began coming ashore in their own landing craft at dusk, and the movement continued all night.[12]

This brief description, echoed by other commentators, ignores the confusion and incompetence shown by some of the senior Naval and Marine officers during the afternoon and early evening of the 16th. These events highlight H. M. Smith's cavalier attitude toward the 27th Division and show that, even at this juncture, Corps Headquarters was behaving much as General Richardson had charged.

Unfortunately for the 27th Division, there was no early warning order indicating that the higher command planned to employ it that day. As late as 1225, Admiral Blandy had orders only to cruise far offshore with the division troops. Less than an hour later he was ordered to take his ships to the transport area and prepare to unload offshore on the Blue Beaches. Neither Admiral Turner nor H. M. Smith provided any further details concerning the proposed landing. Admiral Blandy and Ralph Smith were ordered to report to the command ship when they arrived in the area. The supposition was that they would be briefed and given more specific instructions. Gen. Ralph Smith then ordered Brig. Gen. Ogden Ross, the Assistant Division Commander, and Brig. Gen. Redmond Kernan to report to his ship and await further instructions upon his return from the conference. Each regimental commander in turn alerted the battalion commanders. Before any discussions with Turner or H. M. Smith had taken place, Blandy was notified to prepare to unload one RCT and the 106th Field Artillery Battalion. Ralph Smith then designated the 165th RCT as the unit to be landed. No orders to debark the units accompanied the alert. Ralph Smith presumed that such orders would await the conference to be held on the *Cambria.*

The transports arrived in the selected area about 6000 yards from shore at 1615 and soon after Gen. Ralph Smith and some of his staff accompanied Admiral Blandy to the command ship. Meanwhile, Col. Gerard Kelley, the Commander of the 165th, had conferred with his battalion commanders, and, following orders, left for Gen. Ralph Smith's ship, there to await further detailed instructions.[13] One of the officers of Ralph Smith's staff, Henry Ross, the Assistant G–3, recalled the visit to the *Cambria:*

We hit the anchorage and we went over to the flagship because we wanted to know a lot of the information that we should have— what beach do we land at? What do we do when we get there? Who do we report to? What's our mission; are there any guides? We were just told to get moving; Gen. Holland Smith greeted us with, "What the hell are you doing here?" These words I can hardly forget even in my old age. There was nothing that came out of this whole thing except a delay. We went back to the ship.[14]

Gen. Ralph Smith did not recall this rather startling statement of his Corps Commander, but has confirmed that he received no further details or written orders during the brief conference.

The Navy then began what can only be described as a comic opera performance with potentially tragic overtones. Most of the senior officers to be affected by a landing order were away from their commands. Gen. Ralph Smith was on the *Cambria*, General Ross and Colonel Kelley were on board the *Fremont* awaiting Ralph Smith's return, and the battalion commanders were aboard Kelley's transport, when at 1711 the order was given to debark the troops. After a hasty conference, General Ross and Colonel Kelley signaled orders to Kelley's executive officer, Lt. Col. Joseph Hart, to land the 165th on Blue Beach 1 in a column of battalions with the 2nd Battalion in the lead followed by the 1st and 3rd. Kelley had no choice but to stay where he was and wait for Gen. Ralph Smith's return, presumably with more specific orders. When he arrived, Smith had none. He accepted what had been done in his absence and formed a group of twelve men, headed by Gen. Ogden Ross, to proceed as quickly as possible to the beach before the 165th landed to establish an advance CP and make contact with the Marines. This group of officers spent five hours wandering about aimlessly trying to find a way into Blue Beach 1. Finally, at about 0115, they waded ashore.[15] Of that adventure, Henry Ross remembered later:

The flagship had sent us in and notified nobody. I'd like to have a thousand dollars for every time we had a brace of guns pointing down to our landing craft—"Who are you? What the hell are you doing here?" They [4th Marine Division] knew nothing nor did the Navy guard boats who stopped us—they had a brace of .50 calibers—they don't look good when they are pointing at you. It took us just hours to get in to the beach. Finally we got in—nobody there so we started wandering around. We split into three different groups trying to find somebody. Mike, the officer with me, and I finally bumped into a group of men and they asked,

"Who the hell are you and what are you doing here?" I said, "I'm looking for the Division Command Post," and he replied, "Who are you?" So I told him, and one said, "If you go any further you'll be in a Jap emplacement." He then said turn around and go to your left . . . By then we had a general idea of where Division HQ was and finally ran into it. There they gave us instructions. They had been told someone was coming but they had no men to spare.[16]

Jacob Herzog, the Assistant G–2, then a major, was also in the advance party and confirmed Ross's story. He added that at the 4th Marine Division CP they talked to the division commander, who indicated that the 165th should go in on the right of the line in order to later assault Aslito airfield. He recalled the almost total lack of preparation for receiving the 165th. There had been no liaison of any kind. They just said, "God we're glad you're coming in," and didn't do anything particular to help,[17] according to Herzog.

Most of the foul-up in the landing of the 165th was the fault of Turner, H. M. Smith, and their staffs. The planners of the 27th Division had spent agonizing weeks preparing 22 detailed plans to cover the most obvious landing situations. All this work was simply ignored—the Army units were literally thrown onto the beaches with little thought for their commitment. At the very least, Ralph Smith and his subordinates could have expected clear and concise orders from higher authority. Since it was apparent that the 165th would be attached to the 4th Marine Division, that unit's senior officers should have been given as much information as possible regarding landing sites and times of arrival. In exoneration of General Schmidt and his staff, they had clearly not received this information and could ill afford to expend time and men searching for Army units when they were expecting Japanese counterattacks. Had Schmidt been given more details, he undoubtedly could have provided a dozen or so guides without seriously impairing his division's capacity to fight. The Navy, which had ultimate responsibility for the near fiasco of the evening of the 16th, did not even alert their picket boats to expect the 165th. It is a miracle that a series of tragedies did not happen during the long transit from ship to shore.

That afternoon and evening had to have been a nightmare for the infantrymen who were on alert status for hours down in the holds of the transports. Long before the order to land had been given, they were soaking wet from the heat, the closeness of bodies, and nerves.[18] Even after Hart had begun to load his troops onto the boats at 1750, he had to wait until the battalion commanders could join their troops. Because of another series of errors, the 3rd Battalion commander did not reach his transport for hours, and then only to find that there were not enough landing craft to carry all of his unit. Those men of the battalion already loaded cruised around for the entire night and were not landed until midmorning of the following day. The boats circled the transports as darkness fell; then at about 2040 in a rough column they made for the beaches. The way into the beach was crowded with all types of vessels, with only the illumination from the fire of the close-in support ships. Furthermore, the coxswains had not been given detailed instruction and did not really know the route into the beach. These factors, combined with the challenges from guard ships, some of which rerouted the landing craft, meant that the riflemen of the 165th bounced around offshore for many hours. Some of the LVTs were forced to wait by the guard ships because of priority given to other craft carrying ammunition. Then there was artillery fire from the Japanese directed in an almost random fashion at the beach and the boats offshore. Bernard Ryan, then a company commander, recalls:

The shelling kept on, it is unbelievable how much shelling they did and hardly anybody got hit—nobody in our battalion. And as we began going around and getting separated, Dooley [2nd Bn. S–3] said, "Get a boat hook, slow the boats down and let's keep this battalion together—you keep your company together." We made three little circles and then we ran into O'Brien [Laurence O'Brien, C.O., Co. A, 1st Bn.] or someone from another battalion and he said, "This is getting crazy, the men are getting sick." I had gotten sick on every training mission and I was sick as hell by this time. On his own, Dooley said, "Let's go in!" Then we headed toward the picket boats, which had a flashing light toward the sea and we got these all hooked together. They let us by. The only trouble was the coxswain couldn't find an opening, but we scraped ashore and got out and found the Marines were having a counterattack. We did contact some Marines who told us to stay below the sand dunes. The tide was coming in and that meant we were in the water where the bulldozers were working [to pull the pallets ashore].[19]

Every unit commander could have reported similar problems. James Mahoney, the 1st Battalion Commander, did not get ashore until 0400 of the 17th. Paul Ryan, Bernard's brother and also a company commander, had his unit scattered up and down the beach adjacent to Charan Kanoa, hundreds of yards from the targeted beach areas. The first units to land had come in just before 2300. Almost immediately, Colonel Hart, who had been with this first wave, organized patrols to try to round up his command, which was scattered from the Green Beaches in the north to the Yellow Beaches in the south. These search patrols, confined to a narrow strip of beach, were in constant danger of being shot at not only by the Japanese but by Marines who didn't know who they were. Colonel Hart earned the nickname "Jumping Joe" that night for the many times he had to hit the deck while trying to collect his men.

Despite the countless difficulties, Hart did collect most of the men of the two assault battalions and moved them in single file to Yellow Beach 2 by 0500. There they were joined by Colonel Kelley, the Regimental commander. In conference with the 4th Marine Division staff, it was decided that the 165th would take over the extreme right of the line almost directly in front of Aslito airfield. The orders that had launched the 165th into the dismally organized adventure had initially put the regiment ashore to act primarily as a reserve force for the Marine units, which had taken very heavy casualties. Kelley discovered that the 4th Marine Division had plans to begin a general assault at 0730 and that the tired troops of the 165th were to take part in it, even though the men of the 1st and 2nd Battalions were still approximately 2500 yards away from their assigned positions and the proposed H hour was only about two hours away. Kelley had been warned by the 25th Marines' commander that traveling to the assigned area—over about one thousand yards of relatively open ground—would become very dangerous at daybreak, since the Japanese from their positions on the ridge line could zero in on the main east-west road, which bisected the area the Marines had to pass through. The regiment just barely made it past this area when the Japanese artillery opened up. Nevertheless, Kelley had his unit positioned for an attack toward Aslito airfield at the appointed time, with only a minor disruption from Japanese manning a pillbox at Agingan Point (believed to have been completely neutralized the day before).

The 165th relieved the Marines at 0740 and pushed forward across relatively open ground through a small village where they began to receive considerable small arms fire. There was some confusion over artillery support, which was not delivered until just before 1100. The two battalions then began the attack on the main ridge line west and south of the airfield. The attack failed because of the heavy artillery fire brought down on the troops from behind the ridge and from Nafutan Point. From their positions on the ridge, the Japanese could chart every movement made by the attacking troops across the cane fields. Kelley then reinforced his attacking companies and called for more artillery fire on the ridge. After fifteen minutes of this support fire from the 105th Field Artillery Battalion, the 1st Battalion and portions of the 2nd resumed the attack only to be repulsed once more. Later the 249th Field Artillery added its power to those units already firing on the ridge. The cruiser *Louisville* also moved into position to take the ridge under fire from the east. The ridge was pounded for almost two hours. The infantry then attacked again and had fought its way to the crest of the hill just before dark, with B Company of the 1st Battalion taking heavy casualties. The B Company commander decided he could not hold his position and began to pull back, which affected the other attacking companies. By nightfall, the 165th held the northern part of the ridge, while those units on the right had retired from the ridge to roughly the same positions they had held in the morning.

When the attack on the ridge resumed in the early morning of 18 June, the 165th was a much stronger unit than the day before. The 3rd Battalion had come ashore and was placed on the extreme right. There was much more artillery to be brought into action and tanks were now available to support the infantry. The entire regiment attacked at 0730 with twice the men it had on the 17th, only to find little opposition on the ridge line. Once the top had been secured, observers could see large numbers of Japanese retiring toward Nafutan Point. By 1000 the central and southern portions of Aslito airfield were controlled by the 165th while the Marines adjoining them held the rest. The Japanese did not put up a fight for the field, which was one of the main objectives of the Saipan invasion force. Only one wounded Japanese was found hiding in the control tower. Regimental lines were reformed and, in pursuance of Corps orders, began a direct push eastward toward Magicienne Bay. By the evening of 18 June they had reached nearly to the ocean. Only a few yards separated them from their objective when they encountered a different type of terrain—rocks, gullies, and coral formations leading to sheer cliffs approximately 300 yards ahead. This and the coming of night forced them to stop short. However, the next day a series of patrols encountered hardly any resistance and reached the beach line of Magicienne Bay, thus effectively cutting off the Japanese on Nafutan Point from the main elements of Saito's force to the north.[20]

The Marine units during this same period were still taking the brunt of the fighting and making only moderate advances against the Japanese. The 4th Marine Division units in the south adjacent to the 165th had moved to the 0–2 line by the evening of 17 June in that area immediately north of Aslito airfield. However, there had been no advance on the extreme left in the swamp terrain south and east of Lake Susupe. The next day the right wing elements of the division advanced along with the Army to within sight of Magicienne Bay. In the next two days, they would clear the region east of Lake Susupe, take vital Hill 500, and complete their turning movement to the north. The 2nd Marine Division, after reaching the 0–2 line on 17 June, was content to maintain that position against Japanese infiltration attacks, waiting for the 4th Division to complete its northward wheel. On the 20th of June, the Marines held a line across the island from the west coast directly eastward of Mt. Tipo Pale southwestward toward a point east of Hill 500 on the shore of Magicienne Bay. All the area south of that line had been captured, except the small area around Nafutan Point where the Japanese remnants of the southern region were being rooted out by Army troops.

During this period a number of important events not directly connected with the advance of the Marine and Army units were taking place. In the afternoon of 17 June Gen. Holland M. Smith came ashore with all of NTLF personnel not already there and established his CP at Charan Kanoa. Gen. Ralph Smith had come ashore earlier and established his CP. He had command of the casual troops and those of the 105th then in the process of landing, but presumably the 165th remained attached to the 4th Marine Division. Although Colonel Kelley and his regiment cooperated with the Marines, this appears to have been largely a paperwork type of command; General Schmidt and his staff were primarily concerned with the problems confronting the Marines in their own area of operations. The general orders for times and direction of advance came to the Army units directly from NTLF. For all practical purposes, Colonel Kelley was operating a separate command until the 165th was returned officially to Division. Colonel Kelley was left in limbo as to his exact status after Gen. Ralph Smith had landed. In his Operations Report, Kelley wrote:

On the morning of the 18th there existed considerable uncertainty as to the exact status of RCT 165. I was unable to determine (by telephone conversation with Hq. 4th Marine Division) whether I was still attached to the 4th Marine Division or had passed to the command of CG 27th Division. I had my S–3 call D–3, 4th Marine Division to inform that office of the progress of the attack and what I planned to do. This in view of the absence of formal orders from 4th Marine Division Headquarters. As I remember the report of my S–3, the D–3 (or assistant) had stated I was to do as I had been ordered (in connection with my proposed action). He later tempered his remarks when advised that I had received no orders and indicated that we might be under the direction of the CG of the 27th Division. Shortly after this Maj. Gen. Ralph Smith visited my CP and advised me that I should receive notice of my release from the Marines and reversion to the

27th Division. I did receive notice from the 27th Division but never received such orders from 4th Marine Division Headquarters.[21]

This example is indicative of the confused lines of communication between Corps and the Army units. Corps and the 4th Marine staff appeared unable or reluctant to give him a specific answer. Throughout the Saipan campaign, cooperation between Army and Marine units would be jeopardized by *ad hoc* arrangements when what was needed were specific directives from higher authority.

Early in the morning of 17 June, the 105th RCT commanded by Col. Leonard Bishop began to land on Blue Beach 1. There was no problem landing the troops of the 105th, but its support equipment was another matter. There was only one opening through the reef to this beach, vied for by hundreds of landing craft carrying various types of equipment. The LCMs and LCVPs loaded with the artillery, trucks, tanks, and ammunition were kept outside the reef for hours waiting their turn to unload their cargo directly on the beach. The congestion became so bad that at 1100 the Navy ordered that no further cargo be discharged from ships until the backlog had been reduced. Most of the regiment's equipment was still on board the USS *Cavalier* when this order was issued. Admiral Hill later suggested that somehow the failure to land most of the division's vehicles and communications equipment was the fault of the 27th Division officers in charge of the unloading.[22] This was not true; it was nobody's fault that only a finite amount could be moved through the narrow channel in the reef. No blame certainly can be attached to the Navy for ordering all ships to put to sea at 1700 because of an air raid threat. Admiral Spruance's fleet on the 18th had begun the decisive Battle of the Philippine Sea with Admiral Ozawa's Mobile Fleet. All ships were then ordered to stay away from Charan Kanoa until this action was completed. The *Cavalier* did not return until 25 June. Thus the 105th was forced to operate over a week with only a few of its own trucks and borrowed DUKWs to transport the needed food, water, and ammunition to the troops. Their communications network was an entirely inadequate and improvised system.[23] This lack of equipment, water, and rations certainly should have been taken into consideration by H. M. Smith and Corps staff when they evaluated the first week's performance of this regiment of the 27th Division.

The last battalion of the 105th came ashore shortly before dark on 17 June and proceeded to its bivouac area on the right flank of the division. After dark a message was received from NTLF ordering the 2nd Battalion to a reserve position in the rear of the 2nd Division to be used in case an emergency arose. Although the lateness of this order can be partially explained by the critical situations facing Corps staff on the 17th, its timing was typical of H. M. Smith's headquarters. In this case the late order only caused the battalion to make its reconnaissance and counter march through areas "full of snipers and pockets of enemy that had been bypassed by the Marine assault forces."[24] A few days later another late order from Corps would play a vital role in the decision to relieve the Commander of the 27th Division.

The next three days of action against the Japanese defenders of the Nafutan area not only describe what two of the regiments of the 27th were doing, but also illustrate the methodology of their advance—a good example of Army tactics as compared to those of the Marine Corps. Such differing opinions regarding how a strong point should be captured serve as a useful context for evaluating Colonel Lemp's oft-quoted statement that the 105th "manifested a certain amount of inertia" and "might be censured for its lack of spirit."[25] This statement is generally taken out of context to condemn the actions of all elements of the 27th during this period. Colonel Lemp was referring only to the action of two battalions on 21 June and certainly was not condemning even the 105th during the previous days. However, the Marines and particularly H. M. Smith were clearly dissatisfied with the slowness of the Army's advance despite H. M. Smith's statement that "shells are a hell of a lot cheaper than men, and we propose to reduce this thing [Nafutan] and save men and lives."[26] Nevertheless, the Army's method of taking a strong point was to use the maximum amount of firepower, flank it where possible, and, when time was not a major factor, to proceed slowly and methodically toward the points' capture.

All the units of the 105th were green troops. This was their first action and they were assigned one of the most difficult tasks—the reduction of Japanese defenses in the Nafutan area —immediately after the consolidation of the beachhead. Corps continued to underestimate Japanese strength in this region even after the *Banzai* attack of 26–27 June. Ralph Smith's headquarters at first agreed with higher headquarters that there were no more than 300 enemy troops there. After the first two days of fighting, Division became convinced that even after the casualties they had taken, there were at least 500 Japanese there. The ruggedness of the terrain and the improvised use the Japanese made of these natural features were also underestimated. Few representatives of Corps Headquarters ever visited this sector to check their *a priori* conclusions. When they did, it was generally to find fault with such items as fire discipline or the placement of a CP, or to weigh Army methods against those of the Corps to the disadvantage of the former. The NTLF Operations Report on the action at Nafutan hinted at some of the problems encountered by the Army units. It stated in part, after the attack of 20 June:

P.O.W. interrogation by the Division disclosed that many of the caves were so deep as to afford complete protection from gunfire. The Division reported that it found only a few dead Japs in the area it was occupying. What enemy remained in the Division's zone of action were rapidly being compressed down into the very narrow sector of NAFUTAN Point where extremely rough and jungle-like terrain slowed the advance of assault troops considerably.[27]

This same Operations Report revealed that the 165th had encountered a number of mined pillboxes and booby traps. They also had captured an 8″ mortar capable of firing a projectile weighing over thirty pounds. Another report on the same day revealed a Japanese field piece, probably a 5″ gun, firing on the advancing troops from a cave whose entrance could be sealed with moveable steel doors. Thus, considerably before H. M. Smith's complaint about the 27th's advance, some of his staff must have recognized the major reason for the slowness of movement.

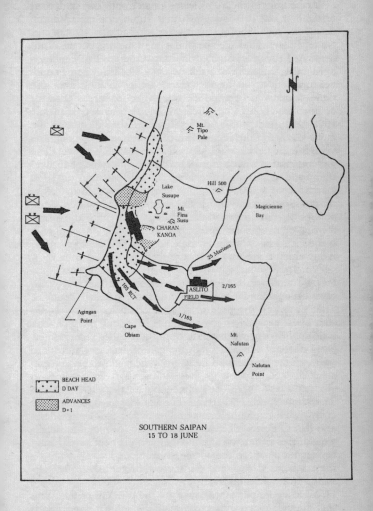

SOUTHERN SAIPAN
15 TO 18 JUNE

In preparation for the concerted attack with two regiments on the 19th, the two battalions of the 105th took their position on the right of the 165th with the 1st Battalion located just south of the airfield and the 2nd's line extending to the south coast. At 1400, the 105th began its first action, advancing eastward under the cover of artillery. They met little enemy opposition, mostly from troops apparently left behind after the main elements had retired eastward. The forward movement of both battalions was halted by Division at approximately 1600 because of the need to reorganize the line due to the rapid advance of the 165th. The 105th dug in for the night on a line roughly even with the eastern edge of the airfield. The forward motion was continued early in the morning of 19 June and made good progress until the 1st Battalion at 1030 reached Ridge 300. This ridge, which blocked further easy progress, ran roughly north and south with the highest elevation to the south. Beyond the ridge to the south and east was the rugged overgrown terrain of the Nafutan Point region. A and B Companies of the 1st Battalion reached the crest of the ridge without difficulty, but were then pinned down by accurate fire from bunkers and strong points beyond. Japanese dual purpose antiaircraft guns from well beyond the ridge also were brought into play. After a one and one-half hour fire fight, Company A retired to reform. Company B also retired after being exposed on the ridge line for a long time. Lt. Col. William O'Brien, the battalion commander, then received permission from Division to shift the axis of his attack and try to approach the Japanese positions from the north where the gradient allowed his units to have tank support. Preparatory to this new attack, there was a fifteen-minute airstrike and then a thirty-minute artillery barrage. The attacking company seemed to be making good progress backed by the tanks when darkness fell. O'Brien felt it better to retire to his point of departure for the night and continue the fight the next day. During the day the 165th to the northeast had done little but consolidate its position and send out patrols through the rough terrain near Magicienne Bay.

At a conference with his staff on the evening of the 19th, Gen. Ralph Smith decided to commit the 165th to the fight for Nafutan the next day. The 2nd and 3rd Battalions would push

Major General Ralph C. Smith 1945 (U.S. Army photo)

Portrait of Gen. Holland M. Smith

Makin Atoll, Gilbert Islands. Men of 2d Bn, 165th Inf. attacking Butaritari, Yellow Beach Two. (U.S. Army photo)

Makin Atoll. Japanese trenches dug outside their main defenses. (U.S. Army photo)

L–R: Lt. Gen. Holland M. Smith with Adm. C. W. Nimitz in back seat of jeep and Adm. King in front seat. Saipan. (U.S. Marine Corps photo)

Aboard an LCVP heading for shore. L–R: Brig. Gen. Kernan, Maj. Gen. Smith of the 27th Division, and his Chief of Staff, Col. Stubbens. Saipan. (U.S. Army photo)

southward and cooperate with the 1st Battalion of the 105th in renewing its drive from the west. He also decided to put the 1st Battalion of the 105th under the command of Colonel Kelley. This was no reflection upon Colonel Bishop, who would later be removed from command of the regiment by General Griner, Ralph Smith's replacement. Bishop was a diabetic who had concealed his condition from all but a few of his staff. The stress of commanding in combat combined with his disease would prove too much, and he would later collapse physically before his relief.

This decision to place one of his battalions under the control of the 165th's commander was believed necessary because the 105th Headquarters was functioning with hardly any communications equipment. Further, Kelley's CP, established in the control tower of Aslito airfield, overlooked the scene of action in the Nafutan region.[28] Col. Robert Hogaboom, Corps G–3, was one of the few members of H. M. Smith's staff to visit the Army units during this phase of the action. In his recollections, he was critical of the 27th Division, one of his points being that the Regimental CP was located 3000 yards from the fighting.[29] Kelley had selected the tower as his CP not only because of its construction, but because it provided him with an excellent overview of the countryside. He was in a better position to follow the course of events there than Colonel Bishop was at his CP.

The three-battalion advance toward Ridge 300 and Mt. Nafutan did not begin until 1200 on 20 June, since it was necessary to move many of the units of the 165th into new positions. The 3rd Battalion of the 165th was on the right, facing Ridge 300, while the 2nd Battalion had its line of advance blocked almost immediately by the nose of Mt. Nafutan. The 1st Battalion of the 105th was to advance perpendicular to the 165th over the same ground traversed the previous day. The regiment's 3rd Battalion had the relatively easy task of maintaining contact with the 1st on its left and moving forward along the southern coast line. The 3rd Battalion of the 165th initially advanced rapidly, but was then caught by heavy fire from the same sources which had halted the 105th the day before. Tanks were ordered up, but communication with them was very poor; twice the tankers became disoriented and fired into their own troops. Another general push forward in this area was tried after a long mortar and artillery barrage, but did not gain the high ground. At nightfall they dug in 100 yards short of the main defenses of Ridge 300. Meanwhile, the 2nd Battalion had also run into difficulty. The Japanese sited along the nose of Mt. Nafutan brought the infantry under fire as it crossed the open ground. Attempts to flank those positions proved fruitless, largely because of the dense undergrowth. The 3rd was likewise forced to be content with only marginal gains as darkness came on. The 1st Battalion of the 105th ran into the same defenses that stopped them the day before and they took up their positions at the western base of Ridge 300. At 2200 hours, the Japanese began a heavy mortar and artillery attack on the Army positions to mask the movement of more men and machine guns directly ahead of the 165th's obvious route of advance for 21 June.[30]

Despite the minimal gains made and the Japanese defenders' knowledge of how to use the rugged natural terrain to their advantage, Corps and Division Headquarters were optimistic that the attack planned for 21 June would be successful. The 106th RCT had landed the previous day and there was hope that the 105th's missing equipment would soon be landed. Gen. Ralph Smith wanted the Japanese and the Nafutan Point area either eliminated or contained so that he would have two RCTs available for action elsewhere. However, he was to be disappointed. Despite heroic actions of the officers and men of the attacking battalions, there was little to show for the expenditure of men and materials at the close of the day of 21 June. Perhaps the most striking action had been that of Colonel O'Brien, whose troops at midafternoon began to advance ostensibly with tanks in support. But the tanks were buttoned up and lost their direction, and, as on the day before, began firing into friendly troops. O'Brien ran through enemy fire, mounted the lead tank, banged on the turret with his .45 to get the driver's attention, straightened him out, and then directed the tank forward while still riding its turret. By nightfall all four battalions had advanced at most only a few hundred yards and the Japanese still held the high ground.[31]

In light of what happened to the 105th in this area a few days later, we should look carefully at the situation at the close of 21 June. Although the Japanese in the Nafutan area appeared to control the battle, in reality they were in a very desperate position. They could not obtain reinforcements or supplies and the artillery, mortar, and infantry attacks had greatly reduced their number. As would be the case later in the year at Peleliu, the defenders in this rugged area could buy time, but were ultimately doomed. It was simply a matter of the attackers exercising patience and viewing this entire region as under siege. The Japanese were not going anywhere; they could not escape. The one thing that should not have been done was to weaken the attacking forces to the extent that they could not operate efficiently in reducing the Japanese strong points. However, that is exactly what H. M. Smith did by his Operations Order 9–44, which was delivered to the 27th Division CP at 1215 on 21 June. Regarding this Operations Order, Ralph Smith later commented, "It was one of the few orders from NTLF during the entire operation which was delivered in time for proper action and dissemination to subordinates."[32] The order read in part, "One Infantry battalion, 27th Infantry Division (to be designated) will operate in the garrison area [Nafutan Point] . . ." The order did not specifically detach the 105th RCT from the 27th Division as H. M. Smith and General Erskine later claimed. There is not even a reference to the name of the regiment in Order 9–44 or in later communications from NTLF. Furthermore, the journal of the 105th for 21 and 22 June does not contain any record that this key order had ever been received from Corps.[33]

Granting that the NTLF staff in this crucial instance was even more confused than it normally was, a fundamental question still must be answered. Why did H. M. Smith and his staff believe that one battalion would be able to achieve what four had not been able to do in two days of fighting? There was the obvious need for more troops, if H. M. Smith was to carry out his plan to drive north from the line that had been established across the island by the two Marine divisions. At first, Corps' plan was to use only the Marines for this attack and hold elements of the 27th in reserve. Later this was changed and the newly arrived 106th and the 165th would be assigned the crucial center sector. Even with the lesser responsibility of providing a reserve force, it would have been necessary to disengage many of the 27th's units then operating in the Nafutan area. It must be remembered that the Marine divisions had sustained heavy casualties, most of which had occurred during their first two days ashore. It is understandable that NTLF would want as many men on the line as possible for the proposed attack on the Tapotchau-Magicienne Bay line. However, the decision to leave only one battalion to press the offensive against Nafutan was based on a series of incorrect assumptions. The first of these, abstracted from the actions of 20 June, was that Nafutan could be taken relatively easily. The second reason tied closely to the first was that the 27th Division units were dogging it; they were not advancing fast enough. It was assumed that if Ralph Smith and Bishop pushed their men in the right way, the task could be completed in a short time. Both of these assumptions, of course, were based on little knowledge of the situation. Very few men from Corps Headquarters had visited this part of the front; looking at their maps they could not imagine how difficult the terrain was in the Nafutan region. The popular prejudice of Marine officers with regard to Army units simply reinforced these conclusions.

The most important of the Corps' presumptions was its estimate of the enemy's strength and of the ability of the beleaguered Japanese to use the natural defenses of the territory to their fullest advantage. The following excerpt from one of Robert Sherrod's notebooks, written on 24 June, contrasts the different attitudes of H. M. and Ralph Smith on this point:

Said Smith [H. M.] to me: "Nafutan Point is still not cleaned up." "How many Japs are down there?" I asked Ralph Smith. "300, maybe 500." He [H. M.] smiled, "I said, 'You know damn well there are not 200'."[34]

Thus, from H. M. Smith's point of view, if there were not even 200 Japanese in the Nafutan area, then one battalion should be able to "mop them up" without difficulty. Of course this estimate of enemy strength was horribly wrong.

After the Point was eventually captured it was possible to determine fairly accurately the number of Japanese defenders. Japanese documents revealed that the 3rd Battalion, 89th Infantry was the base unit, which had been joined by elements of the 47th Independent Brigade, the 25th Anti-aircraft Regiment, and a mixed group that had retreated there after the fall of the airfield. The final recapitulation placed the total number of the enemy at Nafutan on 23 June at 1250 men. Over 350 Japanese would break through the line on the night of the 26th in a *banzai* charge and would be killed in the rear areas.[35] This number alone was nearly twice that believed by H. M. Smith to be facing the 105th. Herein lies the genesis of the idea that the 27th would not fight—later given wide dissemination by Robert Sherrod and *Time* magazine in reporting the supposed failure of elements of the 105th against a "handful" of Japanese.

Confronted with Corps' Operations Order 9–44 and still receiving reports of the hard fighting at Nafutan, the Chief of Staff of the 27th, Col. Albert Stebbins, at about 1430 on 21 June telephoned Colonel Hogaboom, G–3 of the NTLF, and informed him that he believed at least two battalions should be retained there. At 1700, Gen. Ralph Smith telephoned H. M. Smith and recommended that, in view of the difficulties of the terrain and Japanese resistance, the entire 105th RCT should be left in the Nafutan area to finish off the conquest. H. M. Smith reluctantly agreed, but with the stipulation that Colonel Bishop could use only two of the regiment's battalions; the third would be kept in reserve near Aslito airfield to be used if necessary to support the northward movement. By all accounts the telephone conversation between the two Smiths was cordial—there was no yelling or rancor. Written confirmation of the change was not received by the division until 0830 the next day. Since subsequent developments relating to orders given by Gen. Ralph Smith following his phone conversation formed a part of the charges made to Admiral Spruance by H. M. Smith against the Army commander, they will be considered in detail later. Here it need only be pointed out that no specific written orders for use of the battalions scheduled for the attack the next morning were received by Division Headquarters during the evening of the 21st. NTLF tended to operate with more spoken rather than written orders; Gen. Ralph Smith thus believed that his telephone conversation with H. M. Smith had given him authority to issue orders to his subordinate to carry out H. M. Smith's directive. H. M.

Smith had not even specified which battalion should go into reserve and which would be scheduled to attack the next morning. At no time during the telephone conversations, or later in the written directive, did H. M. Smith specify that the 105th had been taken from Ralph Smith's command and attached to Corps. At 2000, therefore, Ralph Smith issued orders to the 27th Infantry Division (less RCT 105) to move to an assembly area near Aslito Airfield, designated by an overlay, there to await orders in NTLF Reserve for operations either in the 2nd or 4th Marine Division areas. In a later key paragraph, the order stated:

RCT 105 (Reinf) will *hold present front line* facing NAFUTAN PT, with two Bns on the line and one Bn in Regtl Res. It will relieve elements of RCT 165 now on the present front line by 22 0630 June. The Bn in reserve will not be committed without authority of Div Cmdr. Reorganization of the present front line to be effected *not later than 22 1100 June and offensive operations against the enemy continued.* Res Bn will maintain anti-sniper patrols in vic of ASLITO AIRFIELD.[36]

These appear to be straightforward orders conveying to his regimental commanders the basic information communicated by H. M. Smith in the earlier phone conversation. Later, H. M. Smith and his Chief of Staff, Graves Erskine, would use these orders as one of their main charges against Ralph Smith. These charges in all probability were thought up at the last minute to justify Ralph Smith's relief. Aside from the main claim that Ralph Smith should not have issued orders to Corps reserve, the charges were essentially petty. H. M. Smith maintained that he had ordered offensive operations to continue at Nafutan and the Division Order had told the 105th to "hold." H. M. Smith believed that this not only was a clear contravention of his orders, but also indicated the lackadaisical manner in which the Army was conducting the Nafutan campaign. Despite H. M. Smith's statements, it now appears that if Ralph Smith's Field Orders 45–A had not been issued, Colonel Bishop would have received no order from higher headquarters to attack on the morning of 22 June.

The action on 22 June was initiated by the Japanese. The

commander of the 2nd Battalion of the 105th in the late afternoon of the previous day had been convinced that there was little resistance to his front and had his two assault companies dig in in the open rather than behind a small knoll to their rear. During the night the Japanese had brought up men and machine guns to the nose of Mt. Nafutan. Alerted, the men of the 105th were in the process of moving back when at daybreak the Japanese opened up on them. Company G was the hardest hit, having six men killed and twenty-one wounded in this action. This company had lost over half of its effectives in twenty-four hours. All cohesion on this front had been lost when the order to replace the 165th was passed down to the company level. The 2nd Battalion of the 105th was ordered to take over the two left battalion areas while the 3rd Battalion covered the two right battalion areas. The 1st Battalion had been designated as a reserve in compliance with H. M. Smith's order. This rearrangement meant that if each battalion held one company in reserve, they would have only two on the line, of which some were definitely understrength. Company G, for example, had only four officers and seventy-two men to replace what had been two companies which were relatively up to strength.[37] After shifting into their new positions, the two companies of the 2nd Battalion resumed their attack against the nose of Mt. Nafutan. Not surprisingly, they gained nothing.

The next day, 23 June, was little different from the previous day. However, Bishop had only one battalion, the 2nd, with which to operate. Companies F and G, after artillery preparation, assaulted the Japanese positions and made some slight gains, which were negated by an accident. The lack of radios, serious before the 105th was left at Nafutan, became critical afterward. Understrength, Company G held a front of 600 yards; the commander had to use field glasses to see what his flanks were doing. Without adequate communications equipment, the action in Nafutan had become even more of a small unit affair. On the 23rd, the 2nd Battalion had unknowingly moved into an area in which there was a large ammunition dump previously discovered by the 165th. Colonel O'Brien of the 165th had ordered the dump destroyed before his unit was ordered to move into reserve. He tried to warn the 2nd Battalion that his men were going to blow up the dump, but could not get through to them. The explosion, larger than had been imagined, came as a complete surprise to the 2nd Battalion. Six men were wounded, vehicles were destroyed, and the Battalion CP was knocked out. Later in the day, another accident wiped out the reestablished CP. A destroyer ostensibly standing offshore to help the troops fired by mistake into the CP area, killing eight and wounding thirty-two.[38]

The situation at Nafutan was definitely not good, since H. M. Smith's order cut the attacking force by over 60 percent. Ben Ryan, then a company commander of the 165th, recalled this changed situation with some bitterness:

The thing is we had them [the Japanese] like water in your hand. We had them up against it. The people who were attacking had patrols out. It was evening before we were asked to pull out of there. Ridiculous. You never refuse an order, but we knew that as soon as we pulled out the Japs would come down where we were and the next guys would have to do it all over again and they wouldn't have as many men. It's like opening your hands up and all the water runs out.[39]

Burdened with the planning for the northward push and with the conviction that there were only a few Japanese at Nafutan, H. M. Smith and his staff could not see the problems confronting the 105th. Gen. Ralph Smith, with two of his regiments in reserve, had not received any further definitive orders from NTLF when, at 1230 of 22 June, he left his own CP and met with Generals Watson and Schmidt, with whom he discussed the battle situation. He then talked with Col. Russell Ayers of his 106th, some elements of which had been used in mopping up areas to the rear of the 2nd Marine Division. Gen. Ralph Smith accompanied by his G–3, Colonel Sheldon, and Lt. Col. John Lemp, a War Department observer acting as assistant G–3, then visited H. M. Smith's headquarters some minutes after 1500. A staff conference was in progress. It was here that H. M. Smith, despite Ralph Smith's protests, reverted to his original plan of leaving only one battalion behind in the Nafutan area supported by a tank company. Note that neither he nor his chief of staff designated the battalion to be left, nor did he tell Ralph Smith that this unit was to be directly under NTLF control. After the conference, in a cordial exchange, H. M. Smith expressed to Ralph Smith the first hint of criticism of any unit of the 27th. He had earlier been complimentary about the actions of the 165th in taking Aslito Airfield. Now, after drastically reducing the force at Nafutan, he was surprisingly critical. General Ralph Smith later described this conversation thusly:

After the conference, Gen. Holland Smith spoke to me about the capture of Nafutan Point. Said he had been told the Commanding Officer, 105th Infantry, had stated he did not intend to force capture of Point but planned to "starve 'em out." Said he did not wish to be unreasonable but that Colonel Bishop (CO, 105th Infantry) must not be permitted to delay. If he couldn't do it, to send somebody who could.

I pointed out difficult terrain and Jap positions in caves and said rapid advance was impracticable if undue losses were to be avoided and if Japs were to be really cleaned out. I said that continuing pressure would be applied and that I thought the Point could be cleaned up in a couple of days more. I was sure Bishop had made no statement that the Japs were to be "starved out" rather than "driven out."[40]

Bishop later denied that he had ever made the statement attributed to him and that the officer who had reported this to H. M. Smith had misinterpreted his remarks. Whether or not he did, the statement was a fairly good summation of the plight of the Japanese, which would gradually become desperate as continuing attacks wore them down.

In retrospect, it is difficult to understand why H. M. Smith was upset with the course of events in the Nafutan area. He had only one understrength battalion committed there; the Japanese could not influence in any decisive way the outcome of his planned push north. H. M. Smith's chief of staff, although not guilty of words committing the Army units to a campaign of attrition, agreed in the main with Colonel Bishop. Gen. Ralph Smith, after his conversation with H. M. Smith, went to Erskine's office and there conferred with him about the details of the 27th's contribution to the northern offensive. He later reported the following:

I stated that I thought at least 500 Japs were still at Nafutan Point; while we had them pocketed, I doubted that they could be eliminated promptly if we diverted too much of our own forces away from that area. Erskine felt that, if necessary, we should merely contain them in the Nafutan area with a minimum of force and put all our strength to the north. The Japs in the Nafutan pocket could then be dealt with later. He thought the one battalion could hold them there.[41]

During this conference with Erskine on 22 June, Ralph Smith had pointed out that it was possible for the Japanese to break through the thinly held lines of the depleted battalions of the 105th. The next day Ralph Smith, most concerned that the reduction of the Nafutan Point area was being left to only one battalion, sent a message to H. M. Smith reminding him once again that this unit was not sufficiently strong to carry out H. M. Smith's wishes. He warned that a Japanese breakthrough of the thinly held lines was probable and asked that H. M. Smith alert the Seabees and Air Force personnel to take steps to provide security.[42] It should be stressed that Ralph Smith was correct. On the morning of 27 June, what he had warned about did occur.

The fighting at Nafutan from 24 to 26 June became repetitious. Units of the 105th probed the Japanese defenses for weaknesses and then made direct assaults. All of the fire power available to the Army there was used for each assault, either on the flanks of Ridge 300 or on the nose of Mt. Nafutan. This included tanks, mortars, and self-propelled guns. The Japanese counterattacked a number of times and there was hard hand-to-hand combat, particularly on 24 June. Corps' continuing complaints about the slowness of the 2nd Battalion to wind up what was considered a mopping up operation were likewise repetitious. In order to speed it up, H. M. Smith on 24 June made another decision. He appointed Col. Geoffrey M. O'Connell, the acting Base Commander, to take charge of the attack at Nafutan. Once again he was bringing in an Army officer with no prior experience with either the unit he was to command or the situation at the front, and demanding that the officer change what H. M. Smith perceived to be a bad situation. Fortunately, O'Connell was a reasonable, intelligent officer who recognized his limitations. Upon his arrival at Nafutan in the early morning of 25 June, he conferred with the battalion commander, Lieutenant Colonel Jensen. O'Connell's later comment that he walked the battalion through the rest of the campaign has been taken by some to mean that it was deficient and the opposition such that he could just go through the motions of command. Nothing could be farther from the truth. He was simply stating that, although officially in command, he did not try to be too obvious in exercising that position. His was rather a joint command with the regular battalion commander.

After a hasty survey of the situation, O'Connell managed to attach two batteries of the 751st AAA Gun Battalion with their 90mm guns and four 40mm guns. With the fire power backing them up, the 2nd Battalion attacked at 1000. By 1700, Ridge 300, the main position which had held up the Army's advance for a week, was taken. It was then discovered that originally the Japanese had twenty mutually supporting machine guns, fifty mortars, and ten 5″ dual purpose guns in these strong points along the ridges. Over 300 Japanese dead had been found on Ridge 300 and in adjacent valleys, although it was known that many more had been killed. Whenever possible, the Japanese retrieved their dead to conceal the actual losses suffered.[43]

The continuing pressure on the Japanese caused their commander, Captain Sasaki, to abandon Mt. Nafutan proper and concentrate his forces in the strong points along the two ridge lines. Even before this, on 23 June, Sasaki had conveyed to his subordinates a plan to escape from the ringing forces and to inflict as much damage as possible to Americans near Aslito Airfield. On the night of 26 June, he put this plan into effect. The terrain at Nafutan and the position of the units of the 105th dictated the details of the breakout. The units left to Colonel O'Connell simply did not have enough men to adequately cover the main front. At the time of the attempted breakout by the Japanese, O'Connell had only 556 officers and men to control the movements of the battered Japanese forces in the Nafutan area.[44] Sasaki divided his troops into three columns—one to advance along the east coast, another to move down the valley west of Nafutan's nose, and a third to work its way along the south coast before driving north. The movement began just before midnight. At about 0200 of 27 June, the Japanese struck the 2nd Battalion, killing four and wounding twenty before being beaten off. Other Japanese penetrated as far as Aslito Airfield, where they destroyed one plane and damaged another before being killed by service troops. At 0500 other Japanese attacked the supply dump of the 25th Marines. The major role in mopping up the scattered Japanese units was given to the 3rd Battalion of the 105th. Combined with Marines of the 25th Regiment, all stragglers had been taken care of by midday. In all, 367 Japanese were killed in this last desperate measure.[45]

The Japanese themselves had done what the troops of the 27th Division had not been able to get them to do; they had left their defensive positions and come out into the open where they could easily be killed. They had also done what Ralph Smith had feared and had warned about before he was relieved. They had slipped by the attacking troops in order to create confusion and havoc in the rear areas. Finally, at 1640 of 27 June, Nafutan Point was officially declared secure.

It is interesting to measure what Gen. H. M. Smith had to say about the Nafutan Point operation against what actually happened. In time, his opinion came to be the accepted version of the fighting there, as well as providing him with one of the excuses for relieving the commander of the 27th Division. He wrote:

The battalion from the 105th Infantry (which was subsequently awarded the Army's Distinguished Unit Citation for its performance on Saipan) failed to show the aggressiveness which its mission demanded, and it even permitted, on the night of June 26, a column of some 500 well-armed and well-organized Japanese, the last such on the Point, to march, in *column of twos,* right through the lines with hardly a shot fired. All these Japanese had to be killed before daybreak by Marine cannoneers and riflemen from the 14th and 25th Marines.[46]

The major reason Nafutan was not neutralized sooner was because H. M. Smith took away more than half of the assault troops. As anyone familiar with the Pacific War knows, the Japanese were masters of infiltration. To believe that they marched in parade-ground style in columns of two past sleeping Army troops is to do an injustice to both the Japanese and American infantrymen. By the time H. M. Smith wrote his book *Coral and Brass,* he obviously had come to agree with Ralph Smith on the numbers of Japanese present in the pocket. But in June 1944, he had claimed there were fewer than 200 men there.

One further rebuttal to H. M. Smith's statement concerns the repulsion of the Japanese attack. The Japanese were not eliminated by daybreak. Search patrols were still flushing the enemy all during the morning of the 27th. One may forgive H. M. Smith's pride in his Marines, but they were nonetheless not the only units involved in that day's actions. However, if one can assume that the feelings H. M. Smith expressed in his book over three years after the event were also present on 23 and 24 June, then the relief of Ralph Smith becomes more understandable.

If H. M. Smith was as perturbed over the poor performance of the Army units as his later actions suggest, then at first he concealed those feelings very well. Nothing in the evidence suggests that, prior to the 106th and 165th taking their positions in the northern attack, H. M. Smith on Saipan had ever decisively communicated his reservations about the 27th Division to its commander. Ralph Smith had no reason to suspect how deeply ingrained H. M. Smith's distrust of him and all units of his division was. However, after 24 June that antipathy became very obvious. Colonel O'Connell, who attended Corps conferences, reported the open contempt for the 27th Division expressed by members of the staff with "constant reference being made to one thousand Americans being held up by a handful of Japs." General Erskine was particularly blunt, remarking that "with a couple of companies of the Marine Reconnaissance Battalion I could overrun the area in half a day." After the *banzai* attack, he promised O'Connell that "if the Peninsula isn't taken today, a lot more people are going to lose their heads." On 27 June after the conference, the avuncular H. M. Smith, whose remarks about the 2nd Battalion had generally been condemnatory, called O'Connell to his headquarters, and as the Colonel recalled, stated in effect:

I do not wish to be unreasonable, but I want you to drive that battalion and if you can't take the whole area today at least show me substantial gain. I am in a peculiar position here. I have served with the Army in the last war; I have served in the War Department General Staff. I have many friends in the Army, yet here I am—confronted with the necessity of relieving Army commanders. I want you to do all in your power to prevent the necessity of removing more.[47]

H. M. Smith should not have been worried at that point. He should have known that a combination of the unrelenting attacks by the Army and Captain Sasaki's death wish had brought organized resistance at Nafutan to an end. Colonel O'Connell had done what was expected of him, although it is doubtful whether the 2nd Battalion achieved its goal any faster for him than it would have for its own commander. What did O'Connell think about his sudden elevation to combat commander, the sagacity of H. M. Smith, and the efficiency of the NTLF? Approximately two weeks after the fall of Nafutan, he wrote General Richardson his opinions. He stated:

I am convinced that neither General [H. M. Smith or Erskine] had any conception of the nature of the terrain, the degree that the Battalion was extended to cover the area, the stength of the Battalion or any details concerning the operation.[48]

From all available evidence, the snide and ultimately damaging statements by H. M. Smith and his staff were never directly voiced to Gen. Ralph Smith before his relief. That decision by H. M. Smith came as a complete surprise to the Army general, who still believed in the possibility of friendly cooperation between the services. Ralph Smith had expressed this earlier in a recording he made for broadcast the day after the capture of Aslito Airfield. He said:

It irritates me a little to read these stories back home because a soldier and a Marine get into a fight in a saloon that the relations between services are at cross-purposes. Nothing could be further from the truth out here in the field. In this landing we came in behind the Marines. Because of the conditions under which we were landing we had very little of our supplies ashore. . . . for the first part of the operation we were entirely dependent upon the Marines. And I want to take this opportunity to stress the very cordial feeling that exists between the outfits. One of the 165th's officers remarked to me this morning that Saipan had sealed the blood brotherhood between the services.[49]

Five days later, he would be relieved by the commander of the NTLF, opening a controversy that still troubles "the blood brotherhood."

8 | SAIPAN: THE RELIEF

Part I

ON THE DAY THAT GEN. RALPH SMITH WAS ORdered to move his two Regimental Combat Teams into the assembly areas preparatory to taking their position in the center of the line, the two Marine divisions were having difficulty carrying out the optimistic goals set for them by H. M. Smith and his staff. The order for that day specified that the 2nd Marine Division on the left and the 4th Marine Division on the right should advance to the 0–5 line by nightfall. In order to do this, both divisions would have to move ahead approximately 4000 yards across very difficult terrain. General Schmidt commanding the 4th Division realized the difficulty, perhaps even the impossibility, of reaching that goal, and established an intermediate one, a line approximately halfway to 0–5 which he designated as 0–4A. At 0600 his attack began with the 24th Marines on the right, the 25th on the left, and the 23rd in reserve. At the same time General Watson's division also attacked with all three regiments on the line. The 2nd on the extreme left along the western beaches could have advanced quickly against little opposition except that it was tied down by the slower advance of the 6th Marines on its right and the 8th Marines, who had the unenviable task of attacking the southern slopes of Mt. Tapotchau and the plateau to the east which the Army would later call Death Valley. The dividing line between the Marine divisions ran almost up the center of that depression.[1]

The 24th Marines on the far eastern part of the line ran almost immediately into terrain problems. In what would become almost a litany for all units attempting to push northward, the operations reports indicated that these would be as bothersome as Japanese resistance. The Marine historian of the campaign noted that the 24th faced broken terrain with many small valleys and declivities which made it difficult for units to keep in contact. He wrote, "At one moment adjacent units would be firmly tied in. At the next, one flanking unit would disappear and a gap would be created."[2] Despite such difficulties, the 24th Marines reached the 0–4A line by 1330, where they halted and waited for the 23rd Marines on their left to advance to this intermediate line. This reserve regiment had been committed just before noon to try to bridge the growing gap between the two original assault regiments. Like the 25th Marines earlier, the 23rd Marines found their forward progress slowed by Japanese resistance and the "troublesome terrain." Its advance was stopped approximately 200 yards south of the 0–4A line and the Marines dug in just before dark. The 25th Marines in the meantime had attacked at 0600 along a fairly narrow front against four roughly parallel ridges ahead of them. The first of these was taken within thirty minutes; the Marines then beat off a counterattack and killed ninety Japanese. By noon they had captured the second ridge and had thrown into the fight all the regiment's reserves. Increasing difficulty in maintaining flank contact with the 24th Marines necessitated Schmidt's commitment of the 23rd Marines. Further advance in the afternoon was halted by Japanese rifle and machine-gun fire from the eastern slope of the main north-south ridge line on their left and from a wooded area to their right front. By nightfall almost all units of the 4th Marine Division had reached General Schmidt's 0–4A line. However, they were over 2000 yards short of where Corps planners had intended them to be on the morning of 23 June.[3]

Most of the fighting in the 2nd Division's sector was in front of the 8th Marines, who were supposed to tie into the 4th

Division in an area in front of what was now called Death Valley. The terrain ahead of them, which would soon become the responsibility of the Army's 106th RCT, was described as "a nightmare of sheer cliffs and precipitous hills" where the "main challenge was to maintain contact and coordination" between units.[4] By 1300 the 8th Marines had reached a ridge line about 1200 yards from the peak of Mt. Tapotchau. Here they were brought under heavy enfilading fire from a hill located just before the entrance to Death Valley in the 4th Division area, as well as from in front, and the Marine's forward movement was halted. The 6th Marines had far less resistance but could not advance too rapidly if contact was to be maintained with the left flank of the 8th. The major gain, however, was in this sector where, against strong resistance, the crest of Mt. Tipo Pale was reached by midafternoon. The sheer cliffs on the north side of this mountain and hidden Japanese positions in front stopped further movement forward. By nightfall some of the day's gains were given up, as the right of the 2nd Division's line was bent back in order to keep contact with the 25th Marines. In order to do this, the 2nd Battalion of the 8th Marines when dug in faced almost due east.

From the fighting of 22 June, we learn that Corps appreciation of the difficulty of advancing in the central areas was faulty. Even before the 27th Division took over this portion of the line, H. M. Smith and his staff, tied to their poor maps at Charan Kanoa, could not envision how bad the terrain really was. Even though the early invasion had caught General Saito before he could complete his defenses, the Japanese were prepared to take every advantage offered by the hills, cliffs, caves, and foliage of central Saipan. The 0–5 line projected to be reached by the Marine divisions on 22 June would not be gained until four days later. Another fact, which would have been obvious to Corps had they had observers near the front lines, was the difficulty the Marine units had experienced in maintaining flank contact. It should not have surprised H. M. Smith that Army units also would find it hard to keep in touch with those next to them.

While the severe fighting on the 22nd was progressing, Corps was preparing to commit two regiments of the 27th to the drive northward. Just how this would be done was still unclear at the time Gen. Ralph Smith visited General Erskine's headquarters late in the afternoon, at approximately 1600. He found General Erskine concerned because all the 4th Division had been committed and the Marines were very tired. Erskine was nevertheless optimistic because he believed the Japanese were withdrawing and there appeared not to be too much opposition. It is difficult to see how he arrived at this conclusion, given the results of the action on 22 June. This optimism, however, carried over to Corps Operation Order 10–44, which later would give more specific instructions for the attack scheduled to begin at midmorning the next day. It called for not only the seizure of line 0–5, but quick advancement to 0–6, another line over 3000 yards to the north.[5] Ralph Smith later recalled his discussion with the NTLF Chief of Staff thusly:

I asked whether he had any plan for 27th Division for 23 June. He said he was considering employment of the 27th Division to relieve 4th Division. I said Division artillery must be advanced to enable the artillery battalions to support attack in area east and north of Tapotchau; also, right of Division must be covered in direction of Chacha village and Kagman Point since front was too wide for troops available to Division unless the right was protected. After some examination of terrain map, Erskine decided to pass 27th Division through left two regiments of 4th Marine Division, continuing right regiment 4th Marine Division in line to cover right flank of 27th Division. 27th Division artillery being under Corps control, I said it must get reconnaissance out at once for forward positions. Erskine agreed and while we were talking I had my G–3, Lieutenant Colonel Sheldon, phone Division artillery to send forward reconnaissance parties for new positions for 104th, 105th, and 106th Battalions, in general area of Target areas 144 and 1 '5, artillery to plan to move at daylight to forward positions. Colonel Lemp phoned to Division CP to have CO's 106th and 165th Infantry and Commanding General, Division Artillery, report at CP 27th Division for orders.[6]

Before General Smith left, Erskine sketched out the rough boundaries for the divisions on his map and the G–3 of the 27th Division made a quick overlay of this. Erskine then gave

Ralph Smith a draft operations order to begin work with and promised a more detailed final order later that evening. He also promised to forward a better overlay later, presumably at the same time he provided the final operations order. However, this quick sketch made at Headquarters would be the only data that Ralph Smith and his staff had for planning the next day's movements. The exact time the forward movement of the 27th Division was to start on 23 June was not firmly fixed. Erskine stated that the attack could be launched at 1000, but Ralph Smith objected, pointing to the lateness of the hour and the fact that there had been little time for reconnaissance by his units and the artillery had to be moved into position. As Ralph Smith recalled, "Erskine agreed it would be close, but said he would set the hour tentatively at 1000 and we could let him know if attack could not be made on time." The 27th's commander promised to "exert every effort" to meet the "tentative" time.[7] It was agreed that movement of the 27th toward relief of the Marine Division's center sector would begin at daylight of the next day, since it would be time-consuming and dangerous to try to move three miles into those positions during darkness. Guides were to be provided by the 4th Division for the relief of the Marines on line.

Gen. Ralph Smith arrived back at the Division CP at 1710 and outlined the situation to the Assistant Division Commander, Gen. Ogden Ross, the Chief of Staff, Colonel Stebbins, and the G–3, Lieutenant Colonel Sheldon. When Colonels Kelley and Ayers arrived at 1730 they were brought up to date on developments and a close study was made of the overlay and possible routes of advance to their new positions along the one available good road leading to the front. The Liaison Officer from the 4th Marine Division was reminded to have guides available at specific places by 0700 on 23 June. After the regimental commanders left, General Smith discussed in detail arrangements for supporting fire from Division artillery with his DIVARTY commander, General Kernan. The staff continued to work on details of the movement and planned attack for the next day while awaiting the orders from Corps which Erskine had promised earlier. At 2130, having received no such directive from NTLF, General Smith decided to send written orders to the regiments to confirm those oral instructions already given their commander. He used as the basis for that field order the draft from Corps which Erskine had given him earlier.[8] He also sent the message to the 105th confirming what was already known, that the 2nd Battalion was to assume responsibility for the entire Nafutan area. Later, H. M. Smith would charge Ralph Smith with infringing on NTLF prerogatives by issuing any order to the 105th, since it was in Corps reserve and should have received orders only from H. M. Smith. This is a disputed point. Ralph Smith and many of his staff claim that at no time prior to 23 June were they informed that the 105th had been taken over by Corps. Indeed, Ralph Smith was guilty of issuing an order to a unit not yet under his command. However, this was to the 106th, not the 105th. He had assumed in his discussions of the afternoon that this regiment would be immediately released to him, since it was planned for him to use it at 0700 the next morning. Presumably, this point should have been covered in the definitive NTLF order promised by Erskine.[9] That order from Corps was not delivered to the Division CP until just shortly before midnight, and Ralph Smith learned that the 106th would not be released by Corps until 0600. The NTLF message certainly arrived very late, if H. M. Smith genuinely expected the 27th to begin implementing it at dawn. Except for slight differences in wording with regard to Nafutan Point, the NTLF Order was the same as Division's Field Order No. 46 dispatched to the regiments two hours before. The final NTLF Operations Order had filled in the name and number of the battalion selected by Ralph Smith for action at Nafutan and had inserted the words "at daylight" to indicate when that battalion, the 2nd Battalion of the 105th, should begin its assault. When this change was noticed at the 27th Division CP, attempts were made, without success, to contact the 2nd Battalion commander. One should keep in mind the sad state of the 105th's communications equipment, and the fact that the battalion could probably not have initiated action "at daylight" since it was necessary for the understrength companies of the 2nd Battalion to take up new positions, which could only be done during daylight.

If Ralph Smith's actions and those of the 27th Division staff on this evening are to be measured by that of the staff of

NTLF, then the Army should not be faulted. Smith had waited almost five and one-half hours for Corps to act, but the promised Operations Order had not come. If the various units of his division were not to operate totally on the basis of the discussions held at his CP, then he believed a Division Field Order had to be issued. The staff at Corps Headquarters had been negligent in confirming in writing within a reasonable time what was expected of the Army units on 23 June—yet another example of how the Corps operated. Erskine admitted later that he liked to operate with a minimum amount of written instructions, relying on generalized oral directives and allowing the division commanders the greatest discretion in carrying them out. Erskine confirmed his abbreviated method when he later recalled:

I used to issue abbreviated orders; no use going back and getting it mimeographed and writing an order for the next day that would be three inches thick . . . you had the basic order: all you had to do in this particular case was "continue the attack, no change in boundary, artillery support will be this and that, gunfire support will be so much . . ."[10]

He then indicated how General Griner, who replaced Jarman, reacted to the first such order he had received from Corps. He remembered:

The first time Greiner [sic] got one of these orders—and sometimes we used to write on a page or a page and a half—he called me up and said he didn't understand the orders. I said, "What is it you don't understand?" He said, "You said to continue the attack, do you know where you are now?" I said, "Well, just go North, I don't give a goddamn, and you can go just as fast as you want." And we went over each item over the telephone. He said he's never seen an order like that. I said, "Well, I graduated from the same school you did, and I know how you liked to put all those commas and periods and so forth in there, and frequently put in question marks. There are no question marks around here. You got your objective, go get it. If there is anything else you want to know about this attack tomorrow morning, you call me on the telephone."[11]

With this understanding, the technical charges leveled against Ralph Smith by H. M. Smith and Erskine as reasons for his removal become doubly ludicrous. One last point should be noted with regard to the 105th at Nafutan. If, as H. M. Smith claimed later, that unit was Corps responsibility, then Corps should have been in direct contact with the unit commander. Any failures in this area after 22 June had to be the direct fault of Corps. Corps had done nothing to convey instructions to the 105th before midnight. If Ralph Smith had not issued his order earlier that evening, no action would likely have been taken at Nafutan the next day.

Other observers have criticized H. M. Smith's and Erskine's plan of attack, based partially as it was on continuing ignorance of the main land features of central Saipan, the locus of General Saito's defense. As is apparent now, and was known by some Marine and Army senior officers at the time, the main Japanese defense positions were based on the hills, valleys, and cliffs between Chacha Village and Mt. Tapotchau. Corps' plan was to attack directly at that strength and force a passage northward. With the major axis of the Japanese lines running north and south along the high ground, any troops attacking north would be under flanking as well as direct fire as long as the Japanese held the high ground. Some critics have suggested that the central area should have been isolated, with the main effort northward being along the west coastal plain, where there were few defenses and progress could have been rapid. Once the Tapotchau-Purple Heart area was sealed off, the escape route to the north could have been blocked and the Japanese hill defenses reduced slowly and methodically as was done later at Peleliu. Such a plan would have taken time, however, and H. M. Smith wanted the Saipan phase of the Marianas operation finished quickly so that the Tinian and Guam invasions could be launched. Another factor, of course, was the sanguine view of H. M. Smith and his staff that the Japanese were pretty thoroughly beaten and all that was needed was a forceful push to have the resistance in central Saipan collapse.

Suggestions of alternate—and perhaps more appropriate—strategies are useful in analyzing the battle for Saipan, despite their being generally after-the-fact conclusions. The reality, however, is that H. M. Smith and Erskine decided to press northward with the bulk of the three available divisions stretched across the island. One criticism of Corps plan is clearly quite valid. This was summed up succinctly by Henry Ross, then the Assistant G–3 of the 27th Division. He commented:

One sure way of getting washed out of Command and General Staff College was to split a hill mass in half. This is exactly what the Marine order called for. They split Mt. Tapotchau and that became the dividing line between the divisions on that side. That is utterly ridiculous but that was the way it was.[12]

One of the complaints the Marines leveled at the 106th on 23 June was that the Army unit did not maintain flank contact. Corps had placed the responsibility for contact with the eastern units. Seemingly unknown to Corps, Erskine had sketched lines on his overlay, placing the nearly sheer cliffs on the east slope of Mt. Tapotchau in the 106th's area. Even had all gone according to Corps' optimistic plan, it would still have been nearly impossible for the Army unit on the flat land to maintain continuous physical contact with the Marines on the top of the cliffs.

The dominant feature of the terrain confronting the Marine and Army units operating in the center of the line was Mt. Tapotchau. Its peak was over 1500 feet high, rising steeply from the coastal plain to the west. Although difficult terrain intervened, the mountain's summit could be reached along its ridge lines to the west and northwest. Most of the mountain was squarely in the zone of action of the 2nd Marine Division. The eastern side of the mountain, where the dividing lines between the divisions had been drawn, was a sheer cliff falling away approximately 600 feet to a plateau of open farmland. This plateau, later dubbed Death Valley, was approximately three-quarters of a mile wide at its greatest extremity, and was almost completely bare. The plateau was bordered on the east by a range of low-lying, interconnected hills of which none was over 150 feet high. These formed a long ridge line that began at the narrow southern end of the plateau at Love Hill and continued in a northeastern direction as the eastward limit of the plateau for almost a mile.

Saipan's few good roads were generally narrow, which made it difficult for needed supplies to reach the front lines. There was one road ganglion in the 27th's zone of action. One road running roughly east and west from Chacha Village ended at RJ561, south of Love Hill, where it met a main road through the plateau region linking the central areas to Tanapag Harbor. Another road junction near the entrance to Death Valley branched to the right and skirted the hill and ridge line to the east. There was good cover from RJ561 for about 400 yards northward, before the wide open spaces of the valley proper were reached.

The entire area between the north-south highway and the base of the Tapotchau cliffs was overgrown with scrub trees, about ten feet high, that had the appearance of a typical American willow swamp. On the east of the road, extending to the southern limits of the line of hills, were several small tree lines that looked much like a Midwestern apple orchard. At the northern limits of the vestibule is a slight rise in ground covered by a solid line of the same little scrub trees.[13]

After being alerted that their units would be put into the line the next morning, Colonels Kelley and Ayers made their plans for the attack, which was scheduled for 1000 on the 23rd. Because of the narrower front assigned to the 106th, Ayers decided to attack in columns of battalions with the 3rd Battalion in the lead. Kelley, on the other hand, decided upon a two battalion front with the 2nd under Lieutenant Colonel McDonough on the left tied into the flank of the 106th and the 1st commanded by Major Mahoney, responsible for advancing on the eastern slopes of the ridge line tied to a battalion of the 4th Marine Division, which held the line as far as Magicienne Bay. Kelley, who had sent patrols earlier through part of the area to be traversed in getting to the front line, did not make a personal reconnaissance because of the lateness of the hour. Ayers, however, who had arrived on Saipan only two days before, undertook a hasty reconnaissance of the projected routes of travel, until forced to turn back because of darkness.

There were also individual efforts to make early contact with the Marines who were being relieved. One such attempt was made by Bernard Ryan, commanding the reserve company of the 2nd Battalion. He recalled:

In the afternoon [22 June] Dooley, the S–3, said "Ryan, you are going to be in reserve so I want you to take my jeep, drive up there and try to contact Vandegrift [Bn. CO, 4th Marines] and find out what the situation is because we don't even have any maps that are accurate." I didn't get started until late 'cause the jeep was late; finally I got going but had to pull off the road for ammunition trucks and I never got to the Marines. We were going up the side of a hill and all of a sudden I realized I didn't know where we were and it was getting dark. So we came to a road and I told the driver to pull in there but turn the jeep around and face it downhill. We took turns sleeping. We were parked by a rock under some brush and early in the morning we heard noises like mess kits and looked down below us and there were Japanese there. I said to the driver, "Just let it roll," and we got down about a hundred yards, hid behind another rock. Some Marines jumped out from the side of the road and said, "Where in hell have you been?" I told them and one said, "Holy Christ, we were trying to get up there all day yesterday."[14]

Ryan told the Marines about the Japanese and continued his search for the Marine CP. He asked one sergeant where the front lines were and was told, "Shit, we had a counterattack last night, it was above there but this part of the line got veed in and I don't know where it is now." Ryan finally found Vandegrift's CP. He remembered:

I went in, he [Vandegrift] had been wounded slightly; I told him who I was and he sorta pushed me aside—he was busy pulling his troops out, they had been fighting all night. I did ask him what it was like up here and he said, "It's the toughest frigging place we've ever been Captain," and then he left and met Dooley further down the hill.[15]

James Mahoney, commanding officer of the 1st Battalion of the 165th, also recalled a similar type of confusion when in the early morning of 23 June he also found Vandegrift. Mahoney at first located him at the Regimental CP and found that he was "very brusque, had no time for me." After finishing in the Regimental CP, Vandegrift returned to his jeep, paying no attention to Mahoney, and drove off. Mahoney tried to follow in his own jeep but went straight ahead when he should have turned. He recalled then that "everything came down on us and we turned quickly back to the right, the only way you could go, and finally found his CP. He had left nobody to guide, he did not wait for me, and it was just pure luck we weren't killed out there."[16]

These personal vignettes illustrate a number of points. One is that the locations of the front lines on 23 June were not nearly as fixed as Corps believed them to be. The Marines were tired; they had been almost constantly engaged and had taken heavy casualties. Their officers knew what lay ahead—nothing as easy as had been imagined in Corps headquarters—and they wanted to get their men out. The relinquishing of their positions to the Army units was not that well planned and at least some of the Marine officers viewed the relatively fresh Army troops with ill-concealed hostility. As these stories suggest, the move of the 27th Division to the front was not achieved without numerous problems. Leaving their bivouac areas at daylight (0530), the infantrymen had to march over three miles uphill alongside the roads leading west and north. The main road leading north from Aslito Airfield was narrow and congested with supply traffic. At times, deep ditches on either side made movement difficult. Colonel McDonough's unit, the 2nd Battalion of the 165th, took a shortcut, veering left down a pathway toward a main road junction. The After Action Report of the 106th related what happened then:

An error on the part of the guides furnished by the 4th Mar. Div. resulted in the 165th Infantry and the 106th Infantry mingling columns on the same road, which made it impossible for the 3rd Battalion to arrive on its line of departure at such time to attack at KING hour. The original line of departure (the front line of the

4th Mar. Div.), as indicated the previous day, was found to be in enemy hands at the time of relief.[17]

Company K, the right flank company of the 106th, was the unit delayed over half an hour. It was not on line at 1000 when the attack north had been scheduled "tentatively" to begin by General Erskine. This gap in the line, however, did not delay the start of the day's action. Despite all the difficulties, units of the 27th began the attack as promised by Ralph Smith at 1000.

The critical problem relating to the question of the accuracy of maps being used by Corps and Division must be examined further. Henry Ross, the Division's Assistant S–3, even after forty years became angry when he talked about the maps available to Division. He recalled one instance where he had been on a reconnaissance with others and was frustrated because he "didn't believe we are where we say we are and where people say they are." He suggested that they "throw the damn map out and start all over again. What do we have W.P. [white phosphorus] for? Send a round out 1000 yards from where the troops are and find out where we are. Damn it, they wouldn't do it."[18] The NTLF staff had plotted a line on its position map late in the afternoon of 22 June. At 1000 the next day the Army units presumably would move from this line forward. According to the Army historian attached to the 27th Division, Gen. Ralph Smith, Major Mahoney of the 1st Battalion of the 165th, and a War Department observer, Colonel Lemp, this line on the situation map in H. M. Smith's headquarters was incorrect.[19] The Marine units that had occupied a ridge line just before the entrance to Death Valley had received heavy Japanese fire in the late afternoon and had pulled back to a safer position approximately 400 to 500 yards south. When the attacking companies of the 106th and the 2nd Battalion of the 165th relieved the Marines in this dangerous area, they found themselves a quarter of a mile behind where Corps said they were. Thus, at the close of the day's difficult fighting on 23 June, although the troops of the 27th had made some headway in all sectors, it appeared to H. M. Smith and his staff that there had been no advance whatsoever. This situation could have been easily rectified if, during the afternoon or evening of the 23rd, Corps had sent a staff member to visit Gen. Ralph Smith's headquarters. As will be seen, H. M. Smith, if it ever crossed his mind to do so, decided against this fundamental procedure and acted as if Corps fully understood the situation.

The fighting on the 23rd in the zone assigned to the 27th Division was too confused and complex to follow in any detail. It must be remembered that, although the Marines had provided guides for the Army, there had been little information exchanged. The Army's battalion and company commanders were called upon to attack in strange territory with poor maps and with little or no information about where the Japanese strong points were. Company K of the 106th, which was late in arriving on line because of the traffic tie-up, was simply led by the guides into the foxhole positions of the Marines who had already pulled out. Another point to keep in mind is the location of Division and Corps supporting artillery. Most of the guns available for support were located directly in the rear of the attacking Army units. Their lines of fire were in most cases almost parallel to the Japanese defense lines on the east side of Tapotchau and along Purple Heart Ridge. Artillery used during the day proved ineffective. The cave positions of the Japanese could be reached most effectively by moving the guns forward for a chance at direct perpendicular fire into these positions. Even when this was done, the Marine units on either side, particularly the 4th Division, complained that their advanced patrols were being hit by the covers. Thus, the army units were asked to advance through the wooded areas at the opening of the plateau onto a flat plain—where the Japanese held the high ground on either side and had carefully prepared artillery, mortar, and machine gun positions in caves. This was a situation roughly comparable to that of the Russians at Balaclava, when Lord Cardigan led his Light Brigade in its disastrous charge.

The first unit to move out at 1000 was Company L of the 106th, which had the unenviable position of holding the left of the 27th's line abutting upon Tapotchau's eastern cliffs. These were about 40 feet high at the jump-off point, rising to over 100 feet by the time the main plateau area was reached. These cliffs retreated to the left and formed a little cove-like

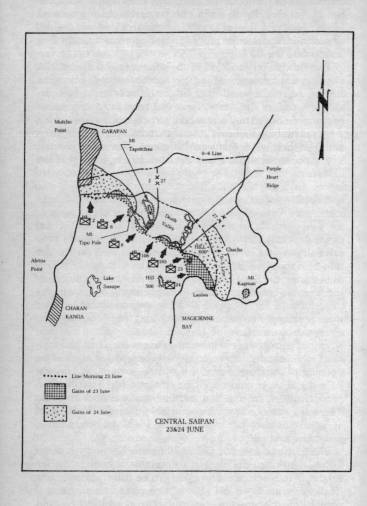

Line Morning 23 June

Gains of 23 June

Gains of 24 June

CENTRAL SAIPAN
23&24 JUNE

indentation in the mountain wall, later named Hell's Pocket. In front of this pocket was a circular park-like area covered with a grove of trees. In the midst of this area there was a 100-foot high rock about 20 yards wide at the top that was covered with vines. There were two caves in this rock, called Queen Rock by the Army, and the whole eastern face of Tapotchau was pockmarked with caves, each with some type of weapon hidden in it. Company L moved out on time and cautiously advanced toward Queen Rock without receiving any fire. But when the troops started across Hell's Pocket, just before 1100, the Japanese began a heavy mortar barrage—the start of a rain of fire on their sector that would continue throughout the day. One of the shells struck a Japanese ammunition dump near the advancing infantrymen. The resulting explosions, in addition to the harassing fire coming from the front, rear, and flanks, held up further advance until about 1400. After that the company commander was primarily concerned with making contact with Company K of the 106th on his right, a process that proved tedious and dangerous. It had just been completed when all the units of the 106th were halted by orders from the battalion commander.[20]

Company K of the 106th, through no fault of the commander, had been held up by traffic on the access roads and reached the line of departure a half-hour late, which had a domino effect upon all the units of the 165th to the right. Lieutenant Colonel McDonough, commander of the 2nd Battalion, was concerned about advancing across open ground without having his left flank secured. He received permission to hold up his advance until Company K arrived on line. On the extreme right of the 27th's line, Major Mahoney decided to wait for the 2nd Battalion to begin its attack before moving forward. Finally, at a few minutes before 1100, Company K began to advance through the dense scrub growth in front, supported by Company I. Almost immediately they were hit by mortar and small-arms fire. They discovered by chance that the Japanese had cut fire lanes through the brush. Anyone venturing into a fire lane was likely to be cut down from machine guns pre-set in the caves. The company commander brought up self-propelled guns to try to neutralize the Japanese positions. By moving forward slowly, K Company reached the point where the highway on its left entered the main part of the valley by 1500. The rest of the afternoon was devoted to making flank contact with Company L on its left. At 1715, the 2nd Battalion of the 106th was moved into position on the left of the 3rd Battalion units, which had borne the brunt of the day's fighting.[21]

The left elements of the 2nd Battalion of the 165th moved directly ahead at 1055, when it was clear that the flank was no longer exposed. The two assault companies advanced quickly to the tree line on the southern edge of Death Valley without drawing much fire. This quick movement once again opened the left flank, since K Company of the 106th was moving very slowly through the scrub. A patrol at 1230 reported K Company's position over 100 yards to the rear and moving slowly. Colonel Kelley thereupon ordered the 2nd Battalion to advance without regard to this open flank. After artillery preparation, the left platoons moved into the open at 1315 to be met immediately with devastating fire from the front and left flank. These units were immediately pinned down, as were those facing more directly upon the southern extremities of Purple Heart Ridge. The Japanese, under cover along the ridge, opened up. Colonel Kelley halted the attack and called for artillery fire against the cliff line on the west and Purple Heart Ridge. As already noted, artillery fire from such rear positions did little except raise the ire of the 23rd Marines advancing toward Kagman Point. The regiment's light tanks were busy supporting the 1st Battalion and self-propelled guns appeared to be nearly worthless, since it was difficult to identify the Japanese positions. The battalion's action only increased the volume of Japanese return mortar fire. Nevertheless, these guns from both cannon companies continued to work over the high ground on the flanks of the 27th until dark.

The 1st Battalion on the division's right wing also encountered heavy opposition. They had relieved the Marines along the Chacha road early in the morning and were prepared to attack at 1000. This was postponed because the 2nd Battalion was delayed and the general attack did not begin until 1055. However, Captain O'Brien of A Company had sent out two patrols earlier to locate Japanese positions that could cover this main terrain obstacle directly ahead of them, a small hill about 75 feet high called Hill Love. This hill was separated from the main part of Purple Heart Ridge by a little valley about 100 yards across that had been planted with sugar cane. O'Brien hoped to flank Hill Love on both sides and thus isolate it before trying a direct attack. The attempt to advance brought down heavy fire from all types of weapons concealed along the ridge line. An enemy round also struck one of their ammunition dumps in this area, which helped to pin down the entire company. By 1700, Company A had advanced to a point only twenty yards north of the base of Hill Love. Company C, located on the extreme right, was also brought under fire from the same positions as Company A. The Japanese could also interdict the road from their positions. The boundary of the 27th Division with the Marines ran along the slope of a hill. Company C not only tried to move ahead, but also tried to push down the Chacha road toward the town, although without success. One of their main problems concerned the Marine units on the right, which had also been taking fire from Purple Heart Ridge. By midafternoon the Marines debouched over the crest of the hill line dividing the divisions and, thus protected, proceeded eastward toward Kagman Point, breaking contact with Company C of the 1st Battalion of the 165th. Because of this move the Army had to be very careful not to fire into the Marine zone of action. Artillery support was denied Major Mahoney's troops; he received complaints from the Marines even for the rifle fire directed at Japanese plainly visible to his right front. Attempts to negate the Japanese positions along Purple Heart Ridge, particularly on the south slope of Hill Charlie across the small valley from Hill Love, with tanks and self-propelled guns proved fruitless. Mahoney ordered the two assault companies to dig in for the night along the north edge of Hill Love and ordered up the reserve company to a position along the south slope.[22]

Note what the Marine divisions on either side of the 27th Division were doing on 23 June. The Corps Operations Order for the 4th Marine Division was as usual very optimistic. The 23rd Marines of the left supposedly tied into the 27th and the 24th Marines on the right were to advance to an intermediate line 0–5A and then move to 0–6, which included the Kagman

Peninsula. These objectives were not reached, the Kagman area not being secured until 25 June. The 24th Marines moved rapidly along the rather flat coastal areas, meeting little resistance and being slowed only by the necessity of maintaining flank contact with the 23rd, which was having trouble taking Hill 600 directly in its path. There were not many Japanese defenders on the southern portion of the hill, but the gradient was difficult to climb. Using fire power and grenades, the 2nd Battalion had captured the summit of Hill 600 by noon. However, advance northward was held up by Japanese defenders along the north slope and by fire from the southeast slope of Purple Heart Ridge. The closer Marine units got to the Mt. Tapotchau–Purple Heart centrum, the more difficult it became for them to advance. If one compares the amount of territory captured by the 4th Marines in the vicinity of Hill 600 and that taken by units of the 27th, there is not too much disparity. H. M. Smith refused to face the fact that General Saito's main defenses lay directly ahead of the 27th Division and the flank units of the Marine divisions.[23]

The 2nd Marine Division was ordered by Corps to continue its forward movement to the 0–5 line. Unfortunately, that line was drawn approximately 100 yards north of Mt. Tapotchau, the main part of which lay directly ahead of the 8th and 29th Marines. Aircraft reconnaissance had shown that the only practical way to the top of the mountain was along a ridge near the right boundary of the division. But this could be undertaken only after taking a rocky cliff dominating it from the northwest. The advance toward the objectives moved forward slowly, held up by the concern of the 29th's commanding officer about his open right flank. The Army's 106th RCT had not made contact. After attempts to contact the left elements of the Army unit, which was pinned down in Hell's Pocket at this time, General Watson ordered the attack forward. He moved a reserve battalion in on the right, facing east to protect that exposed flank, and by midafternoon the rocky cliff had been captured. However, on the left, the 1st Battalion of the 8th Marines ran into a hornets' nest of about thirty Japanese with six machine guns dug into the walls of a ravine. Although all available weapons were directed at reducing this strong point, it was still in Japanese hands at dark. Once again, the rapid advance envisioned by Corps could not be achieved, even by Marine units, due to stubborn Japanese resistance in prepared positions in the challenging terrain near Mt. Tapotchau.[24]

Much would be made later of the 27th Division's failure to maintain physical contact with the Marine units. The difficulty of doing so in broken, hilly terrain has already been noted, when only Marine units held the much less rugged area south of the Chacha road. The Marine historian of the Saipan operation states that the Marine gains at Hill 600 "had been executed without benefit of contact with the 27th Division on the left" and therefore General Schmidt "ordered the 23rd to hold up its advance until Army elements tied in."[25] This leaves a false impression of responsibility. Corps had ordered that responsibility for maintaining flank contact lay with the units to the right. It was therefore the responsibility of the 4th Division to maintain contact. It is questionable whether on 23 June this was as important as H. M. Smith seemed to believe. But if he later complained (although erroneously) about his Marines taking fire from their exposed left flank, then it was the fault of the Marines, not the Army.

No such defense can be raised for the 27th Division not keeping contact with the 2nd Marine Division on their left. It was clearly the Army's responsibility to do this. H. M. Smith, however, would later make more of this failure than was required. As noted, the dividing line between the Army and Marine Divisions lay along the eastern cliff line of Mt. Tapotchau. At the time of the attack at 1000, Company L of the 3rd Battalion pushed forward and became involved with the Japanese to their front. At first, visual contact between the Marines on the high ground and the infantrymen was maintained, but it was lost before noon. The company commander of Company L did not have the men to hold his position and regain visual or physical contact with the Marines on the high ground above and to his left rear. Colonel Ayers should have been aware of this and should have moved one of his battalions not yet committed to this flank with the express purpose of regaining contact. In the late afternoon, a Marine patrol led by Major Chamberlin of the 8th Marines finally reached the CP of the 2nd Battalion, which had finally been moved into the line. Chamberlin suggested that an Army company be sent back with him and maintain the needed contact between the units. Major O'Hara, commander of the 2nd Battalion, considered the potential opposition facing him, and did not want to give up an entire company just to maintain liaison. While this discussion was going on, Gen. Ralph Smith arrived at the Battalion CP on an inspection tour of his front. After listening to the arguments of both officers, he agreed with the Marine officer and ordered Company F to accompany Chamberlin back toward the Marine areas. In light of H. M. Smith's later statements about what a danger this open flank posed to his Marines, it is well to turn again to the official Marine historian for the denouement of this affair. He wrote:

Although this company [Company F] was inserted in the line on the right flank to assist in protecting the exposed area, the situation otherwise was not materially improved, since the company *was then out of contact with the rest of the 27th Division. Company F remained on top of the cliff* for several days, performing all assigned missions in an excellent manner.[26]

The last major significant action of the first day's fighting for the 27th Division began at dusk. At 1930 the Japanese began a major attack down the valley with approximately two companies of infantry supported by six tanks and continuous mortar fire from the cliffs. The first tank broke through the Army lines, but the others were quickly knocked out. That one tank, however, did a great deal of damage since one of its shells landed in the middle of another Japanese ammunition dump near where the 3rd Battalion of the 106th was located. Although the tank was soon destroyed, its one lucky round caused a spectacular explosion that killed four men, wounded twenty-seven, and forced two companies of the 106th to pull back away from the explosions. By midnight the attackers had been driven off and the companies most directly affected had moved back to their earlier positions.[27]

Part II

Attention must now be focused on Corps Headquarters, and specifically on H. M. Smith, to determine his actions during the afternoon and evening of 23 June. In attempting this general reconstruction of events, one is hampered by much of what has been written in defense of Smith's decisions. A recent biography of H. M. Smith presents a picture of a good, perhaps even noble, man beset by troubles, the most serious being the lack of activity of the 27th Division and its meek commander who would do nothing to change the dilatory habits of its units. It is worth quoting this author's litany of H. M. Smith's problems. He wrote:

In addition to the failure of the 27th to attack on time and move forward, the battalion on Nafutan Point had again failed to show any gain. Combined with the immediate situation was the slow, halting, long extended advance on Nafutan Point, the chronic tardiness in beginning an advance, the frequency with which ground gained was given up at night, the uninspired leadership of battalion commanders who stayed behind the lines, the general lack of aggressiveness, the poor performance of the 106th Infantry on Eniwetok, the even poorer performance of the 165th on Makin, and the apparent refusal of Ralph Smith to remove the inefficient officers responsible.[28]

One might be tempted to dismiss the above paragraph as nonsense. However, to do the author justice, he has probably recreated reasonably well from H. M. Smith's dispatches, letters, and publications what was going through the Marine commander's mind at the time. Therefore, each of these statements should be examined carefully and measured against other evidence not tainted by H. M. Smith's prejudices.

The charge that the 27th Division did not move forward "on time" has already been dealt with. It should be noted here that the time of attack was set "tentatively" by General Erskine and that only one unit of the 27th was not in position, despite difficulties partially caused by Marine guides getting lost, to attack north on 23 June. It is well established that the front line of the 4th Marine Division as shown on the Corps situation map was incorrect, and that the 106th had to fight to move forward to that theoretical line. It has escaped the notice of most critics of the Army units in the Nafutan area that the one battalion of the 27th in action there was no longer Ralph Smith's responsibility. Even if H. M. Smith's charge against that unit of the 105th on 22 and 23 June was correct, it was his responsibility to correct it. He had reduced the number of men available for the capture of that area to only one battalion, which he placed directly under Corps' control. One of the charges later made against Ralph Smith was that on 21 June he had dared issue an order to the 105th to do what Corps had previously informed him would be the objective of that unit. What would H. M. Smith have done if Ralph Smith had dared remove the officers in charge of the Nafutan offensive and replace them with others? If the 2nd Battalion of the 105th was behaving poorly at Nafutan, it was H. M. Smith's responsibility, not Ralph Smith's, to correct it.

H. M. Smith's biographer, in his analysis, shifted his target from what was then happening on Saipan to Eniwetok and Makin. The performance of units of the 27th at these two atolls has already been detailed. It is questionable whether H. M. Smith could analyze the 27th's performance in the Gilberts and Marshalls objectively. However, any reference to earlier campaigns is irrelevant. The 27th and its commander should have been evaluated on the basis of its performance on Saipan. It is probably not beside the point here to investigate just how much control Ralph Smith exercised over the 27th prior to the attack of 23 June. The 165th upon landing was attached to the 4th Marine Division until 18 June. The 105th upon landing, with most of its equipment still at sea, remained under his control only from 17 to 21 June. The 106th, which when landed became Corps' reserve, was not returned to him until 0630 on the day it was to attack northward. Ralph Smith never commanded all three of the 27th's regiments together on Saipan. He thus had only a limited time to evaluate the performance of the division's officers under combat conditions. This, of course, included Colonel Ayers, who had been awarded the Navy Cross for his "performance" on Eniwetok.

H. M. Smith's state of mind on the afternoon in question

was, despite facts to the contrary, probably reasonably well captured by his biographer. He had decided to get rid of Ralph Smith by the time of his staff conference at midafternoon. If one believes the recollections of those involved in these deliberations, hardly a dissenting voice was raised. This included General Erskine, who claimed to have been a good friend of Ralph Smith and who had been one of Smith's students at Leavenworth. He recalled that he "always considered him [Ralph Smith] to be a very brilliant individual, particularly in the intelligence field." However, he didn't think he was a "field type soldier" and that Ralph Smith wasn't really the "tough son of a bitch" it took to command on the battlefield. He concluded that he "was sort of heartbroken over the final outcome of our association."[29] He had certainly given Ralph Smith time to prove himself as a "battlefield" leader. Less than twenty-four hours had passed from the time Erskine had provided Ralph Smith with the preliminary order and rough overlay of the area to be taken over by the 27th Division to the point of considering his removal. The only two senior Marine officers who would later go on record as questioning what H. M. Smith was about to do were John C. McQueen, then G–3 of V Amphibious Corps, who in an understatement commented that he thought the relief "a little premature," and his associate, Joseph Stewart, who was attached briefly to the 27th and found the officers and men of that unit to be "first rate."[30]

By late afternoon, H. M. Smith had decided that the cure for his troubles with the Army was to relieve Ralph Smith. One could reasonably ask if it would not have been proper to send one of his staff forward to the 27th Division CP and to have that officer survey the situation and discuss with Ralph Smith the presumed failures of his unit to live up to NTLF expectations. This would have been particularly appropriate in light of H. M. Smith's many previous statements about the need for senior commanders to get out in the field and see for themselves what was going on. It has been documented that Erskine also felt the same way. H. M. Smith's biographer has the Chief of Staff replying to anyone complaining of a lack of information with the question, "Have you been out to find out the answer yourself?" This question, if not answered in the affirmative, presumably would bring Erskine's wrath down upon the poor subordinate.[31] Why, then, did not this "friend" of Ralph Smith find out for himself if the charges against the 27th and its commander floating around NTLF headquarters that afternoon were correct? Corps, as had been its practice from the day that the 165th landed, continued to maintain its aloofness from the Army units.

Gen. Ralph Smith later confirmed the reluctance of the Corps staff to visit the Army front. He stated:

So far as I know during the period I was on Saipan Gen. Holland Smith's personal activities were limited to the beach and contact with the Navy. I recognized that as a Corps Commander he had many responsibilities that would hold him in this area and considered it entirely proper for him to depend on reports of staff officers as to conditions in front; however, I do not know of any staff officers from his headquarters who visited the front area except the aide who, on the afternoon of 24 June, came up to a position under mortar fire to deliver to me the order for my relief. I repeat, I did not see any of his staff officers, and I did, there at the time and since, inquire of my subordinates whether or not they had seen NT and LF staff officers and the answer has been negative.[32]

H. M. Smith was consistent in his behavior when he decided to send as his emissary to Ralph Smith the senior Army officer on Saipan, Maj. Gen. Sanderford Jarman.

General Jarman, who was the base commander designated to take command of the island after its capture, has been described by those who served under him as an extremely intelligent and capable officer. He was older than any of the other senior commanders on Saipan, having graduated from West Point in 1904. There is an odd tie between Ralph Smith, Erskine, and Jarman. Erskine had been one of Ralph Smith's students at Leavenworth; he had also been one of Jarman's. While attending Louisiana State University, Erskine had been encouraged by Jarman, who was then in charge of officer training, to enter the Marine Corps. Despite the many favorable comments that can be found about his character and intelligence, there was one thing General Jarman did not have—

experience at commanding a large body of troops in a combat situation. His duties throughout the war had all been in administrative positions. Even had he had combat experience, he was sadly handicapped with regard to the Saipan operation, having taken no part in the planning sessions for the invasion and not having been kept up to date with details of the assault and advance of the Marine and Army units. He had simply been preparing himself and his staff for the important but relatively mundane task of directing the administrative machinery once the island had been secured. He was removed from this behind-the-scene operation by the actions of H. M. Smith, who wanted to use Jarman as a cat's paw to deal with Ralph Smith.

After the midafternoon Corps staff conference attended by Jarman where the presumed problem of the 27th Division had been discussed, H. M. Smith requested that Jarman meet him at his quarters. There he unburdened himself to the Army general, relating all the problems he believed he had with the 27th Division and Ralph Smith. He was concerned with what he believed to be the failure of the 27th to keep pace with the flanking Marine divisions. H. M. Smith then asked Jarman for advice. In a letter to Lt. Gen. R. C. Richardson, Jarman stated that he told the Corps commander that he could give him no advice since he felt that it was not "up to me to make any recommendations or decisions for him." H. M. Smith went on to say that "If it was not an army division and there would be a great cry set up more or less of a political nature, he [H. M. Smith] would immediately relieve the division commander."[33] H. M. Smith then asked Jarman if he would go forward, examine the situation, talk to Ralph Smith, and perhaps get him to spur his division forward. There is no indication that Jarman demurred from this request, but he must have thought it curious since this was obviously a task that H. M. Smith or one of his staff should have undertaken.

That evening General Jarman visited the 27th Division CP and had a long conversation with Ralph Smith. He conveyed H. M. Smith's opinion that the 27th "was not carrying its full share." Jarman, in reporting this conference to General Richardson, then included a series of comments often quoted by

H. M. Smith's defenders to show that Ralph Smith agreed with Corps assessment of the situation. Jarman wrote:

He immediately replied that such was true; that he was in no way satisfied with what his regimental commanders had done during the day . . . He further indicated to me that he was going to be present tomorrow, 24 June with his division when it made its jump-off and he would personally see to it that the division went forward. . . . He thanked me for coming to see him and stated that if he didn't take his division forward tomorrow he should be relieved.[34]

During the long years of silence by Gen. Ralph Smith after his relief, this statement was allowed to stand as a relatively accurate account of the central core of the discussion. Gen. Ralph Smith, however, vehemently denies Jarman's version of this meeting. He claims that when he made his statements concerning the lack of progress of the 27th, he was not in any way condemning his men, but was reflecting upon the Japanese resistance being more tenacious than had been expected. He simply had said in passing that he wished they could have moved farther that day and hoped the division would do better the next day. His displeasure over the day's action was therefore significantly different from H. M. Smith's. The damning sentence that if he didn't move the 27th forward the next day he should be removed, was a misquotation. Knowing H. M. Smith from past experience in the Gilberts, he had actually told Jarman that if there was not a significant improvement in the situation the next day, "they'll [Corps] think I should be relieved."[35]

General Jarman returned to NTLF Headquarters and reported his conversation to H. M. Smith and stated that Ralph Smith ought to be given one more chance to move his units forward before any decision about his relief should be considered. Although General Jarman had been brought into the affair largely against his will and was on friendly terms with Ralph Smith, one should look carefully at this attempt to moderate H. M. Smith's opinion. It should be apparent that General Jarman knew almost nothing about the conditions at the front. What he had learned had come from his attendance at the Corps staff meeting and from being briefed by Ralph Smith. He visited Ralph Smith's CP in the evening, and thus had no chance to see for himself the terrain through which the 27th was attempting to move. Whether he intended it or not, his report, which was a reaction to H. M. Smith's near-paranoia, would later appear damaging to the Army.

It is difficult to know what was driving H. M. Smith the evening of the 23rd. Even had the 27th been guilty of his charges, a more rational approach would have been to view the Army units as inexperienced, since some of the officers and men were going into combat for the first time, and they were not Marines. Even had staff contact with the Army been minimal, he should have known from the 4th Marine Division reports that the terrain in the 27th's sector was difficult. The 4th Marine Division Operational Report for the 23rd was restrained when discussing its interaction with the Army units on its flank. The only comment that could have been taken as a negative was that "several times during the progress of the attack, troops on the low ground were pinned down by MG, mortar, and AT fire from the hills in the Army zone of action."[36] This was hardly news, since the 27th was being pinned down by fire coming from those same hills and H. M. Smith should have been aware of what his own Marines were reporting. But if he was, he chose to ignore it. By the evening of the 23rd he had worked himself up to a near frenzy. Robert Sherrod, the correspondent who had been accorded special treatment by H. M. Smith and who was a friend and later staunch defender of the Marine commander, wrote in his notebook that at 1700 on the 23rd, "Old Man, H. M. Smith, is upset as hell. Army won't fight."[37] Thus, even while the action was continuing in the 27th's sector, it is likely that H. M. Smith had made up his mind that the only way to correct what he perceived as a dangerous situation was simply to remove the offending commander.

Another question which should be raised here (and has not been addressed by other commentators on the Saipan controversy), is what role did General Erskine play in this drama? By his own admission he had a great deal of influence on H. M. Smith's decision to relieve his "good friend," Ralph Smith. Before the end of the war, Erskine became known in the

Corps as a commander who had absolutely no compunction about relieving subordinates. If he did not believe they were getting the job done he would remove them at "the drop of a hat." In the Oral History interview he gave long after the events on Saipan, this future commandant of the Marine Corps had a considerable amount to say. General Erskine's recall was sometimes faulty, but this is what he said:

Then after we'd gone up about halfway up the island we brought in the 27th Division. They landed; of course they had no opposition in landing, but once they got into position they just didn't fight. And I talked to Ralph about this on the telephone and also personally—I went down to his headquarters—and I said, "I have a hell of a goddam problem; I give the orders and they don't carry them out."[38]

The General in this passage was being vague. He did not state when or where these supposed infractions of his orders took place and what their consequences were. If the conversations took place, they obviously had to refer to the Nafutan Point situation. There is overwhelming evidence that the first time Corps became perturbed about the slowness of advance was on 21 June. The next day, the 105th was removed from Ralph Smith's authority and placed under Corps. Perhaps that explains why Erskine referred to the culprits who would not obey his commands as "they." If so, there was little Ralph Smith could do to help him out of the situation unless Corps wanted to return the 105th to his command.

General Erskine then went on to develop a conspiracy theory. He had earlier related that General Richardson had always been cool toward him and H. M. Smith's staff, not even being courteous. He had dismissed Richardson as just "an old hard-liner" who carried out "the theme song of the Army."[39] Erskine revealed in his interview his dark suspicions when he wrote:

I thought at the time—and I still have the feeling—that the Army had given him [Ralph Smith] some instructions to use his own mind to make up decisions rather than to take direct orders from us. In other words, I didn't think he was really pushing the way he should. And it wasn't in his own heart, but he was carrying out a plan which I blame Richardson for, to not get too much under the control of the Marines.[40]

In other words, on 23 June, the only day by which to judge Ralph Smith's performance in the northward push, the commander of the 27th Division was deliberately disobeying orders to move quickly through the plateau, the so-called Death Valley, because he was secretly following a plan devised by Richardson in Pearl Harbor to embarrass the Marines. Such a charge would be too fantastic to comment on if it did not come from the man who was Ralph Smith's "friend" and who was also the Chief of Staff of NTLF. According to Erskine's own words, he thought this at the time of Ralph Smith's relief and he goes further, indicating that it was he who pointed out to H. M. Smith the Army's deficiencies when he decided upon a "showdown." Erskine had talked to Gen. H. M. Smith, presumably sometime on 23 June, and "told him we had to do something about this goddamn thing [presumably the Army's lack of forward progress that day] and he agreed."[41] Given General Erskine's own admissions, it seems safe to assume that his attitude had considerable weight with H. M. Smith, who already had shown as early as the Gilbert's operation that he distrusted the 27th and disliked its commander.

Much has been made of the fact that Ralph Smith was not officially relieved of command until midafternoon of the 24th and thus, presumably, his actions and those of the 106th and 165th on that day played a part in his removal. Nothing could be farther from the truth. H. M. Smith had already decided the night before to get rid of a man whom, despite his outward show of friendliness, he must have disliked intensely. Erskine sent Ralph Smith a telegram at 0836 on 24 June that was supposed to jog Ralph Smith into the type of action the Corps believed necessary. That message was not received at the 27th Division CP until 1030, four hours after Ralph Smith and some of his staff had left for the front lines and about the time that H. M. Smith was packing up some of his charts to call on Admiral Turner to request that the 27th's commander be removed. It is not an exaggeration to point out that, even if the 27th had been able to achieve a major breakthrough during the afternoon of the 24th, its commander would still have been relieved. Aside from the dubious choice of sending a telegram rather than a staff member to inform Ralph Smith of what Jarman had already conveyed the evening before, the telegram could have achieved nothing except perhaps show that Corps had done everything possible to move this weak, intellectual, and ineffectual commander to do his duty. Despite the fact that the telegram served no functional purpose and contained a number of erroneous implications, it does show H. M. Smith's and Erskine's attitudes. It stated:

Commanding General is highly displeased with the failure of the 27th Division on June 23rd to launch its attack as ordered at K hour and the lack of offensive action displayed by the division in its failure to advance and seize objective 0–5 when opposed only by small arms and mortar fire. The failure of the 27th Division to advance in its zone of action resulted in the halting of attacks by the 4th and 2nd Marine Divisions on the flanks of the 27th in order to prevent dangerous exposure of their interior flanks. It is directed that immediate steps be taken to cause the 27th Division to advance and seize objectives as ordered.[42]

Long before Ralph Smith could do anything to show that Corps' opinion of the 27th was incorrect, H. M. Smith and some members of his staff were on their way to Admiral Turner's flagship, the *Rocky Mount*. There H. M. Smith related how disappointed he was in the progress of the 27th and confided that the only solution was the removal of its commander. H. M. Smith found a sympathetic listener in Turner, who also had formed a low opinion of Army units and who assured H. M. Smith that the Marine general had full authority on his own to relieve Ralph Smith. However, H. M. Smith must have realized the gravity of what he was proposing and wanted support from the Navy for his action. Turner suggested that since Admiral Spruance was in the area that they take the problem to him. Turner alerted Spruance and he, H. M. Smith, and his staff members went on board the *Indianapolis*. Robert Hogaboom, then NTLF G–3, was also present. He recalls that H. M. Smith made his presentation; Spruance listened, asked questions, and made the decision to relieve General Ralph

Smith. Spruance's chief of staff later added more information about this conference when he recalled that H. M. Smith was "very indignant . . . disgusted with the general performance" of the 27th Division and "irritated . . . beyond measure with its failure to attack." He also recalled that H. M. Smith had "indicated his disgust with the performance of the 27th Division."[43] After Admiral Spruance had made up his mind on the basis of the one-sided presentation, General Erskine was asked to write the order for the relief. It "authorized and directed" H. M. Smith to remove Ralph Smith from command of the 27th Division.[44]

H. M. Smith had obtained what he wanted—authorization to relieve an unwanted commander, and he also could share the responsibility with the Navy senior commanders for the action. Although Admiral Spruance would continue throughout the postwar years to insist that it was he who made the decision, few people either in the Army or Marine Corps were fooled.[45] H. M. Smith, commander of the NTLF, the man ultimately responsible for actions on Saipan, backed by senior members of his staff and Admiral Turner, had come to Admiral Spruance with their litany of complaints and suggestions for the solution of what appeared to be a major problem. Admiral Spruance, while technically in command of the Saipan operation, had been primarily concerned the week previous with meeting the Japanese fleet and securing one of the brilliant naval victories of the Pacific War. He had to depend upon the judgment of his subordinates in the matter of Ralph Smith. He could not even appear to be neutral and ask the Army commander to confer with him in order to hear a defense against the charges. If he had done this, no matter what his ultimate decision, it would have undercut the authority of the NTLF commander. The decision was made; Ralph Smith would be relieved.

Even once his wish had been granted, it appears H. M. Smith still wanted reassurance that he had been correct. He must have suspected that he had started something more serious than just the removal of a commander charged with incompetency. His friend and occasional confidant, Robert Sherrod, in his notebook for 24 June jotted down one of H. M. Smith's defensive outcries:

Growled old H. M. S., "By God, I told him [Ralph Smith] to attack and he issued an order to hold. I've got a duty to my country. I've lost seven thousand Marines. Can I afford to lose back what they have gained? To let my Marines die in vain? I know I'm sticking my neck out—the National Guard will be down my throat —but I did my duty."[46]

There is no reason to question the authenticity of the above quotation. While it certainly reveals H. M. Smith's state of mind, it is totally inaccurate in describing the actual situation on Saipan. The order to "hold" referred to the Nafutan area and even if one accepts the argument that Ralph Smith's order to the 105th should not have been issued, it was directed at only one battalion which was taking over a line previously held by four. It seemed logical to ask the battalion commander "to hold" while consolidating his lines before attacking. The Japanese in the Nafutan area, even accepting the Army's estimate, were at that time less than one thousand men and thus posed no significant threat to Army or Marine units. The only reason H. M. Smith could lose "what they have gained" in the Nafutan area would have been because he had so weakened the attacking force that, in effect, he invited the *Banzai* charge that was to happen two days later. The statement to a senior correspondent of the powerful *Time* sounds very much like a public relations gesture. Here was the avuncular figure mourning his Marines, doing his duty, and saving others from dying in vain presumably because of the 27th Division and its commander. On closer examination, this part of the emotional statement proves as faulty as the rest. Four thousand of those Marine casualties occurred during the first two days, when they were attempting to gain a foothold on the beach. From D day onward to 23 June, with the exception of the relatively minor actions in the Nafutan area, the fighting had been borne by the two Marine divisions. The two regiments of the 27th had been committed to the drive north only on the day before Ralph Smith was relieved. Those units could not be held responsible for seven thousand Marine casualties, and it was much too early to ascertain whether these men would have "died in vain."

Almost a month after relieving Ralph Smith, H. M. Smith,

under pressure of General Richardson's reactions sought vindication from the Commandant of the Corps by adding a new reason for the relief of his subordinate. He wrote to General Vandegrift:

R. Smith is a weak officer, incapable of handling men in battle, lacks offensive spirit, and tears would come into his eyes on the slightest provocation. My duty was clear. My action was approved by every Army officer with whom my staff or I discussed the situation . . . I would have relieved Schmidt or Watson under the same circumstances but God be praised they fought like true Marines.[47]

To be very blunt, this was character assassination, pure and simple. Ralph Smith, a veteran of combat in two wars who had demonstrated his personal bravery in each, was certainly not a "weak" man. He is remembered by the officers and men of his division as a competent, caring commander who was not afraid to be up front pushing his units forward. The worst allegation in this spiteful letter, however, concerns tears coming into Ralph Smith's eyes "on the slightest provocation." In an effort to confirm the author's own judgment of this hyperbole, a number of officers of the 27th Division were given this quotation and their comments were solicited. Each responded vociferously that they had never seen "tears" in Ralph Smith's eyes and most had unprintable comments concerning the author of such a distortion. One veteran of the 27th, Headquarters, commented:

Rubbish. The Division General Staff officers with whom I came in contact (mind you, I was a lowly 3-striper in the G-1 Section) not only had the finest respect for Gen. Ralph Smith but an abiding disdain for Gen. H. M. Smith, whom they considered a grossly uninformed, thoughtless boor more interested in personal glory than the welfare of his men—Marines or any other service.

Any tears in General Ralph Smith's eyes were probably tears of rage and frustration at having to deal with H.M.S.[48]

While H. M. Smith and many of his staff were conferring with their naval superiors, the direct attack against the Japanese positions in central Saipan was continuing. At 0800 all units began the assault. In the 27th Division's sector the 1st Battalion of the 165th to the east of Purple Heart Ridge launched a three-company attack on the ridge. Company A moved directly ahead, crossing a canefield at approximately 0800, and was halted by heavy concentrations of fire from the heights. Company A found it could not advance during most of the day, even with the support of tanks. Company B, working on the left flank through the canefields, managed to advance about 50 yards before it too was brought under devastating fire from the same positions as the day before. Company C on the right, however, made significant gains by using the same small hill line for a mask as the Marines had the previous day when they broke contact with the Army regiment. By sidestepping and using the hill as a shield, Company C passed through the 4th Marine lines. By midmorning they had bypassed the pocket of Japanese resistance in the south and reached the northern nose of Hill Xray-Yoke. Maintaining firm contact with the Marines on their flank, they established a firing line to deny the Japanese freedom of movement on the eastern slopes of Purple Heart Ridge. General Ralph Smith, who was on the front lines, witnessed this small success and ordered the 3rd Battalion of the 165th, which had been in reserve, to follow the same general route as C Company. This route took them past Hill Q, then a turn left to descend to the bottom of Shrine Valley. From there, they were to attack straight up the eastern slope of Hill Xray-Yoke, reach the crest, and tie in with the 2nd Battalion attacking from the west. The battalion was in position to make the attack by midafternoon, when all forward movement elsewhere had been halted. They moved methodically through the underbrush on the lower slopes before Company K made a dash up the slope of the hill, reaching within fifty yards of the crest before a hail of fire from the defenders just before dark drove them back to their original attack positions.[49]

The 2nd Battalion of the 165th also began its advance at 0600 in a column of companies, with the immediate goal of mopping up the lower fringes of the ridge line. Advancing through heavy undergrowth, the leading units had moved along the western slopes of Hill Charlie and moved on toward

Xray-Yoke when they were confronted by a gulch forty feet deep and fifty yards wide. The first men to try clambering down the slope were immediately killed. The battalion commander then tried a series of flanking movements, one of which took the reserve company through the exposed valley floor at the base of Hill Xray-Yoke. These movements eventually were successful. The battalion was prepared to begin its direct assault up the western slope of the hill when news of a Japanese tank attack down the valley caused a postponement. When the hostile tanks had been knocked out by men of the 106th, another such attack was believed imminent, just as the 2nd Battalion was once again ready to advance. They were then informed that the 3rd Battalion was soon to begin its attack to the east. It was decided to wait instead of attacking directly at the face of friendly forces on the other side.[50]

The 3rd Battalion of the 106th had the most difficult task of all. It was responsible for attacking on the valley floor where the Japanese had established some strong points. The most difficult problem facing them was the concentrated fire from both the cliff side of Mt. Tapotchau and Purple Heart Ridge. In a two-pronged attack, one company attempted to forge ahead while another directed its attention to the cliffs to the west. They were supported by two platoons of medium tanks. In one fire fight in the valley, three tanks were seriously damaged and thirteen men wounded in a few minutes of action. After two hours, the 106th had moved forward only about fifty yards. At this time Colonel Stebbins relayed the message to the battalion commander from the 2nd Marines that the 106th had not moved forward fast enough. Gen. Ralph Smith also was aware of the 2nd Marines' complaints and sent his oft-quoted messages to Colonel Ayers voicing his displeasure that the 106th's failure to advance and also to maintain contact with the Marines was "most embarrassing."[51] Responding to Stebbins' criticism, Lieutenant Colonel Mizony, the battalion commander, ordered Company K supported by mortars, tanks, and heavy machine guns to move ahead and capture a Japanese strong point situated behind some rocks. Halfway to the objective, the entire cliff face to the west seemed to belch fire. Within minutes, the company lost eight killed, including the company commander, and had fourteen wounded. One of the supporting tanks was knocked out and two others damaged. The company was stopped cold. Mizony decided to try withdrawing his men under a smoke screen. This did not work well; ten more men were wounded before the company could be extricated. General Smith, who had arrived at the Battalion CP, then ordered Mizony to commit his reserve, I Company. This unit also was struck by a heavy concentration of enemy fire, losing its commander and most of its non-commissioned officers. Before I Company could be brought back to its line of departure, it had nine killed and fourteen wounded. The tank support units, which had entered the valley in the morning with ten tanks, had only two operating by 1000. Shortly after noon the Japanese launched an attack down the valley with nine tanks supported by infantry. Before these were knocked out, three got within a few feet of I Company's lines. At approximately 1500, the 1st Battalion began relieving the 3rd, which during the attempt to force the valley corridor had lost 137 men.[52]

The 2nd Battalion of the 106th, pressed up against the cliff line, had difficulty moving forward; they not only faced fire from Japanese positions but also had to try to maintain contact with units on either side. The 3rd Battalion's failure to move forward in the valley restricted any advance by the 1st. They also had problems trying to meet the unfair criticism of the Marines on their left about an open flank. On orders from General Ralph Smith, the battalion commander, the night before, had dispatched F Company to operate as liaison between the Marines and the 106th. However, the terrain continued to prevent this. As a result, F Company operated for four days as a *de facto* part of the 2nd Marine Division and had contact with G Company on their right only by radio.[53]

The close of fighting for 24 June showed only a few minor advances for the division. The most important movement had been that of the 1st Battalion of the 165th on the right flank of Hill Xray-Yoke and by the 2nd Battalion eliminating the Japanese positions on Hill Charlie. This latter gain would make a major flanking movement possible on the east side of the ridge, because Chacha road would no longer be under close-in mortar and machine gun fire. Obviously, Corps neither appreciated the difficulty of the terrain, the savagery of the fighting, nor the gains made during the day by the Army units. The Marine divisions moving through less difficult terrain had not made spectacular gains. The 4th Division managed to move out into the relatively flat land of the Kagman Peninsula to what they had designated as line 0–5A. This constituted an advance in some places of over 2500 yards, but they were still more than 4000 yards short of the 0–6 line which Corps had designated as their target. The 2nd Marine Division advanced on either side of Mt. Tipo Pale, located roughly in the center of their sector. The left units of the 2nd encountered some resistance from the Japanese in a few positions, but by nightfall had advanced almost 2000 yards along the coast to the out-skirts of Garapan. The right wing elements of the 2nd advanc-ing along the ridge lines toward Tapotchau, however, were lucky to have moved forward approximately 500 yards. They still had not taken the mountain from which the Japanese could view developments everywhere in central Saipan. The Marines were also 500 yards short of the 0–5 line in this re-gion. Marine units nearer the central highland region assigned to the Army found it much more difficult to advance than did those near the east or west coasts.

One last curious report about the problems posed by the terrain in front of the 27th Division should be made. It has already been shown that the Corps staff seemed reluctant to visit the Army areas even during the crucial day of 23 June. The historian assigned to the 27th Division, who later was called on to take over a company during the latter stage of the breakout from the pocket, recalled that General Erskine paid a visit to Division Headquarters a few days after Ralph Smith was relieved. He recalled:

He [Erskine] took a look around and said, "My God I never realized that it was anything like that. Had we known what was going on up here we could have changed things."[54]

H. M. Smith and his Corps staff had already made *a priori* conclusions about the 27th Division and its inability to fight. They apparently didn't want to be bothered with visiting that front to ascertain the situation for themselves. Instead, H. M. Smith believed he had found the solution.

The 27th Division's commander, unaware that no matter what was done during the 24th, the decision to relieve him had been taken, was constantly up front the entire day. Jacob Herzog, the Division Assistant S–2 remembered:

He [Ralph Smith] and I had spent the whole day at the front line together. He showed a tremendous amount of bravery—took charge in reorganizing things, talking to company and battalion commanders, and getting the front organized, primarily for the next day's attack. When we got back it was very late in the day.[55]

Lt. Edmund Love, the Army historian, was also aware of Gen. Ralph Smith's activity during the 24th. He relates that he had taken up a position near the 165th's CP just off Chacha road, where he could watch what was going on and also interview some of the officers and men walking along the ditch who had taken part in the fighting. He confirms that the General passed his vantage point five or six times during the day even though this stretch of road was under continual harassing fire. Love stated:

Ralph Smith four times that afternoon came walking along that ditch. He was right up where the fighting was. He knew what was going on and not one single man from V Amphibious Corps ever got up there to check.[56]

Even Gen. Ralph Smith, who is very reluctant to discuss any possible heroism on his part, recalled, "I pretty near got killed up there during the forward reconnaissance. In fact, one of Kernan's colonels did get killed up there in that area during the afternoon."[57] It could be that this part of the general's recollections referred to the shelling of the CP of the 1st Battalion on Hill Q in the early afternoon when he was holding a conference with Kelley, Ayers, McDonough, and Mahoney, among others. During this incident six men were killed and sixteen wounded. Later in the day, there were thirty-two more casualties in this same area as a result of shelling.[58]

Gen. Ralph Smith's reconnaissance trips and conversations with his commanders had impressed upon him the near impossibility of forcing the valley directly. By early afternoon, he had decided on an alternate attack plan for the next day. Since the Chacha road was now relatively safe, he intended to leave only the 2nd Battalion of the 106th behind to contain the Japanese in the pocket between Mt. Tapotchau and Purple Heart Ridge. The other two battalions of the 106th would be pulled out at daybreak and marched east down the Chacha road to the bend in the road. They would pass through the Marine areas to the east of the 165th, then move northward until they came to the S Road and then, moving left, they could reach a position in Death Valley beyond Hill Able. While the 106th was deploying in the valley, the 165th would move northeast of Purple Heart Ridge and deploy along the S road, ultimately tying into the left flank of the 106th. Those Japanese defenders along the ridge from Hill Xray-Yoke to Hills Oboe, King, and Able could then be worn down by attrition from the 2nd Battalion of the 106th and the division reserve.[59] Ralph Smith did not know it at the time, but he would not be the man to carry out these plans.

General Erskine, who was possibly the *bête noir* in this drama, admitted that it was he who suggested that General Jarman replace Ralph Smith. It would have been more logical if Smith had to be relieved to have his place taken, at least temporarily, by the Assistant Division Commander, Ogden Ross, who was privy to all the positive and negative aspects of the division and their situation on the 24th. However, this would have meant the appointment of a Brigadier to command the division and, moreover, one who was a National Guard, not a regular officer. Erskine reported that he told H. M. Smith:

Why not put Sanderford Jarman in command? It will give him a good feel, being island commander here, and with his rank and experience I see no reason why he shouldn't be in command.[60]

H. M. Smith agreed and Jarman was informed of the decision. It has already been established that Jarman's major asset was his intelligence. He didn't need to be a genius to figure out that the Army was being singled out for punishment without good reason, or that he was going to be H. M. Smith's cat's paw in this affair. Despite what Erskine said, Jarman knew that while he might have the rank, he didn't have the experience. General Jarman told his brash ex-student that he didn't want the job. He said, "Hell, I am the island commander here." Erskine passed on H. M. Smith's decision to him and said, "So you are it. If you want any briefing or anything here, say what you want and I'll give it to you, but that goddamn outfit's got to get going or you'll get the sack."[61] Perhaps dredging his memory, General Erskine was exaggerating a little about giving Jarman what he wanted. There were still two battalions of the 106th in Corps reserve and he did not release these, nor would he immediately do so for Jarman's successor. Erskine seemed amazed that Jarman's "attitude sort of changed from that moment on. We were not the same boy scouts we were the day before, as old LSU buddies. There was a cooler atmosphere right there."[62]

Gen. Ralph Smith, shortly after the shelling of the 1st Battalion's CP, was walking toward Hill Love along the Chacha road at approximately 1530 when a jeep drove up and one of H. M. Smith's aides handed him an envelope containing his relief order. He opened and read the message as the aide drove hurriedly off to the west without waiting for a reply. He then walked back into the CP and went over the plans once again for the shifting of the regiments for the next day's attack, without saying anything to Ayers or Kelley about his relief. After this conference, the General rejoined Major Herzog, got back in his jeep, and returned to Division Headquarters, arriving there at approximately 1700. Here he found General Jarman, who had been waiting for more than an hour.[63] Jarman knew very well that he was being placed in a completely untenable situation. It is doubtful whether he considered Corps' criticism of Ralph Smith justified, but no matter what his feelings, he now was the commander of the 27th Division. He had been informed by Erskine to get that "goddamn outfit" going, but Erskine for all his promises had not told him how. Jarman knew nothing about the situation at the front lines and he asked Ralph Smith to fill him in. Before going into any detail on his plans for the next day's operation, General Smith called NTLF Headquarters and talked to Erskine. He indicated his willingness to stay on with the new commander until the next morning to offer his advice and

expertise for that day's action. Erskine approved the request.
The two generals then conferred on Smith's proposed attack
plans. As Gen. Ralph Smith recalls, "I had all my maps there
and I showed him what my plans were to push through the
area of the 4th Division on the right and envelope the resistance that was holding us up."[64] Jarman accepted these pro-
posals completely because, as Gen. Ralph Smith noted, "that
was about the only plan going."[65]

H. M. Smith, however, was not finished with his attempts to
humiliate Ralph Smith. Despite Erskine's promise to allow
Smith to act as a reference tool for the new commander, H. M.
Smith had a call placed through to Division Headquarters at
approximately 2230 ordering Ralph Smith off the island. He
was to report to Blue Beach by 0330 of 25 June for transport
to Pearl Harbor.[66] In compliance with this order, he packed
his equipment and with one aide made his way to the beach.
The "Pilot's Log Book" of Floyd Harris, a Navy lieutenant
and pilot of a Martin PBM patrol plane, lists five passengers
taken aboard at 0500 25 June 1944 for a routine 9.8 hour
flight to Eniwetok.[67] One of those passengers was Gen. Ralph
Smith. The main chapter in the one-sided antipathy between
the Smiths which dated at least to the Makin operation was
closed. But, much as H. M. Smith had suspected, the issues
raised by his curt dismissal of the Army commander were far
from resolved.

9 | SAIPAN: THE BREAKOUT AND TANAPAG

Part I

GEN. RALPH SMITH'S DEPARTURE FROM SAIPAN in the early morning of 25 June did not signal the end, but rather the intensification of the controversy. Gen. H. M. Smith was probably aware that he had allowed his anti-Army bias and his personal antipathy toward the commander of the 27th Division to override a more prudent view of the situation. He must have known that his precipitous action would bring a quick reaction from General Richardson in Hawaii, and might even jeopardize his far from friendly relations with Admiral Nimitz. However, the decision, backed by Admirals Turner and Spruance, had been made, and he was prepared to defend it. In so doing, over the next quarter century, he would confuse his own personal predilections with those of the Corps. He would never admit that he had perhaps acted hastily, his decision being based on scant information of the conditions at the front. He and his defenders would claim that he acted only for the good of the Corps, to protect his Marines, and to get someone to command the 27th who would make it "toe the mark" and "fight as it should."[1] Presumably, he had found such a man in the elderly major general who had earlier been satisfied with being base commander designate. One must ask, however, if General Jarman really did get the 27th moving any faster than the departed previous commander.[2]

Following the scenario outlined the previous evening by Ralph Smith, General Jarman ordered Colonel Ayers' two battalions of the 106th to move eastward toward Chacha Village and then to turn northward flanking the southernmost positions of the Japanese on Purple Heart Ridge. Once in position along the S Road, the 1st Battalion followed by the 3rd would attack west against the hill line dominated by Hill Able in the north and Hill King in the south. Meanwhile, the 2nd Battalion of the 106th, which had been left behind to guard the southern entrance to Death Valley, would attack north once again on the floor of the valley and clean out pockets of Japanese resistance there. The three battalions of the 165th in a coordinated fashion from their flanking positions would attack Hills Oboe, Xray-Yoke, Love, and Charlie. If all went according to plan, Colonel Kelley was to send his northernmost battalion, the 2nd, on toward the S Road and there link up with the 106th, which would be moving west through the corridor in the northern end of Death Valley.

Despite the logic of the plan and the bravery of the men of the 27th Division, the major objectives were not attained during 25 June. In retrospect, the reasons are obvious. The Japanese had no intention of giving up any part of their defensive positions on Purple Heart Ridge or in the cliff line of Mt. Tapotchau across the valley. The concerted fire from the cliff area did not abate even after the 8th Marines, aided by F Company of the 106th, had taken the crest of the mountain. Although bypassed, the Japanese defenders continued to pour fire onto any Army unit attempting to advance through the valley. It was also later discovered that the area which the 1st Battalion of the 106th was to attack was one of the strongest on the island. General Saito's headquarters and the communications nerve center for the defense of Saipan were located in this vicinity. Called How Position, it was defended by one battalion of infantry, over twenty machine guns, dug-in tanks, anti-tank guns, and a few larger artillery pieces. It was one of these which periodically took the junction of the S Road and Chacha Road under harassing fire and caused some Marine commanders to blame the Army for slowness in advancing to

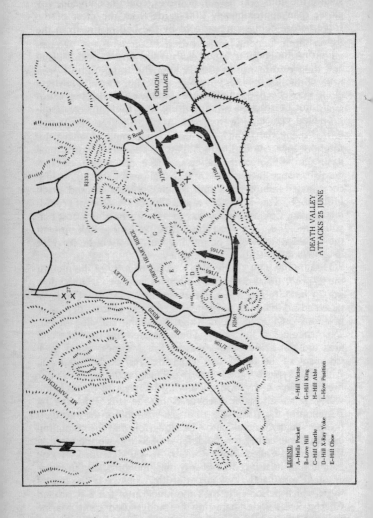

DEATH VALLEY
ATTACKS 25 JUNE

LEGEND
A—Hells Pocket
B—Love Hill
C—Hill Charlie
D—Hill X-Ray Yoke
E—Hill Oboe

F—Hill Victor
G—Hill King
H—Hill Able
I—How Position

silence the guns. The 106th, however, could not advance any closer than approximately 200 yards from the crest of the ridge before being stopped cold by the hail of fire from the defenders.[3]

During the day the 165th had mixed success. Its 2nd and 3rd Battalions had little success in trying to take Hill Oboe. The reasons for the lack of success were the same as elsewhere —the very effective Japanese fire coming from positions which could not be reached by supporting fire from tanks and self-propelled vehicles, or from the units' own mortars. At one time the 2nd Battalion was forced to fight in three directions, meeting enemy fire from north, west, and south.[4] During all the days of the slow reduction of the Japanese positions in central Saipan, the regiments of the 27th attacked with a minimum of artillery support. Such support was generally refused the attacking units, since any misjudgment on the part of artillery fire direction would drop the full concentration on Marines advancing on either flank. Thus the Army units, denied artillery support, had to take the Japanese strong points with minimum supporting fire power. The attrition rate on the attackers can be seen in the number of tanks lost in the different assaults. On the morning of 16 June, the 762nd Tank Battalion had seventy-two tanks available for action. By the evening of 23 June, this unit had only ten Shermans and eighteen light tanks fit for duty.[5]

Halted in the south, the 165th had made significant advances in the area east of the Japanese defense line along Purple Heart Ridge. At 1030 Colonel Kelley learned that the Marines had moved beyond Chacha Village and were advancing north and east into the Kagman Peninsula with very slight opposition. This left a gap between the Marine units and the Army. Since H. M. Smith made such a point of undefended flanks, this open flank, by H. M. Smith's own order, should have been the Marine's responsibility. It was, however, covered by Kelley, who moved his 3rd Battalion from near Hill Victor to fill the gap. By nightfall this battalion had reached a point approximately 500 yards north of Chacha Village. Late in the day, the 165th received additional strength when Corps released the Battalion of the 105th to him. Kelley moved this unit to the left of his 3rd Battalion, well north of the S Road.[6]

The 2nd Battalion of the 106th had the whole area of southern Death Valley to protect. General Jarman believed that the pressure of five attacking Army battalions from the east would divert the Japanese attention and allow the 2nd Battalion to secure a large portion of the southern part of the valley floor. This, of course, did not happen. Japanese resistance was as strong as ever. About the only success made by midafternoon was the destruction of an ammunition dump. At about that time, General Jarman, on an inspection of the front, arrived at the Battalion CP. After surveying the situation, he ordered Major O'Hara, the battalion commander, to use two companies to attack along the inner slopes of Purple Heart Ridge, working their way north along the low ground on the westward side of the hills.[7] He brought up a platoon of Sherman tanks and committed a battery of 155s and one of 105s to take the Tapotchau cliffs under fire. Major O'Hara and his company commanders protested that the proposed attack late in the afternoon would leave practically no troops to guard the southern exit of the valley, and that there was a good chance of the two companies becoming isolated in the valley at dusk. Despite the protests, the attack began at 1630 and, as Major O'Hara had warned, the Japanese, undaunted by the supporting artillery, pinned down the Army units. Darkness then became a major factor; the companies were running low on ammunition and the attempt to move back from their exposed positions was almost thwarted by roving bands of Japanese, who had slipped back on the valley floor.[8]

Attention has been focused upon this affair, since it was the first major independent action initiated by General Jarman. Before this, he was merely an instrument carrying out an agreed plan whose author, Ralph Smith, was on Kwajalein awaiting transport to Hawaii. It would be charitable to General Jarman to say that his order to the 2nd Battalion of the 106th was questionable. As his subordinates had warned, it certainly did not work. He had fallen prey to believing, as did so many at Corps, that Japanese resistance in this area was minimal, the major problem being the Army units' lack of aggressiveness. If one grants that Jarman's order here was probably a mistake, then his later actions toward Colonel Ayers become difficult to reconcile with the reality of the situation in central Saipan. Since H. M. Smith and others have used the Ayers incident to bolster their case against Ralph Smith and the 27th Division, the basis for that relief should be carefully examined.

Accepting the brief account of the actions of the 1st Battalion of the 106th on 25 June as related by Lieutenant Colonel Lemp and by the Marine official historian, the only rational conclusion is that this unit was lost, stumbled around, and finally found itself deep within the Marines' zone of action and subsequently took many casualties.[9] Such an account reaffirms the Army commanders' ineptness. This being the reason for General Jarman, an Army man, relieving his subordinate, it reinforces H. M. Smith's defense of his attitudes toward the 27th. A close reading of the action reports of the 106th and the account of the day's activities given in Edmund Love's detailed history of the 27th Infantry Division, however, leads to the inescapable conclusion that the 1st Battalion was not lost. This was the same unit which had by noon moved against the strongly defended How Position and advanced to within 200 yards of the crest of Purple Heart Ridge. They did take heavy casualties, not because they were lost north of Chacha Village, but from long-range and short-range Japanese fire as they attacked the strongest Japanese position in the Purple Heart defense chain. The major question in this operation concerns how they got into position to launch the attack. Briefly, the answer is that it was a command decision made by Colonel Ayers.

The 1st Battalion commander, Lieutenant Colonel Cornett, arrived at the point where his unit was to leave the Chacha Road and strike north, only to find that elements of the 165th were fighting in the area through which the 1st was ordered to pass. In addition, inadequate scouting reports had misled Generals Ralph Smith and Jarman into believing the northward descent from the road at that point was less steep than in reality. Cornett did not believe he could get his vehicles down the hill. Faced with the two problems, he requested permission from regiment to move further east to the junction of Chacha and S roads and move northward from there before launching his attack toward Purple Heart Ridge. This permission was granted by Colonel Ayers. Unfortunately, this decision placed the battalion squarely in the Marine area and added to the congestion at the Cross Road numbered 189. The Japanese, from their vantage points on the high ground, then brought more artillery fire down on this locale, causing even more confusion. The Marines in the area complained of the Army's encroachment and these complaints eventually reached General Jarman. Late in the afternoon he decided to abandon the flanking movement by the 106th and ordered its two battalions back to the original positions south of Death Valley, where he proposed the next morning to have them follow the route then being taken by the 2nd Battalion.[10]

General Jarman was clearly under great pressure. General Erskine's remarks to him would have left no doubt that the Marine leadership at Corps had already judged the 27th Division; if he didn't change things to their satisfaction he would be sacked as summarily as was Ralph Smith. Jarman had been thrown into a strange situation where he did not even know most of his subordinates. He had no time to acquaint himself directly with the situation at the front, and had gratefully accepted Gen. Ralph Smith's plans for the attack on 25 June.

Now a portion of that plan had failed and it appeared to him that one reason for its failure was the lack of leadership displayed by Colonel Ayers. Jarman likely overreacted, since he must have been influenced by H. M. Smith and Erskine's negative attitudes. The move to Cross Road 189 probably should not have been authorized by Colonel Ayers, at least not until he had cleared this with Division. It was a mistake, but an action which was probably necessary if the plan of attack for the day was to be carried out. The most serious black mark against Colonel Ayers that day was when General Jarman discussed the matter with him, Ayers appeared not to know what had happened or where his units were. As the 27th Division's historian said, Ayers never gave the impression of being in command of a situation, an assessment shared by General Watson in his appraisal of Ayers at Eniwetok. During the conversation between General Jarman and Ayers on the evening of the 25th, Jarman severely reprimanded his subordinate for allowing the encroachment into the Marine areas. He informed Ayers that he would give him one more chance. If he did not handle his regiment better, he would be relieved.[11] The next morning, when the 106th was slow in moving back to the foot of the valley and beginning its attack, Jarman acted. He ordered Ayers to the Division CP, relieved him of command, and replaced him with the Division Chief of Staff, Colonel Stebbins. He also sent down Maj. Henry Ross to act as the regiment's Executive Officer.[12]

Did this change in command result in any substantial improvement in the situation of the 27th Division? It is no reflection upon the extremely capable Stebbins to note that the relief of Colonel Ayers produced the same results as the earlier and more celebrated removal of Gen. Ralph Smith. The reason for the lack of immediate improvement in the attackers' position did not lie with the commanders, nor with the men of the 27th Division, notwithstanding H. M. Smith's prejudices to the contrary. Rather, it was due to the nature of the terrain, General Saito's carefully prepared defenses, and the fatalistic tenacity of highly skilled Japanese soldiers. As Marine and Army units would discover even more forceably later at Peleliu, Okinawa, and Iwo Jima, if the Japanese held the high ground in broken terrain dotted with manmade and natural caves, it was pointless to rush these prepared positions in direct frontal attacks. The Japanese had to be rooted out of their positions in painstaking and time-consuming maneuvers which utilized the maximum of firepower and patience on the part of the commanders of the attacking forces. It is little wonder that Colonel Ayers was later somewhat confused. He had been given a Navy Cross on Eniwetok, presumably for his ability to command his unit, and on Saipan he was to be removed after three days for an ostensible lack of command presence.[13]

General Jarman's plan for 26 June was to have the 3rd Battalion of the 106th assault Hill Oboe from the west and then proceed to capture Hill King to the north. The 2nd Battalion would follow and mop up. All went well at first in this sector; the crest of Oboe was reached before noon. But then the advance companies were caught in the saddle between the two hills. In a matter of minutes, the lead platoon had six men killed and seventeen wounded. It was forced to withdraw and could not advance any farther all day. Partially due to heavy losses, the 1st and 2nd platoons were reduced in effectiveness to only twelve men each.[14] The 2nd Battalion of the 106th remained relatively quiescent; its commander made no attempt to move it out into the valley, instead waiting for the 3rd to gain its objectives. General Kernan, the division artillery commander, and Colonel Sheldon, the G–3, visited this front at about 1000 and reported to General Jarman that the 2nd, and elements of the 3rd, appeared to be in a demoralized state and something should be done to get them moving. General Jarman waited until these two staff members returned to the Division CP and then, true to his promise the evening before, summoned Colonel Ayers and relieved him. On the eastern portion of Purple Heart Ridge, the 2nd Battalion of the 165th made substantial gains, taking Hill Victor without much trouble. Even here, after its capture, no significant further advance could be made because of the concentrated Japanese fire which continued, despite artillery and mortar support for the advance. Before dark the infantrymen retired from the crest and dug in on the south slopes of Victor. Meanwhile, the 1st Battalion across the valley was vainly trying to clear Hell's Pocket. Despite the attached cannon company's firing of over 400 rounds in direct support, the Japanese still held the pocket as stubbornly as when the 27th first attacked the strong point.[15]

On the evening of 26 June, Corps detached the 1st and 3rd Battalions of the 165th and the 1st Battalion of the 105th from Jarman's control. These were placed under General Schmidt of the 4th Marine Division, which had by this time secured the Kagman Peninsula and finally had arrived at the 0–6 line. Corps still retained control over the two battalions of the 105th. Thus, for the attack of 27 June, General Schmidt had nine battalions on line while Jarman had only four, of which two had taken a severe beating from the Japanese. General Jarman, for that day's operation, altered his previous day's plan. According to the new plan, the 3rd Battalion, which had suffered the most casualties, would move north to King Hill, then pivot left and attack across the valley toward Mt. Tapotchau's cliffs more than 1000 yards distant. With the help of the 2nd Battalion of the 165th attacking from the east, King Hill was taken by 1130 and the pivot across the valley began. The attacking companies deploying down the steep slopes met fire from the cliff areas as well as from Hill Able in the rear.

Nevertheless, by 1530, the units had reached the western edge of the valley and sent out patrols to contact Company F, which had been advancing with the 2nd Marines on the top of the cliff. Tanks were brought up to resupply the infantry units with water and ammunition before nightfall.

Meanwhile, the 2nd Battalion of the 106th was stalled by strong enemy resistance in the saddle between Hills King and Able. In the fighting, Major Brusseau, who had replaced Colonel McDonough as commander of the battalion, was killed. Without substantial gains, the unit dug in where it was for the night. Across the valley the 1st Battalion was finally making headway in reducing resistance in Hell's Pocket. Early in the morning of 27 June, two companies climbed the high ground to the west while one attacked directly ahead. All forward movement, however, was stalled by the Japanese, who manned defenses in a deep crater within the pocket. This was finally overrun by midafternoon. The attackers found twenty-five Japanese dead who had earlier manned two machine guns and three captured U.S. BARs. The attacking units moved approximately 100 yards farther into the pocket before preparing defenses for the night.[16] The major advance of all units in central Saipan was by the 4th Marine Division and the attached Army battalions. These nine battalions advanced beyond Hashigoru Village and finally reached the 0–6 line. Some commentators have noted that the shape of the American lines resembled a U, with the Marine units farther in advance and the 27th Division lagging behind. This configuration became true only at the close of 27 June, three days after Gen. Ralph Smith was relieved.[17]

In evaluating the performance of units of the 27th Division, it is important to keep in mind the strength of the Japanese forces. When the 27th first entered the valley and assaulted the ridge lines, the Japanese units were at full strength. By the close of 25 June, they had sustained such heavy losses that they could no longer expect to hold for long even such excellent positions as Hill Able or Hell's Pocket. General Saito, in a message to 31st Army Headquarters in Guam, estimated that he had slightly over 1000 men on line as of the morning of 26 June. Reserve, supply, and hospital units had also suffered heavily. Supplying the forward troops was very difficult; what they needed most was water. There had been little water available at the beginning, and American bombardment had eliminated most of its sources.[18] During the evening of the 27th, General Saito began withdrawing his battered units from the valley northward to his final defense line in the north. Thus, the cracking of Japanese defenses in front of the 27th Division was due in part to the severe reduction in Japanese defenders. Nevertheless, they managed to slow down the general advance of the Army units on 28 June by holding tenaciously to Hill Able. During the day's fighting, Colonel Mizony was killed, as well as two company commanders of the Third Battalion of the 106th. The regimental commander of the 165th was also wounded during the morning attack.[19] The strongpoint of Hill Able was not taken until 30 June. By then the Army had broken out of the valley and cleaned up Hell's Pocket. Finally, after a week of hard fighting, a continuous line once again stretched across the island with the two Marine divisions on either flank of the 27th Division in the center.

At 1030 on 28 June, the new commander of the 27th Division took over from General Jarman. As soon as the information of Gen. Ralph Smith's relief reached him, General Richardson had moved quickly to restate the Army's control of its own units. He named Gen. George Griner, then commander of the 98th Division, to relieve Jarman. Later H. M. Smith complained of this discourtesy, bemoaning the fact that he was not consulted in the choice. Perhaps under normal circumstances he would have been, but for two factors. The first concerned the reasons for and the manner of Ralph Smith's removal. The second had to do with the available Army major generals in the central Pacific area. Despite the fact that General Griner was never fully accepted by the officers of the 27th Division, he was a competent commander. It is doubtful whether H. M. Smith and his staff could have improved on the selection process.

General Griner had not been briefed by Gen. Ralph Smith, the only senior officer in Hawaii who knew firsthand of the situation on Saipan. General Richardson, fuming from the slight to the Army, could not give Griner any more than general details. He, like Jarman a few days before, was coming into a combat situation with minimal knowledge of the enemy situation or of the unit he was to command. Unfortunately for the reputation of the 27th Division, Griner was briefed by H. M. Smith and his staff. As would have been the case with most reasonable officers, he left Hawaii with the feeling that "where there was smoke there was fire"; that H. M. Smith would never have relieved the 27th Division's commander without reasonable cause. H. M. Smith very soon explained to him the cause: "I gave him [Griner] a full account of the action of the 27th and expressed the hope that he would reorganize the division and develop among the men a better fighting spirit."[20]

General Griner later elaborated on that conversation. As he recalled, he reported to H. M. Smith at approximately 1730 on 27 June to find the Marine general indignant that Griner's orders did not direct him to report to the commander of the NTLF. He was partially mollified by Griner's assurance that the omission was unintentional and he was then reporting. H. M. Smith then spent about an hour discussing the alleged deficiencies of the 27th, going as far back as the Makin operation which he claimed would have been unsuccessful without his "own personal leadership of frontline elements." In his opinion, Ralph Smith should have been dismissed then instead of decorated. H. M. Smith repeated over and over that he had warm relations with the Army, had served with Army units in France, and that many of his friends were Army men. Despite this, he related how the Army infantry "had frozen in their foxholes on Nafutan Point" and that a full regiment could not eliminate a small enemy force there which could have been "disposed of by a handful of Marines." Griner pointed to the fact that one Army battalion was then holding a front 3000 yards wide at Nafutan, but this made no impression on H. M. Smith.[21] General Griner had learned during his briefing by H. M. Smith that he had only four battalions under his command, the 165th being attached to the 4th Marine Division, one battalion of the 105th under Island Command at Nafutan, and another battalion of the 105th in Corps reserve. Not surprisingly, he asked for their return. H. M. Smith replied "that when the conduct of the 27th justified, it would be given its organic elements."[22] In other words, there was to be no relief for the 27th Division attempting to force Death Valley until

Corps decided that they deserved to get back their own units. Perhaps recognizing the need to give the hard-pressed units of the 27th some relief, a fifth battalion was returned on 29 June. However, the 27th Division was not a complete division until Death Valley had been cleared, and on 4 July the last battalion of the unit was reattached.[23]

H. M. Smith's briefing and General Griner's own prejudices would prevent Griner from appreciating his division's qualities until after the Saipan campaign was almost concluded. He then became only a reluctant defender of the division against the false impressions created by Robert Sherrod's *Time* article. These attitudes, more than anything else, made most of his subordinate officers angry and explain why he was generally disliked by many of them throughout the Saipan and Okinawa campaigns.[24] However, even General Griner's *a priori* conclusions could not blind him to certain facts. By the close of the campaign for central Saipan on 30 June, he had only a shell of a division. Of the four battalions available to him on taking command at midmorning of 28 June, one, the 3rd of the 106th, was shot to pieces, having approximately 100 riflemen available. By the time the breakout from Death Valley was completed, twenty-two company commanders had either been killed or wounded; Colonel Kelley, commander of the 165th, had been wounded, Colonel McDonough, commanding the 2nd Battalion of the 165th, was wounded and evacuated, and his successor, Major Brusseau, was killed, as was Colonel Mizony, commander of the 3rd Battalion of the 165th.[25]

Later, in recollections of the various campaigns in the central Pacific, H. M. Smith placed great emphasis on casualty reports. This was noted at the time by a number of officers. Brig. Gen. E. B. Colladay perhaps phrased this best when he wrote of H. M. Smith's appraisal of the 27th Division after Griner had assumed command: "He [H. M. Smith] emphasized the fact that the 27th had few casualties. I got the impression then as later while I attended the morning conferences that General Smith's idea of a good fighting division depended entirely upon the number of casualties they sustained."[26] H. M. Smith later defended his relief of Gen. Ralph Smith by stating that the 27th's inactivity on 23 June was endangering the lives of his Marines and the 27th had taken few losses. His biographer is even more explicit on this point, trying to establish a ratio of friendly-to-enemy losses to decide comparative effectiveness of Marine and Army units during the Marshalls campaign.[27] If one views casualty figures as the measure of a given campaign's difficulty, then there is no doubt that, leaving aside all other evidence, the much-maligned 27th Division had the most difficult role in the fighting between 23 June and 30 June. During this period they had suffered 1465 casualties, as compared to 1506 for the 4th Marine Division and 1016 for the 2nd Marine Division.[28] Even these figures are misleading, however, since at no time did the 27th Division have available in their advance through Death Valley more than six battalions, while the Marine divisions had a full complement of subordinate units. The 4th Marine Division's strength after 27 June was also bolstered by the three Army battalions. In a very real sense, some of the elements of the 27th almost bled to death in the attack through the valley while H. M. Smith and his staff at Corps denigrated their efforts, and branded them as men who would not fight. Some Marine officers would later modify their views toward the action of the 27th Division during that crucial week. One of the best examples of this change was General Schmidt, who stated of the Army's struggles in Death Valley that "no one had a tougher job to do."[29] General Erskine had also remarked that Corps had not been aware of the true situation or it would have acted differently. However, the black mark cast by H. M. Smith's snap judgment and his unguarded, intemperate statements would remain part of the legacy of the 27th Division.

Another set of events, occurring long after the relief of Gen. Ralph Smith, has become linked to the earlier events by the actions of H. M. Smith in July 1944 and later in his memoirs. This concerns the *gyokusai* attack launched by the Japanese during the early morning hours of 7 July against the positions held by units of the 105th Regiment.

The advance northward after the breakout from the valley was ordered. Compared to the harsh fighting of the previous week, it was rapid against only minor enemy resistance. Garapan Town, a complete wreck from the shelling, was taken with little opposition. General Saito's troops, greatly reduced in numbers, low on ammunition, and forced to subsist on what could be scrounged from the countryside, nevertheless had established a strong defensive line just north of Tanapag. This line was anchored in the west by units defending a deep gulch nicknamed Harakiri Gulch, approximately 50 feet deep and 400 yards long, through which ran a secondary road. The Japanese had mined portions of the Tanapag Plain immediately to the front. The land sloped down to these positions near the coast from the central highlands of northern Saipan, which provided relatively secure areas for the remaining Japanese troops. In the drive northward, the 2nd Marine Division was pinched out after the capture of Garapan and the west flank of H. M. Smith's drive north became the responsibility of the 27th Division. In retrospect, this seems strange, since H. M. Smith later downgraded its abilities back as far as the Makin operation, claiming that he had taken it to Saipan only because no other division was available and had roasted three divisional commanders for the 27th's poor performance. If all he claimed was true, he would presumably have kept a proven Marine division in the line and pulled back into reserve such a lackluster outfit as the 27th. Such, however, was not the case. By 6 July the 27th had apparently won at least enough favor with H. M. Smith to have the last elements of the division returned. On that day the extreme left flank of the line was held by the 105th RCT, commanded by Colonel Bishop.[30]

Even after 40 years, it is difficult to sort out the elements which went into the tragedy of the night of 6–7 July, let alone apportion ultimate responsibility. H. M. Smith and members of his staff later claimed that Corps had warned of the possibility of a counterattack. Smith recalled that in his visit to General Griner's Headquarters the afternoon of 6 July he had specifically warned of such a possibility.[31] In his defense, General Griner pointed out that the 400 yard gap which would later play an important role in the night's affair was not present at that time. It was caused by orders from Corps to move Colonel O'Brien's 1st Battalion into line and attack from the established positions north of the main east-west road. Colonel Bishop argued against committing his reserves at such a late hour, but was overruled by General Griner. The attack north was begun at 1715 and had moved ahead approximately 500 yards against slight opposition before nightfall. The 2nd Battalion of the 105th then occupied the area west, while O'Brien's 1st spread approximately 200 yards east of the railroad line. The 3rd Battalion had not been able to advance northward, since its main objective had been to seal off the west end of Harakiri Gulch. Thus a gap approximately 400 yards wide existed between the 1st and 3rd Battalions.[32] O'Brien in response placed all his antitank weapons in a position to cover the gap until expected reinforcements from the 165th could arrive to fill in the line. Unfortunately, General Saito had come to the conclusion that all was lost at Saipan and that the only honorable option left for him and his troops was to die for the emperor in such a way as to cripple the enemy. He had obviously been planning this last attack for some time, since it was not to be merely a *banzai,* but rather a *gyokusai* attack. In rough translation, *gyokusai* means "breaking the jewel" or a total destruction of the units involved. General Saito alone could not order this, but had to clear it with Imperial Headquarters in Tokyo. Having received permission, he issued his final order at 0800 on the morning of 6 July. He called on all his units to attack and take "seven lives to repay our country." He promised to lead them in the charge to gain "eternal life of the Emperor and the welfare of the country."[33] Saito, old and sick, did not lead his men, but committed suicide before the attack. Vice Admiral Nagumo, after dining with General Saito during the evening of 5 July, returned to his headquarters and presumably committed suicide himself at about the same time as Saito.

The first intimation of a possible suicidal attack had come to Corps two days before on 4 July, when a naval airforce civilian employee under interrogation had revealed such a plan. Corps gave little credence to his story until it was confirmed on the late evening of 6 July by a captured Japanese private who, under interrogation by Sgt. Hoichi Jubo, the Nisei interpreter of the 3rd Battalion, placed the time of the attack at 2000. Lt. Benjamin Hazard, in charge of the Prisoner of War Interrogation Point at Tanapag, continued to question the prisoner and was in constant contact with Col. W. M. Van Antwerp, the Division G-2, until after midnight. Van Antwerp, for his part, had immediately contacted Corps with the initial information. There were fourteen separate calls logged from Van Antwerp

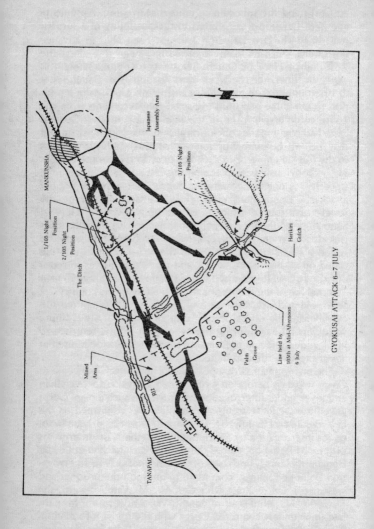

GYOKUSAI ATTACK 6-7 JULY

to Corps and the subordinate units that evening. All units of the 27th Division were alerted to the possibility of a surprise suicide attack.[34]

Colonel O'Brien, by now concerned about the gap on his right flank, called Regiment and asked for reinforcements to plug the line. However, Colonel Bishop had earlier reluctantly committed all the units of the 105th. Col. Leslie Jensen, the Regimental Executive officer, after receiving O'Brien's call, had then called Division and asked for support, but was told that no units were available and the battalions on line would have to make do.[35] All this appeared to be worry expended for no reason once 2400 arrived with no attack by the Japanese.

The reason the *gyokusai* did not go off as scheduled was because of the difficulty of drawing men together from all parts of northern Saipan and concentrating them near Makunsha.[36] The main force of the Japanese suicide attack began to move south from there at 0400, and within an hour had hit the 1st and 2nd Battalions below Makunsha. Other units struck the 3rd Battalion guarding Harakiri Gulch while the Japanese in the exposed gap continued southward unopposed until stopped by headquarters troops and Marines.

The attacking forces were desperate but totally dedicated men. Many, particularly naval personnel, were well armed, but some had only sticks with bayonets attached, clubs, or knives. Some had tied grenades to poles. All were united in their desire to kill the enemy before dying. Major McCarthy, commanding the 2nd Battalion and one of the few officers to survive the attack, later recalled:

It was like the movie stampede staged in the old west movies. We were the cameramen. These Japs just kept coming and coming and didn't stop. It didn't make any difference if you shot one, five more would take his place. We would be in the foxholes looking up, as I said, just like those cameramen used to be. The Japs ran right over us.[37]

It took less than half an hour to overrun the positions of the 1st and 2nd Battalions. Most of the officers and men of these units stood, fought against overwhelming odds, and died. One such was Colonel O'Brien, who met the Japanese charge in the same manner as he had when leading the tanks at Nafutan. After exhausting the ammunition from his .45 he manned a machine gun, although seriously wounded, until he was killed. For this action he was posthumously awarded the Medal of Honor. Another member of the 105th similarly honored was Sgt. Thomas Baker, who was directly involved in a series of hand-to-hand actions. Although gravely wounded, he refused medical attention. Propped against a tree, he had only a pistol and eight rounds—when found, there were eight Japanese dead in front of him.[38]

Survivors of the initial attack retreated back to Tanapag Village, where Major McCarthy with a few other officers managed to set up a perimeter, and fought a bitter house-to-house battle with the Japanese. They held out until a platoon of medium tanks arrived in midafternoon. Meanwhile, the Japanese pouring through the gap had reached the 3rd Battalion, 10th Marines (artillery). The presence of this unit, located approximately 500 yards to the rear of the front lines, is another illustration of the laxity of liaison between Marine and Army units. General Griner stated that the Marine artillery battalion had the day before emplaced their guns without his knowledge and certainly without the intention of supporting the units of the 105th directly ahead of them.[39]

The 3rd Battalion had been ordered to join units of Marines located on ridge lines to the east. The unit commander decided not to try pulling his guns up the hill on a bad road that afternoon, since the hour was late and part of the movement would be in the dark. Instead, he placed his guns behind the 105th to wait until the next morning. Apparently he did not feel it necessary to notify the Army of his presence. General Griner stated that not only was he unaware of the presence of the Marine artillery, but the commanders of the 105th were as well. After the action, this Marine unit was singled out by H. M. Smith for a special commendation and eventually received a Presidential Unit Citation for the defense of their position.[40] Griner complained to H. M. Smith without any effect that Smith's citation made no mention of Army units and, by inference, would lead one to believe that the beleaguered Marine artillery battalion was relieved after "holding

out until 1500" by Marines rather than by infantrymen of the
106th. Even more distressing to Generals Griner and Richardson was the fact that this was the unit Robert Sherrod (who
never visited the 27th Division CP after the engagement)
chose to headline in his *Time* articles of 19 July and 18 September as having halted the Japanese attack.

Sherrod's article in *Time* of 19 July 1944 made heroic reading and could not have been a better advertisement for the
Marines if H. M. Smith himself had written it. It said in part
that the Marine artillerymen

fired point-blank into the Japs with fuses set at four-tenths of a
second. They bounced their high explosive shells fifty yards in
front of the guns and into the maniacal ranks . . . When the order came to withdraw they sent this answer back, "Sir, we would
prefer to stay and fight it out." They did.[41]

Such brave words indicated that these Marine gunners were as
heroic as any who had ever worn the uniform. General Griner
specifically acknowledged that the Marine artillery battalion
had fought hard and well; they suffered 136 casualties, and
over 300 Japanese dead were found in the area of their positions. However, the fact remained that the Marine unit, like
the two battalions of the 105th, had been overrun. Edmund
Love, the historian who was on the ground soon after the
Japanese suicide charge and who helped interview the Army
survivors, stated that no one remembered the Marine artillery
unit firing their guns. Investigators from the CP of the 3rd
Battalion of the 105th claimed that no rounds of 105 ammunition had been fired; the ammunition and used brass was still
neatly stacked in piles.[42] One of the most telling stories concerning Marine participation is told by Oakley Bidwell, at that
time G–1 of the 27th Division. He had been given the task by
General Griner of making an accurate count of the bodies,
both American and Japanese, and supervising the burial details. After making his first visit on 8 July to witness the car-
nage, he remembers:

On my way back to our CP, I was accosted by an almost hysterical
Marine lieutenant colonel. "You army bastards," he screamed,

"you let them slaughter my battery." He led me to a sickening sight. Slung between trees were dozens of green Marine Corps jungle hammocks. Most contained the bodies of young men whose throats had been cut. Nearby were the battery's 105mm guns. I did not see a single empty shell case. The guns had never been fired.[43]

Without denigrating to the slightest degree the bravery of the men of the 3rd Battalion, 10th Marines, the story given credence by H. M. Smith and publicized by Robert Sherrod appears to distort what happened somewhat. The following seems a reasonable summary of what probably occurred to the Marine unit.

Only one battery, Battery H, was in a position to fire, but the Marines of that unit after a few rounds were forced to retreat so hurriedly that they left behind the breechblocks and firing locks to their howitzers. They joined the remnants of Batteries I and G and fell farther back to establish a defensive perimeter, where they held on until relieved at midafternoon by elements of the 106th. The 27th Division's artillery in direct support during this period had poured as much fire into the advancing Japanese as possible. During the height of the attack, in the hour after it had begun against the 1st and 2nd Battalions, 2666 rounds were expended.[44] The 3rd Battalion of the 105th during the early morning hours had met attacks from two directions. The Japanese in Harakiri Gulch attempted a breakout to the west, while many of the Japanese in the main attack struck the Army's positions on the high ground, blocking entrance into the gulch. Some of the most vicious small-scale fighting occurred in this locale.

Division and Corps reacted tardily to the disaster of the *gyokusai*. Not until four hours after the first Japanese attack did General Griner order Colonel Stebbins to attack northwest to halt the Japanese advance through the gap. Stebbins began a slow, deliberate movement forward at approximately 1000. He remained concerned throughout the day about the Japanese who might be bypassed in his advance. By midafternoon the 106th had recaptured the Marine artillery positions and relieved McCarthy's troops at Tanapag. Stebbins' decision to halt the advance at 1600 approximately 200 yards short of the morning front line has been criticized; it meant that many isolated infantrymen had to be evacuated by water.[45]

If Division's response had been slow, that of Corps was snail-like. At approximately 0930, it approved the attachment of the 3rd Battalion of the 6th Marines to the 27th Division to help clear out the Japanese in the Tanapag area. Yet, one and one-half hours later, General Griner's request for the release of Marine tanks to his command was refused. General Griner noted later that "headquarters [Corps] did not accept my version of the importance of the action then in progress."[46] About noon H. M. Smith did authorize the transference of 1000 rounds of 105mm ammunition to the Army batteries, who were running dangerously low. By nightfall most of the ground lost had been regained, and the 3rd Battalion had even cleaned up Harakiri Gulch.

During the morning of 8 July the Japanese made a series of unconnected suicide attacks against the dug-in units of the 106th. The heaviest fighting occurred along the beach lines of the 1st Battalion. By 0700 the attack had been contained, with heavy losses to the Japanese and negligible casualties for Colonel Stebbins' troops. H. M. Smith had decided even before the Japanese attack to replace the 27th Division with Marine units. Despite General Griner's protests that such a move would make it appear that the 27th was not in control, the 2nd Marines passed through the lines of the 27th for the mop-up of 8 July. The 2nd Marine Division and the 165th, which had been relatively untouched during the action of 7 July, had a field day in slaughtering the scattered remnants of the Japanese force. The next day the 4th Marine Division completed its drive to Marpi Point, and at 1615, on 9 July, Admiral Turner declared Saipan secured. All that was left was to clean out hidden pockets of Japanese. After 13 July this was left to the 27th Division, since the Marines were sent to capture Tinian. Not until 6 August, after a series of organized sweeps, was the island totally pacified. In the period after Admiral Turner declared the island secured until the 27th Division left Saipan on 4 October, an additional 1972 enemy soldiers were killed.[47]

The battle for Saipan, one of the most crucial engagements of the war, was over. The cost had been high. V Corps had lost 3119 men killed and 10,992 wounded or missing. Since body counts apparently played an important role in H. M. Smith's evaluation, one should note that the 27th Division in its 22 days of combat had lost 1053 killed, a figure surpassed only by the 4th Marine Division, which had lost heavily during the initial assault and had been in action for four more days.[48] At the NTLF conference of 15 July it was confirmed that 17,801 Japanese had been buried. Of that number, 6468, or more than 35 percent, had been buried by units of the 27th Division along their front.[49]

While the *gyokusai* attack had obviously shortened the campaign for northern Saipan, its defeat had been purchased by the near destruction of the 1st and 2nd Battalions of the 105th. Those units, in slightly more than 12 hours of fighting, had sustained losses of 406 officers and men killed and 512 wounded. In the 1st Battalion, only one officer, Lt. John Mulhern of B Company, was unscathed. Major McCarthy of the 2nd Battalion survived, but all his staff and company commanders were either killed or wounded.[50] General Griner, finally angered by the attitude of H. M. Smith and his staff, detailed his G–1 to conduct a very close count of enemy dead and their precise locations. By contrast to what was believed at Corps, the Japanese had lost 4311 men killed during the days fighting. Of this number, 2295 Japanese were counted in the areas where the 1st and 2nd Battalions fought. There were 322 Japanese dead in the positions of the Marine artillery units and 1694 bodies were found in the areas of the 105th CP and where the 1st and 2nd Battalions of the 106th fought later in the day.[51]

It is difficult to put such cold, unfeeling casualty figures in terms which better explain the effects of the suicidal *gyokusai* attack. Lieutenant Hazard, then in charge of Prisoners of War Interrogation for the 27th Division, recalled that on the morning after, the entire plain seemed to be covered with bodies. Howard Cook, a lieutenant and forward observer with the 249th Field Artillery, said that when he moved up to the positions which had been held by the 105th he saw nothing but dead bodies.[52] Robert Sherrod, if nothing else a master of the language, wrote of this visit forward: "The whole area seemed to be a mass of stinking bodies, spilled guts and brains . . .

They are thicker here than at Tarawa."[53] Oakley Bidwell who supervised the burials, remembered:

I don't think I can draw a picture more horrible than my memory of Tanapag Plain. It appeared to be virtually solid dead soldiers. A creek ran through a shallow ravine, emptying into a beautiful turquoise-blue lagoon. The creek and its banks seemed filled with bodies. And while I watched, a huge crimson flower grew out of the mouth of the creek.[54]

Bidwell also recalls General Erskine's visit to the Plain. Erskine, Ralph Smith's former student, had believed one had to be a "tough son of a bitch" to command combat troops. According to Bidwell, the Chief of Staff "took two steps, a long breath" . . . and promptly and efficiently lost his breakfast before returning immediately to his car and driving rapidly off. Dante could not have described a more harrowing sight than the aftermath of the *gyokusai* attack.

The trials of the 105th on 7 July and the days immediately following clarify a number of things. One is that the Japanese attack was a surprise. Despite the warnings by intelligence officers, it caught almost everyone off guard. The exception at the front perhaps was Colonel O'Brien, who had earlier requested reinforcements. Even with those available, it is doubtful whether the line could have been held against the massed Japanese attackers, who sought only to kill, without regard for whether they were killed. The second salient point is that it took Division and Corps hours before a suitable counterattack could be launched. A third fact, and perhaps the most important, concerns the bravery of the men of all the units involved. Words cannot adequately express the feelings of the men of the 27th Division when confronted by the fiction created by Robert Sherrod in his infamous *Time* articles of 19 July and 18 September. In the latter he accused the 105th, the "greenest" of the Army regiments, of breaking and allowing the Japanese through until stopped by the actions of a Marine artillery battalion. It is no disservice to those Marines involved to point out the inaccuracy of Sherrod's account. They too fought gallantly, but a large number of the Marines were also surprised and many were killed as they slept. No one artillery battalion halted the Japanese; they were not even stopped by three battalions of Army artillery firing more than thirty rounds per minute. However, despite the inaccuracy of Sherrod's report, it soon became a part of the myth of Marine supremacy and later gained the full support of H. M. Smith, who applauded the "accurate report of what had happened."[55]

One of General Richardson's main criticisms of the assumption of Corps command by Marine officers was that they had no training in operating at higher command levels. That charge is certainly true if one surveys the liaison between NTLF and the 27th Division on Saipan. Corps remained ignorant of the problems of the 27th attacking through Death Valley. That ignorance could have been dispelled easily by a reasonable liaison effort with the division. If this had been done, the relief of Gen. Ralph Smith probably would not have occurred. The *gyokusai* attack on 7 July is another glaring example of Corps' ignorance of the real state of affairs. H. M. Smith and his defenders have taken great pains to prove that Corps was aware that a possible attack might be launched. H. M. Smith's biographer points to the warnings given to General Watson of the 2nd Marine Division about keeping the right of the 2nd Marine Division strong, and of how H. M. Smith during his conference with General Griner on the 6th had pointed out the possibility of a Japanese counterattack. He then discusses the "fatal gap" developed because of "lackadaisical leadership" that allowed the Japanese to pour through. He leaves the impression abstracted from Spruance's investigation team that, had one or two companies from the 3rd Battalion moved into the gap, all would have been well. General Griner dealt with the first of these points, underscoring the general rather than specific nature of H. M. Smith's warning, when he wrote, "He [H. M. Smith] did warn of the expected enemy counterattack, as he had done at every previous conference, by Japanese Marines, the best troops the Japs have."[56] The gap which developed in the Army lines was because of the orders given to move the division ahead. Once Colonel O'Brien had been alerted to the possible danger of a suicide attack, he requested reinforcements, which were denied him. One has the impression from reading H. M. Smith's biography that if two of the companies of the 3rd Battalion of the 106th had been swung in a northwest direction, thus filling the gap, the Japanese attack could have been contained. This is a complete misreading of the *gyokusai*. The main attack struck where the defense line was strongest and overran the dug-in positions of the two Army battalions. The only way the Japanese forward motion could have been stopped on that morning was by a defense in depth, which would have been able to bend back only a few dozen yards before the Japanese could be contained.

A further indication of how far Corps was out of touch concerns its evaluation of the attack. Robert Sherrod, no friend of the 27th, reported that at a correspondents' briefing by Corps at 0800 on 7 July Corps described a breakthrough by two Japanese companies accompanied by two tanks.[57] Division was by this time aware of the nature of the breakthrough since, by then, over one-third of the 105th had been wiped out. If Corps really believed that there were only two companies of Japanese to deal with, H. M. Smith's actions in refusing to release Marine units to the Army become understandable. There was no need to commit his Marine units "piecemeal" if the enemy to be dealt with was so weak. From H. M. Smith's prejudiced point of view, even two Army battalions should be able to contain two companies. Even by the next morning, 8 July, Corps was still underestimating the number of Japanese involved.

The NTLF summary for 6–7 July labeled General Griner's second estimate of the numbers involved "of doubtful accuracy." At 0936 on 8 July, Corps sent a message to Admiral Turner containing the following information: "These two battalions were overrun by a considerable force estimated to be at least 300 to 400 Japanese supported by 2 tanks."[58] General Griner protested such underestimates vehemently. He placed before H. M. Smith the actual burial count made by his officers. He recalled that on 8 July he had invited General Erskine to come forward or send one of his staff officers to observe the scene of the *gyokusai*. Erskine had declined then, and it was not until the officers appointed by Admiral Spruance arrived that anyone from higher authority had visited the scene. Griner noted that he had been the only general on the ground soon after the attack was contained and this had hap-

pened in his command area. He complained to H. M. Smith,
"I submit that my personal observations be given more credence than is indicated by the record."[59] General Griner's
complaints of the Marine reactions to the disaster prompted
Admiral Spruance to appoint a two-man commission to ascertain the facts concerning the *gyokusai*. On 9 July the commission investigated the on-site conditions and reported later that
between 1500 and 3000 men had been involved in the attack,
certainly not very specific statistics. However, these figures
were taken from General Griner's report to Corps which at
0900 on the 7th indicated 1500 Japanese were involved; later
at 1300 this was updated to 3000 with the note that "the
estimate was unconfirmed and of doubtful accuracy." Despite
this information, which had been supplied by General Griner,
H. M. Smith sent his message on the morning of 8 July to
Admiral Turner giving the figure as "300 to 400." Eventually
H. M. Smith reluctantly accepted the lower figure estimated
by the Spruance team, noting that he thought 1500 a liberal
estimate. The more careful body count by Colonel Bidwell
made on General Griner's orders was ignored by H. M. Smith
and his supporters, since this would indicate even more definitely how serious the early morning Japanese attack against
the 27th Division had been. On 15 July, Corps Headquarters
specifically refused to change its earlier reports to Admiral
Turner, stating that the more than 300 freshly killed Japanese
in front of the 10th Marine constituted a large part of the
attacking force.[60] The Spruance team had also reported that
"technically there was no breakthrough of the 27th Division.
Although the front line was penetrated to a depth of 1500
yards, the division reserve had at last contained the attack." It
further stated that "there is no question but that our troops
fought courageously."[61] This last statement must be measured
carefully by what was later reported by Robert Sherrod in his
Time article and, most importantly, by H. M. Smith's intemperate outbreaks during the day of the action.

If the officers at Corps really believed that 300 to 400 Japanese had overrun two Army battalions, H. M. Smith's outburst
against the 27th Division becomes more understandable even
if still inexcusable. Robert Sherrod, a friend and admirer of
H. M. Smith, recorded a portion of these unwarranted and

uncalled-for slurs against the men of the 27th Division uttered by H. M. Smith during the evening of 7 July. He wrote that H. M. Smith said:

They're yellow. They are not aggressive. They've held up the battle and caused my Marines casualties. I'm sending the 2nd Division through them tomorrow and I hope the 2nd doesn't get into a fight passing through. I'm afraid they'll say, "You yellow bastards" as they pass through.[62]

H. M. Smith that evening had truly earned his sobriquet of "Howlin' Mad." From this moment onward H. M. Smith's angry and ill-informed comments, bolstered by the near fictional accounts of Sherrod, would be accepted by the rank and file of the Marine Corps. The 27th Division was thus stigmatized as "yellow bastards."

Long after the Tanapag Plain battle, H. M. Smith was still searching for a scapegoat, trying to show that he had known what was going to happen and blamed the events on the 27th and their commander. He told Robert Sherrod:

In the heat of battle there is time to inquire only into the immediate cause or causes when a unit displays a lack of combat effectiveness. Griner's failure to be prepared for the banzai was due to his disloyalty or inefficiency.[63]

Part II

It has been necessary to go into some detail concerning the actions on Saipan after Gen. Ralph Smith's relief since they have been linked by the myth-makers with earlier events. They have become confused in the minds of many Marines who served on Saipan. Some are still convinced that the stories they heard of poor Army performance all occurred while Ralph Smith commanded the division. He is thus blamed for the supposed failures of the Army at the Tanapag *gyokusai* which occurred twelve days after he had left the island. After dismissing such beliefs as rank ignorance, one must now inquire as to what had been going on in Hawaii and Washington during this period as a reaction to the summary dismissal of Gen. Ralph Smith.

The many articles and books written after 1944 refer to the events on Saipan as "The Smith vs. Smith" affair. This too is misleading. At no time was Ralph Smith ever involved in a power struggle with his commanding officer. He was surprised and shaken by his relief, but did not create a scene on Saipan and left quietly on the regular morning plane to Kwajalein. Although he believed vehemently that he had been treated unjustly, at no time after leaving Saipan did he ever question H. M. Smith's right or authority to relieve him. He did not initiate the furor that came from the media quarrel between the Hearst and Luce publications. Unlike H. M. Smith, he did not rush into print immediately after the war to justify his actions. His defense during that period was taken up by the Army historian, Edmund Love, who was concerned more with vindicating the good name of the division than in focusing on the single injustice of the relief of one general officer.

Ralph Smith, a soldier for almost twenty-eight years, swallowed any bitterness and obeyed orders, one of the first of which came from General Richardson. Upon reporting to the commander of Army units in the Central Pacific on 27 June, he was told to take as much time off as possible and write a report of what had happened.[64] Despite the difficulty of recreating such a detailed report with none of the official division papers at his disposal, Ralph Smith produced a sixteen page report covering 15–24 June. There were also eighteen pages of annexes to the main report. The report was held up until copies of orders to and from the 27th Division and journal entries for the division and subordinate units became available. When the work was completed on 11 July, it was forwarded to General Richardson's headquarters.[65] From there it was made available to Admiral Nimitz and his CINCPOA staff.

Although Gen. Ralph Smith's report was not yet completed, General Richardson decided to act on 4 July. He appointed a board of officers to investigate the circumstances surrounding Ralph Smith's relief. This was a blue ribbon commission, whose chairman was Lt. Gen. Simon B. Buckner. Members were Maj. Gen. John Hodge, Brig. Gen. Henry Holmes, Jr., Brig. Gen. Roy Blount. Lt. Col. Charles Selby acted as the recorder. These members of the so-called Buckner Board met nine times between 7–26 July to consult and examine the documentary evidence and examine witnesses concerning the performance of Ralph Smith and the 27th Division on Saipan.[66] Some of the most important materials examined were Gen. H. M. Smith and Admiral Spruance's memoranda stating the reasons for the relief, Gen. Ralph Smith's newly completed report, General Jarman's report of 30 June, General Griner's certificate dated 12 July, and Colonels Kelley and Ayers' reports. Particularly important were H. M. Smith's written charges against Ralph Smith made to Admiral Spruance. These were supplemented by a letter written by H. M. Smith on 27 June at the request of General Richardson, in which he elaborated on earlier statements. In addition, the Board had available all the pertinent orders and journals, copies of which Ralph Smith had used in preparing his report. The investigation's thoroughness included annexes and appendices to the final report—a document more than two inches thick. Robert Sherrod, H. M. Smith, and others tried to discredit the report by pointing out that no Marines or Naval personnel were called by the Board. Only four Army officers were questioned by the Board, however. One was Gen. Ralph Smith; another was Colonel Ayers. Most of the information provided to members of the board came from written memoranda, orders, and reports. It is doubtful whether Admirals Spruance and Turner, far removed from the events on Saipan, could have added anything to their official statements. Much the same can be said for H. M. Smith and his staff. His written statements, particularly the letter of 24 June to Admiral Spruance, were most definite and specific on the reasons why he wanted Ralph Smith removed. H. M. Smith's direct testimony could probably have only further prejudiced his case against Ralph Smith, since the reasons given for the relief were clearly technical, petty, and not the real reasons for H. M. Smith's actions. Charges of favoritism by the Buckner Board can only be sustained if one believes that these men would ignore a mass of evidence at hand to protect one of their own. H. M. Smith's biographer attempts to make such a case by suggesting that

Richardson would do anything to have the Army supplant the Marines as the major factor in the Central Pacific. He intimates that Generals Buckner and Hodge also had good reason to whitewash their colleague.[67] Yet despite General Richardson's well-established position *vis à vis* the Marine Corps, he took no direct part in the deliberations and did not sign the Buckner Report, although pressed by Admiral Nimitz to do so. Most written attacks on the Board's veracity overlook the fact that this was an Army investigation, convened to determine whether one of its senior generals had performed poorly. Gen. George C. Marshall justified Richardson's actions, writing that:

In appointing the Army Board to examine persons and records within his jurisdiction, General Richardson followed Army precedent. The Board had no judicial authority. It served to advise him as senior army commander in the theater on the aspects of the case from the point of view of Army officers.[68]

A careful reading of the Buckner Board's deliberations should quiet all criticism as to its fairness. Its findings should further negate the charge of overt, willful bias in favor of the Army. One of the members, General Blount, who had been deputized by the Board to visit Saipan during the investigation, later revealed that he believed the report was a whitewash of H. M. Smith and his staff. He accused Buckner and Hodge of pulling punches in order to appease the Navy. Blount had wanted to file a minority report, using all the materials he had gained during his stay on Saipan, to openly condemn the actions of H. M. Smith and the Navy on 24 June. Some idea of the report he wanted can be gained by his reference to H. M. Smith as a "stupid egomaniac! A perfect ass if ever one lived."[69]

The task given to the Board by General Richardson was twofold: Did the officers who relieved Ralph Smith have legal authority to do so, and was the relief justified by the facts?[70] The first question could be answered almost immediately. No one in the Army chain of command ever accused Admirals Spruance and Turner or Gen. H. M. Smith of going beyond the limits of their authority. It was probably not even necessary for H. M. Smith to confer with Turner and Spruance before issuing an order relieving the commander of the 27th. The Board therefore answered the first charge in the affirmative. The second was much more difficult to answer—all the hundreds of pages in the supporting evidence in the Report addressed the question of whether the facts justified Ralph Smith's relief. The Board had to decide immediately on what grounds H. M. Smith, and by extension Admiral Spruance, relieved Ralph Smith. This was not difficult to establish since H. M. Smith had signed a letter to Admiral Spruance prepared by General Erskine which specifically stated the reasons. There were three:

1. That Ralph Smith on two occasions contravened an order given by Corps with reference to the 105th RCT which had reverted to Corps control. Ralph Smith had no right to issue any order to that unit.

2. The engaged unit of the 105th did not push its advance rapidly enough toward Nafutan Point.

3. Failure of the 27th on 23 and 24 June to begin its advance on time, thus holding up the Marine divisions on its flanks.[71]

Since these allegations have already been covered in previous chapters, it is sufficient here to deal only with the Buckner Board's findings on these points. The first of H. M. Smith's charges was examined and found lacking in substance. Although H. M. Smith might have intended the 105th to revert to Corps control, this was never made clear to Ralph Smith. The second order in question given by Ralph Smith to the 2nd Battalion of the 105th did not substantially alter the preliminary order relayed to him by General Erskine. At worst this incident was simply poor communication between H. M. and Ralph Smith, since the latter was convinced that he still retained control of the unit. Ralph Smith was therefore acting in good faith and his contravention, if indeed it was a contravention, had no effect on later operations.[72] Brig. Gen. Thomas North, in a memorandum later summarizing the Buckner Report for General Handy, stated of this part of H. M. Smith's case, "My impression from the appendices to the report is that Holland Smith added this charge as an afterthought in order to strengthen his case."[73] Gen. Robert Hogaboom, USMC, a member of H. M. Smith's staff, was also very definite in noting that this charge was something probably added by General Erskine and not a serious reason to remove an officer from command. He stated much later: "Certainly this was not any reason for relieving a man because the Division would be remiss if it didn't supervise in some degree what (one of its) units was doing although attached to another Division."[74]

The second accusation concerning the Army unit's slowness of movement in capturing the Nafutan Point area was also dismissed by the Board as having little substance. General North summed up the reasons for the Board's decision when he wrote:

It appears from the records that Holland Smith's headquarters was unfamiliar with the situation. He himself had not visited the area and the staff work at his headquarters was not up to the standards taught by the Army. The exhibits indicate that this unit met far greater resistance than was estimated by the Corps headquarters.[75]

The third charge was also declared unsubstantiated. The Board obviously had gone into all the details of H. M. Smith's proposed drive northward which has been related in Chapter 8 and its findings were as follows:

The bulk of the 27th Division was opposed by the enemy's main defensive position, on a difficult piece of terrain, naturally adapted to defense, artificially strengthened, well manned, and heavily covered by fire. Lt. Gen. Holland M. Smith was not aware of the strength of this position and expected the 27th Division to over-run it rapidly. The 27th Division, instead of massing its personnel in a frontal attack against the strongest part of the enemy's position, initiated a maneuver to contain and outflank the enemy's resistance. The delay incident to this situation was mistaken by Lt. Gen. Holland M. Smith as an indication that the 27th Division was lacking in aggressiveness and that its commander was inefficient.[76]

The memorandum of General North to General Handy also amplified this finding when it stated, "The evidence again indicated that staff work at Holland Smith's headquarters was weak."[77]

The Buckner Board issued its report to General Richardson on 4 August, who then forwarded it to the appropriate higher headquarters. All material relating to the investigations of the Board and its report were classified as either Secret or Top Secret and no part was ever released to the press during the war. Its findings were that Holland Smith had full authority to relieve Ralph Smith from his command; that Holland Smith was not fully informed regarding conditions in the zone of the 27th Division when he issued orders relieving Ralph Smith; that the relief of Ralph Smith was not justified by the facts, and that Ralph Smith's official record or future commands should not be adversely affected by his relief.[78]

The points generally agreed on by both Marine and Army officers of the units involved in this entire affair concerns the veracity of H. M. Smith's charges. Both sides tend to believe that the three charges made by H. M. Smith to Spruance were not the actual reasons for Ralph Smith's relief. The generally accepted reason was simple to express although nearly impossible to prove. H. M. Smith, as early as the Makin operation, had focused on the 27th Division all his pent-up suspicions about the Army. They and their commander came to epitomize what was wrong with the Army. From that time forward, H. M. Smith, despite a few statements to the contrary, could never accept that the 27th was doing a good job. He was convinced on Saipan that the 27th was a bad outfit; at best the men wouldn't fight, while at worst they were cowards and Ralph Smith would not make them fight. So obviously convinced was he that he relieved Ralph Smith only one day after the drive north had begun. If his case resting on the three counts made to Spruance was weak, then the charge that the 27th wouldn't fight was even weaker when the division had such a short time in which to prove itself. This charge would have been even more difficult to prove considering that his Corps staff work with regard to the 27th had been so sloppy. Had H. M. Smith's actual reasons been placed before the Buckner Board, their reaction would probably have been much sharper than it was.

The adverse statements made to the Board by General

Jarman concerning the performance of the 27th Division must be considered, since H. M. Smith's defenders have used them to justify his condemnation of the 27th Division. In a memorandum on 30 June for the Board, General Jarman complained that the troops in Nafutan lacked "offensive spirit"; they would take terrain and then at nightfall give it up to organize a defensive perimeter.[79] To counter this, he issued an order that ground gained would not be surrendered that way. General Jarman exaggerated when he stated that "a battalion will run into one machine gun, and be held up for several hours." There was only one battalion operating in Nafutan during the time Jarman commanded the division, and as the unit reports from this battalion indicate, it was held up by more than a single machine gun. There is no doubt that the 2nd Battalion of the 105th did not charge ahead in a *gung ho* fashion after 25 June. They had learned some sad lessons from the Japanese during the previous days. One battalion attacking against an unknown number of dug-in defenders had to be very careful of its night defenses. It was discovered after the *banzai* attack on 27 June that the Japanese had almost as many men in their Nafutan defenses as the single Army battalion allotted the task of winding up the operation. In a similar manner, General Jarman noted that on 27 June, after he replaced Colonel Ayers, he saw only a few yards advance in Death Valley. He reported that Colonel Stebbins told him the men of the 106th "lacked the will to go forward" and he had to get the unit "personally in hand before they would move." Enough has already been presented of the fighting in Death Valley to cast doubt on the accuracy of this observation.

A final point to be made concerns General Jarman and Colonel Stebbins' statements. Neither man was familiar at first hand with the situation he was describing. General Jarman pushed into command of a division engaged in a fierce struggle, could by 27 June only begin to comprehend the nature of the Japanese defenses and the problems these posed to an attacking force. His knowledge of Nafutan can be questioned even further. The 105th was under Corps control and General Jarman, busy with the northern push, would have had no reason to have personally witnessed the action of the 2nd Battalion. Colonel Stebbins, although previously Chief of Staff of the

Division, had only one day's experience in direct confrontation with the Japanese defenses in Death Valley when he addressed General Jarman about the performance of his command.

General Richardson did not wait for the Board's report before taking further action. When he realized that Ralph Smith's relief was probably uncalled for, he appointed him to command the 98th Division which General Griner had commanded until ordered to Saipan. In a questionable maneuver, Richardson then decided to visit Saipan on 12 July. It is questionable only because of the mixed-up nature of command in the Central Pacific. General Richardson ostensibly had command of all Army units in the huge area, but actual combat control of these units came under Naval command. Richardson's relationship with the 27th Division was thus nebulous. They were still attached to V Amphibious Corps, yet he was responsible for their supply and maintenance. If it had not been for the furor over the removal of Ralph Smith and H. M. Smith's berating of the 27th Division for the relative success of the *gyokusai* attack, Richardson's visit to the island would have occasioned little comment. General Richardson later stated his reasons for his visit; he wished to see the island for himself and he had a number of awards which he wanted to present to men of the 27th Division for previous actions. Despite H. M. Smith's allegations, Admiral Nimitz had been informed of Richardson's proposed visit to Saipan and had done nothing to halt it.

It is difficult to sort out the facts of Richardson's visit; the story presented by H. M. Smith and Admiral Turner is very different from General Richardson's version. Perhaps it is best simply to relate what each had to say. The most lurid report is that of H. M. Smith, who in *Coral and Brass* claims that General Richardson proceeded to usurp authority by holding a review and decorating troops of the 27th while the fighting was still going on. According to this version, he did this without notifying H. M. Smith. But H. M. Smith does not claim, as his biographer does, that Richardson failed to pay him a courtesy call. Smith admits that Richardson discharged this by visiting him and Admiral Spruance. Ever conscious of protocol, H. M. Smith and General Schmidt then paid a return call to

General Richardson. No sooner had they entered his quarters than Richardson began a tirade. H. M. Smith has Richardson saying:

You had no right to relieve Ralph Smith; I want you to know that you can't push the Army around the way you have been doing; you and your Corps commanders aren't as well qualified to lead large bodies of troops as general officers in the Army, yet you dare to remove one of my Generals.

Then after criticizing H. M. Smith's handling of the Saipan campaign, Richardson was supposed to have delivered the final blow by saying, "You Marines are nothing but a bunch of beach runners anyway. What do you know about land warfare?" Throughout this tirade, H. M. Smith reports he remained silent because he had promised Admiral Spruance to hold his tongue.[80]

Admiral Turner was also angry at what appeared to be an unwarranted assumption of authority by General Richardson. H. M. Smith wrote a memorandum to Turner in which he stated what had occurred. Turner then invited Richardson to visit the *Rocky Mount.* When Richardson responded on 14 July, the admiral began to question Richardson's right to exercise any command functions in the area in which he still held command. There is no record of the conversation, but it appears that the irascible Turner had taken the lead in trying to dress down Richardson. He demanded to know by what authority Richardson had even come to Saipan. When informed that Admiral Nimitz had authorized the visit, Turner demanded to see proof. Thereupon Richardson told him that he need not report to Turner on anything. His command of all Army troops in the Central Pacific overlapped those of Turner and H. M. Smith. After this exchange, General Richardson left to pay a final visit to Admiral Spruance before leaving for Hawaii. It appears that Admiral Spruance, wishing to minimize the personality conflict, passed the latest incident off as an example of Turner's bad temper. Soon after he arrived in Hawaii, however, Richardson was confronted by a request from Admiral Nimitz to answer reports from Turner and Spruance criticizing his visit.[81]

In a long memorandum Richardson answered his critics.[82] He stated that his purpose in going to Saipan was to present awards, an administrative action which meant that he was not required to inform H. M. Smith of his plans. He reminded Nimitz that the admiral knew of his plans and had not objected. He maintained that he did not assemble troops on Saipan, stating, "I told the Garrison Force Commander that I had brought these awards to the area and would bestow them if convenient. The necessary arrangements were made. A platoon of military police formed a guard of honor." With regard to H. M. Smith's report of his conversation, Richardson stated that the letter

has been examined and found so grossly to exaggerate and distort the true facts and circumstances alluded to and the particular conversation in question, as to render a detailed refutation thereof unwarranted dignity to which official correspondence is entitled. Suffice it to say I am inaccurately quoted . . .

After the appearance of the *Saturday Evening Post* articles, General Richardson released a statement to the press denying H. M. Smith's allegations that he had denigrated the Marine Corps in any way and he particularly had not called them a "lot of beach runners." Richardson stated that he had never heard that expression until it was used by Holland Smith himself.[83]

Richardson's memorandum of 23 July was mainly devoted to answering Admiral Spruance's short and reasoned complaint concerning command relationships. Clearly, each man had a good case, Spruance claiming that Richardson in an area of specific operations such as Saipan should be treated only as a subordinate commander of Army troops. Richardson's reply was that he was in overall command of all Army units in the Central Pacific, including air units, and therefore could not in his many functions of that office be considered subordinate to any regional commander. Each man recognized that this type of overlapping command required a clarification never provided during the rest of the war.

This minor incident concerning the clash of egos would amount to little had it not been used by H. M. Smith in his book and articles to link Richardson's visit with the relief of Ralph Smith, the Buckner Board Report, and the *gyokusai*. To H. M. Smith it was clear that they were all connected with the 27th Division's poor performance and General Richardson's attempt to cover it up. This interpretation has been picked up by almost every writer who has dealt with Saipan. Based on the foregoing and on the questionable veracity of much of *Coral and Brass*, there is at least reasonable doubt whether the confrontation between Richardson and H. M. Smith took place as the latter reported it. However, there is one fact that is indisputable. This minor conflict further exacerbated relations between the services in the Central Pacific. Taken with the "Buckner Board Report" which was completed within two weeks after Richardson's return, and the Sherrod article in *Time,* the Saipan problem which had first emerged with the relief of Ralph Smith could not be swept aside. Some action by higher authority was needed to end the undignified and potentially dangerous controversies that threatened the concept of unified command in the Central Pacific.

10 | AFTERMATH

THE CONTROVERSIES BETWEEN H. M. SMITH AND his subordinate Army commanders on Saipan at first had primarily local significance. To the senior Army and Navy officers in Washington faced with the multiplicity of problems of the most complex global war in history, the interservice rivalry in the Central Pacific did not call for much attention. The focus was on the European theater, where the Allied Armies had broken through the German defensive lines and were racing toward Paris. Even in the Pacific, high level decisions on utilizing the now potent long-range bomber force, shipping and supply priorities, and strategic planning for the ultimate conquest of Japan were obviously the key issues concerning General Marshall and Admiral King, Chief of Naval Operations, and their staffs. Had it not been for the continuing embarrassing debates in the public press, the Buckner Board Report would probably have been glanced at and filed, a few noncommittal memos written, and the entire affair shelved without comment. General Richardson's patent dissatisfaction could have been stifled by a single terse communication and the entire affair buried and forgotten. Such a position, however, was not possible once two of the nation's major news-dispensing agencies had chosen to make the controversy on Saipan the centerpiece in a debate over military strategy. The problems raised by H. M. Smith's actions, minor though they were, had to be addressed directly and quickly. Although Pentagon officials of both services could not ignore the minor furor, they could investigate and then take action which would satisfy the pride of the Army, Navy, and Marines while simultaneously burying the entire affair as efficiently as possible.

The Buckner Board Report is the key element in the decisions made in Washington. General Richardson in his letter of transmission had made certain specific recommendations to General Marshall. The most important was that in future operations, Army and Marine units should not be mixed. Failing this, if the reputation of Army officers and men was to be maintained, "then every effort must be expended to exclude from the command any officer whose command experience remotely resembles that exhibited by Lt. Gen. Holland M. Smith in this and other operations." In conclusion, Richardson asked General Marshall to "exert his influence in such matters" to preclude the repetition of incidents such as those in Saipan.[1] The official Army historian, Philip Crowl, was correct when he indicated that the chief of staff's office was not overjoyed to get the Buckner Board Report and that General Marshall's chief advisors "tended to take a 'plague on both your houses' attitude."[2] Maj. Gen. Thomas Handy, assistant chief of staff, read the report and sent a long momorandum to his superior on 16 August 1944 in which he summarized it and attached a draft communication to Richardson for General Marshall's signature. The concluding paragraph to the memorandum was the operative one regarding Ralph Smith's career. General Handy wrote:

Far more important than the present case is the potential danger to future operations of the conditions which developed on Saipan. In my opinion it would be desirable that both Smiths be ordered out of the Pacific Ocean area. While I do not believe we should make definite recommendations to the Navy for the relief of Holland Smith, I think that positive action should be taken to get Ralph Smith out of the area. His presence undoubtedly tends to aggravate a bad situation between the services.[3]

The Deputy Chief of Staff, Lt. Gen. Joseph McNarney, agreed with Handy. In a succinct memorandum written three days after Handy's, he outlined his impressions. General McNarney believed that "there was reasonably good tactical direction on the part of Maj. Gen. Ralph Smith." However, he faulted him because he failed to "exact the performance expected by a well-trained division." Specifically, he believed that Ralph Smith condoned "poor leadership on the part of some regimental and battalion commanders"; the units showed hesitancy to "bypass snipers" and use "because of lack of reserves" as an alibi and displayed "poor march discipline and lack of reconnaissance." Each is a questionable point, as addressed in preceding chapters, made by a senior staff officer 10,000 miles from the scene. McNarney's conclusions are nonetheless important, because they led him to the conclusion, partially based no doubt on the politics of the affair, that Ralph Smith was not an acceptable division commander.[4]

General McNarney was even more blunt when dealing with Lt. Gen. Holland M. Smith and V Amphibious Corps. He believed that the staff work of the Corps was "below acceptable standards" and that "Holland Smith lacks one of the most important attributes of command—fairness . . ." McNarney stated emphatically that "Holland Smith is not fitted to command Army forces." This conclusion was based not only on the scant specific details of the Saipan campaign, but also on statements made by a number of officers to the Buckner Board either in direct evidence or deposition. McNarney suggested that General Marshall in his proposed letter to Admiral King include the statement, "I seriously doubt the advisability of again placing Army units under the command of Lt. Gen. Holland Smith."[5]

Before General Marshall could take the recommended actions, relations between the Marines and Army commanders in the Central Pacific deteriorated even further, primarily because of Robert Sherrod's defamatory article in the 18 September issue of *Time*. Sherrod's account of the Tanapag fight had a devastating effect on the morale of the 27th Division, then recovering from the Saipan campaign on the less than idyllic island of Espiritu Santo. General Griner on 30 September informed General Richardson that he could no longer assume the responsibility of leading the 27th into combat unless some attempt was made to restore the division's good name.

He also complained of misleading captions under the photographs in another Luce publication, the 28 August issue of *Life*, which presented the Saipan campaign as if it were totally a Marine operation. General Griner, assisted by Edmund Love, had prepared a long letter to the editor of *Time* rebutting Sherrod's statements. However, due to wartime restrictions, this letter could not be sent without Admiral Nimitz's permission. General Griner suggested that CINCPOA release to the press the report of the investigating team appointed by Admiral Spruance. Failing this, Admiral Nimitz should be asked to clear the Griner rebuttal to Sherrod's article. General Griner closed his letter by placing the blame for the bad publicity directly on H. M. Smith. He wrote, "In my humble judgement, the Army must now frankly face the fact that under the connivance of at least one Marine, we are being scandalized in the public press."[6]

General Richardson wasted little time in following up Griner's suggestions. He went even further and put together a dossier of complaints aimed directly at H. M. Smith and his faulty command of Army troops on Saipan. He collected testimony from a number of Army officers, who had heard H. M. Smith making directly derogatory remarks in public concerning the 27th Division. Richardson's reason for this work was clearly stated. He wanted to "preclude the subjection of Army troops to his [H. M. Smith's] command." Before sending these documents and a covering letter to Admiral Nimitz, he submitted the dossier to the Judge Advocate General's Office in Hawaii for advice. The opinion given by the legalists was negative. Col. E. H. Snodgrass, in terms echoing the opinions of General Marshall's associates in Washington, wrote that the Saipan problems were "water over the dam." He stated the reality of the situation when he observed that the war in the Pacific was moving to a stage where Navy and Marine units would play a less important role, while the Army and its commanders would gradually become the most important factor in the defeat of Japan. His conclusion was that it was "not good policy to aggravate a frictional issue between the participating services because of the objectionable qualities of one Marine officer."[7]

General Richardson took the advice of his legal officer and

decided not to press the matter with regard to H. M. Smith's unfitness for command. He was content to forward General Griner's complaints with enclosures to Admiral Nimitz with the request that, at the very least, General Griner's letter should be released and the credentials of the *Time* correspondent who had written the article of 18 September be withdrawn. In his memoirs, H. M. Smith sluffs over this incident in less than a paragraph. In this short space, however, he manages to give a false impression of what happened to Richardson's request and the reasons for the lack of ensuing action. H. M. Smith does give Admiral Nimitz a parting shot for not defending the former's questionable command decisions by noting that the Admiral was "always inclined to compromise."[8]

Far from compromising, Admiral Nimitz made his position very clear to General Richardson and also to Admiral King. E. B. Potter, Nimitz's biographer, does not do the admiral justice in reporting Nimitz's reaction to the Saipan imbroglio. While doing everything possible to keep the quarrel from escalating, Admiral Nimitz did not disregard "the whole silly dispute."[9] While his letters to Admiral King on this subject were models of circumspection, his displeasure at H. M. Smith's actions, already in evidence before Saipan, had obviously grown considerably. He was also irked by some of General Richardson's actions, but his official memoranda were always correct, as were those of the Army commander when communicating any part of the subject to Admiral Nimitz. There is considerable evidence that Nimitz had liked Gen. Ralph Smith before the Saipan affair occurred and that his feeling of respect continued throughout General Smith's command of the 98th Division. It must have been apparent to Nimitz that, of all the major actors in this minute drama, Ralph Smith was the only one who had remained silent except when ordered to give evidence. Nimitz further believed that the 27th Division had been harshly treated and much maligned. He forwarded Richardson's complaints to Admiral King with the comment, "I am in complete accord with the objections raised by Lt. Gen. Robert C. Richardson, Jr. to the publication of the subject articles which, in my opinion, are contrary to the best interests of the nation."[10]

In the same memorandum, Admiral Nimitz suggested that there was a definite need to remove the stigma attached to the 27th Division either by the Navy Department in Washington or by Admiral Nimitz himself publicly stating their "continued confidence in the courage and battle efficiency of the 27th Division." Nimitz also suggested that General Griner's letter to *Time* be cleared for publication and that the "author or authors" of the September article in *Time* "be identified" and their credentials rescinded so that "they may not again have an opportunity to publish articles of this nature."[11] Edmund Love claims that he later attended a conference with Admiral Nimitz and Sherrod where the Admiral stated in no uncertain terms his opinion of the type of story filed by the *Time* correspondent and made clear his intention of withdrawing Sherrod's credentials.[12] Fortunately for Sherrod's career as war correspondent, decisions made jointly by higher command in Washington negated Nimitz's plans.

The new charges and countercharges reached General Marshall's office before he had made final disposition of Generals McNarney and Handy's suggestions. The seriousness of the Saipan matter was underscored by a long letter from Admiral King, who in his most forthright manner came to the defense of H. M. Smith. He informed Marshall that he too was concerned that the men of the 27th Division shouldn't suffer unjustly and that H. M. Smith had offered to make a statement lauding their bravery. However, he refused to see any necessity of rescinding Sherrod's credentials, because King claimed, the article of 18 September had properly been reviewed by the appropriate authorities. Admiral King did not make any suggestions on how the good name of the division could be upheld by a simple statement from H. M. Smith even as the *Time* article went unrefuted. The Chief of Naval Operations went to the attack by discussing General Richardson's actions, which he considered the real divisive factor in the Central Pacific. He also criticized the Buckner Board as a unilateral investigation which allowed attacks on H. M. Smith's personal character and professional competence without allowing him to testify.[13] It was apparent from this letter that Admiral King was prepared to do battle for the decisions made on Saipan. He, unlike Admiral Nimitz, was not prone to compromise, and had no intention of letting the matter be filed away if there was any chance that H. M. Smith's actions would not be supported by the Pentagon.

General Marshall obviously had already decided not to be drawn into a long, fruitless controversy with the Navy and Marine Corps. He simply wanted to find a mutually satisfying solution so that the whole matter could be concluded. He was also concerned with avoiding such command conflicts in the future. He indicated as much to Admiral King in a return memorandum of 22 November, in which Marshall noted that what had happened in the Central Pacific was not mere healthy rivalry between the Marine Corps and Army. He suggested that both Nimitz and Richardson conduct an investigation of what happened on Saipan with the objective of preventing any reoccurrence of the embarrassing situation in the future. He included in the memorandum General McNarney's statement that "much of this trouble might be obviated if the senior officers had a better idea of the differences between the basic concept of tactical operations and the reasons therefore as taught by the two services."[14] Attached to Marshall's memorandum was a draft of a telegram that he suggested should be sent to Nimitz and Richardson simultaneously by himself and Admiral King.[15] Admiral King replied to this conciliatory communication with another bellicose answer defending the actions of H. M. Smith and once again attacking Richardson for the appointment of the Buckner Board. He also stated he could not concur in any further investigations, since General Richardson had already done enough damage by his "activities during his visit to Saipan."[16] Finding little consolation in the attitude of the Chief of Naval Operations, Marshall unilaterally decided to end the affair. All the papers concerning the Saipan incident were filed away, and not made available to the public until Secretary of the Army Kenneth C. Royal in 1948 opened the Top Secret records, in part to respond to the charges in H. M. Smith's book and articles, and to disprove the charge that the 27th Division lacked "aggressive spirit."[17]

The message General Marshall had suggested he and Admiral King send jointly to their commanders at Pearl Harbor was telegraphed to General Richardson, who understood enough to stop pressing the Army's case in Hawaii. Admiral Nimitz, disappointed that his suggestions to King concerning Richardson and Griner's complaints were not followed, wrote a personal letter to General Griner. In it he expressed his confidence in the officers and men of the 27th Division and their past and future actions.[18] As predicted by Colonel Snodgrass, the war in the Pacific in its concluding phases was primarily an Army show. True, the Marine Corps served bravely and well winding down the Marianas campaigns on Tinian and Guam, spearheading the tragic assault on Peleliu, and participating in the Okinawa campaign and at the bloodbath of Iwo Jima. But the emphasis had shifted. With MacArthur's return to the Philippines, he became the central figure in the planning for the conquest of the Japanese home islands. In a sense Nimitz's star had waned, and with it went the primary role the Marine Corps had played in the Pacific War. The shift of emphasis served to quiet the Hearst Press and its attacks on Naval and Marine leadership. During the last months of the war the American press had enough good news to report from all battlefronts; most papers now refrained from the sniping which had characterized many earlier stories on the Pacific War. The details of the battle for Saipan slipped from most Americans' memories, as did also the controversy between the Army and Marine commanders there; both would be revived only by H. M. Smith, with the publication of his postwar memoirs.

H. M. Smith's career after Saipan was, on the surface, not damaged by his confrontation with the Army. He remained in overall command of the Marianas operation, although leaving most of the conduct of the campaign on Tinian to Major General Schmidt and that of Guam to Maj. Gen. Roy Geiger. However, true to form, he disagreed with the tactics of one of his subordinates, General Geiger, and also had harsh words for the commander and men of the 3rd Marine Division for, as he believed, their lack of aggressiveness. In September, H. M. Smith's suggestions for the creation of a Marine Headquarters above the level of a corps came into being. Called the Fleet Marine Force, Pacific, that Headquarters had as its components six Marine divisions, four aircraft wings, twenty-eight artillery and antiaircraft battalions, twelve amtrac battalions, and all the supply and engineering units needed to maintain those forces.[19] As the senior Marine officer in the Pacific,

H. M. Smith was selected to command this new unified force with his headquarters in Hawaii. There is considerable evidence that H. M. Smith was not happy despite his new command and the plaudits of a large segment of the American press and public. Part of the reason for his feelings had to do with the nature of the command of the Fleet Marine Force. H. M. Smith, on assuming his new position, had become primarily an administrative officer whose headquarters was responsible for the administration, training, and supply of troops in the field. Under normal circumstances, H. M. Smith would clearly not again be allowed exercise command of troops in combat, although Admiral Nimitz allowed for the possibility that he could act as a task force commander if directed to do so. Because of requests by Admirals Spruance and Turner, H. M. Smith acted in such a capacity at Iwo Jima. But even there he recognized that he was not really needed and was, for all practical purposes, a supernumerary. In an ironic twist of fate, H. M. Smith's apparently exalted command had placed him in roughly the same position as that which had plagued his Army nemesis, General Richardson.

H. M. Smith's exaggerated feelings of isolation were reinforced by his suspicions that Admiral Nimitz had not defended him strongly enough after the Saipan affair had become general knowledge. His suspicions of Nimitz's negative feelings were not new. He had believed from the beginning of his command in Hawaii that the Admiral was at best cool toward him. After Saipan, he had a number of indications that his earlier suspicions were correct. One action of Nimitz, H. M. Smith's fitness report for April–July 1944, the period of the Marianas operation, appeared to confirm his conclusions. The Admiral had marked him only "Fair" in loyalty. As a friend later recalled, "He was furious. Just furious!" over such a low rating and the memory of this slight must have continued to rankle him for years afterward.[20] His new position as Commander of Fleet Marine Force, Pacific also minimized his contact with those naval officers—Spruance, Hill, and Turner—with whom he had had the longest contact. The staff which had served him so well was also broken up. Erskine, promoted to Major General, assumed command of the 3rd Division, and Hogaboom went with him as chief of staff. Colonel McQueen took over the same position with the new 6th Marine Division, and the only senior Army officer on his previous staff, Col. Joseph C. Anderson, was ordered to the 98th Division as its chief of staff.[21] Throughout H. M. Smith's later career, he tended to exaggerate the support he had received, as well as any opposition to his plans. In many ways he had considered his staff as a kind of family. The reassignment of personnel had a traumatic effect upon him and, in combination with other developments, helped create the moods of depression and bitterness that would mar his immediate postwar years.

One of H. M. Smith's failings was that he envisioned himself as a tough, no-nonsense fighting Marine. Much of his toughness was for show. There are many instances where his basic kindly disposition showed through. That, of course, is one of the reasons he was so protective of "his" Marines. He had almost a mystical attachment to the Corps. A significant part of his difficulty on Saipan had been that he could not include the Army units within this circle of affection, and when he thought they failed him, he felt they also threatened the Marines. His concept of toughness would also not allow him to admit he was wrong even on small matters, and he would go to great lengths to prove he was correct. Contrary to his view of himself, his greatest talent was in administrative and training positions. His contributions to the theory and practice of amphibious warfare both before and during the early stages of the war are unquestioned. However, he proved at Saipan that he was at best a mediocre field commander. Yet he yearned for another assignment which would give him a chance once more of directing large bodies of American troops against the enemy. In the Central Pacific theater, that meant command of the forces scheduled for the invasion of Okinawa.

H. M. Smith would probably not have been given preference to command the Tenth Army over a number of competent Army commanders of equal rank, even had the memory of his Saipan operations not been fresh in the minds of the Army high command. The bulk of the Tenth Army would be Army rather than Marine units, and it would have been illogical to seek out a Marine as its commander. Despite these facts mitigating against his selection, H. M. Smith was "let down" by the decision to give the command to the Army's Lt. Gen. Simon B. Buckner.[22]

It is not possible to know exactly what role H. M. Smith's actions on Saipan played in the decision to appoint someone else as Tenth Army commander, or even in his being "kicked upstairs" in the noncombat role of Commander of Fleet Marine Force, Pacific. His command decisions on Saipan and the later private and public debate over the relief of Ralph Smith and the actions of the 27th Division obviously had an effect on his later career. There is no clearcut evidence of what General Marshall said about H. M. Smith's actions. It is likely, as some have claimed, that he vowed H. M. Smith would never command Army divisions again. Such a statement would only duplicate what General McNarney had written on 19 August in his memorandum to Marshall. Even if Marshall had made no statement about H. M. Smith's fitness, it is highly unlikely that he would dismiss the opinions of senior Army commanders. Not only did Generals Richardson, McNarney, and Handy reflect upon the unsuitability of H. M. Smith to further command Army units, but so too did every Army general contacted by the Buckner Board or General Richardson.

On several occasions Gen. H. M. Smith had stressed to a number of Army officers the good relations he had always had with the Army before and during the war. Many of those who defended H. M. Smith's actions in Saipan point to these statements and dismiss most of the Army's negative attitudes as a blind following of General Richardson's prejudices. All that is needed to resolve doubts on this point is to quote the candid comments of some of his Army subordinates. Gen. Ralph Smith, as one might imagine, reported his negative attitude most definitely when he wrote to General Richardson:

I feel it is my duty to make of record my urgent and considered recommendation that no Army combat troops ever again be permitted to serve under the command of Marine Lt. Gen. Holland M. Smith . . . So far as the employment of Army troops are concerned, he is prejudiced, petty and unstable. He has demonstrated an apparent lack of understanding of the accepted Army doctrines for the tactical employment of larger units.[23]

Gen. Ralph Smith's opinion has been dismissed by some as the reaction of a disgruntled commander who had been relieved by a superior. But the two Army generals who succeeded Ralph Smith in command of the 27th Division also voiced negative opinions. General Jarman, who was selected by H. M. Smith to rectify the presumed mistakes made by the Army and who receives the best treatment of any Army commander in H. M. Smith's memoirs, had the following opinion of Marine and Army cooperation based on his experiences at Saipan:

[It is my] earnest recommendation that in future operations of any kind where the Army and the Marine Corps are employed, that under no circumstances should Army Divisions be incorporated in the Marine Corps . . . Their basic concepts of combat are far removed [from those of the Army].[24]

Gen. George Griner, who took command of the 27th Division from Jarman on 28 June, had even harsher words for H. M. Smith when he wrote:

Based upon my experience and contacts with Lt. Gen. Holland M. Smith, USMC, it is my firm opinion that he is so thoroughly prejudiced against the Army that no Army Division serving under his command alongside Marine Divisions will receive fair treatment or their deeds fair evaluation.[25]

Gen. Redmond Kernan, 27th Division DIVARTY Commander, wrote that H. M. Smith's attitude endangered "the efficiency and morale of the Division during combat." He closed by stating, "In my opinion, he is unsuited for command of Army troops and I personally desire never to serve under his command again."[26] A final example of how Army commanders felt about H. M. Smith's fitness for combat command comes from Brig. Gen. Clark Ruffner, an observer from General Richardson's staff who had also served as Ralph Smith's Deputy Division Commander at Makin. He wrote to General Richardson:

In my opinion, Army troops should not be placed under command of Maj. [sic] Gen. Holland M. Smith, Marine Corps, for the reasons that he is highly prejudiced against the Army, as demonstrated in his manner, language, overbearing attitude toward Army commanders and his biased remarks and actions in all Army matters. I could not loyally serve under his command in peace or war, especially in combat, and believe no Army units should serve under him.[27]

Letters such as these obviously had some effect not only on General Marshall, but also on Admiral Nimitz, who had the very difficult task of trying to maintain harmony in the Central Pacific theater. Most of these letters and other equally disparaging comments, together with documentation relating to the Saipan controversy, were in the Buckner Board Report, which had been made available to H. M. Smith for his comments. Smith thus knew what most of the Army officers thought of him. Even the expressions of affection and loyalty from the senior Army officer who had been on Corps staff, Col. Joseph Anderson, could not counterbalance all the hostile opinions. It is no wonder that H. M. Smith came to view himself as being attacked unjustly. He had expressed this view most succinctly to the Commandant of the Marine Corps in a letter which he advised should be torn up. He wrote, "Good God! I work my heart out, clean up the Marianas in good style and all I get is—Crap."[28] H. M. Smith took into retirement these same feelings and when he decided to write his memoirs, they influenced his judgment. Together with a writer who did not check the factual base of H. M. Smith's memories, he produced a book which his friends tried to dissuade him from publishing and now admit damaged his reputation. But H. M. Smith has had his revenge. Those highly flawed reminiscences in *Coral and Brass* and *The Saturday Evening Post* over the past thirty-five years have come to be accepted by most readers as fact; H. M. Smith is firmly established as one of the great combat commanders of World War II, while the 27th Division and by extension all Army units in the Central Pacific are thought of as having performed poorly at best.

The 27th Division had taken the full brunt of H. M. Smith's scorn for Army units and their tactics. Even before the arrival of General Griner, Smith had taken every opportunity to belittle the officers and men of the division. Members of his staff had taken their cue from his intemperate statements. Maj. Stephen McCormick, a Signal Corps officer who attended H. M. Smith's morning staff conferences after 28 June, was one of those who witnessed this behavior. General Richardson solicited his report and McCormick wrote that at these conferences

. . . derogatory insinuations were continually made regarding activities of the 27th Division by staff members. It was obvious to an observer that General Smith reflected the staff's attitude, particularly in questions regarding the 27th patrols, with resultant head shaking and facial grimaces.

He concluded that, in his opinion, "the Commanding General and Staff of the NTLF held units of the 27th Division in little esteem, actually a position bordering on scorn."[29] It is no wonder that, within a short period of time, the ordinary Marine who had no opportunity for joint action with the Army infantrymen had become convinced that everything he had heard about them was right. Hadn't old "Howlin' Mad" removed its incompetent commander and later two regimental commanders been fired because of incompetence? The stories in *Time* were magnified and, in the retelling, exaggerated until most Marines actually believed that the men of the 27th "froze in their foxholes" at Nafutan and later at the Tanapag Plain battle and in both places let the Japanese run over them, causing an untold number of Marine casualties. In each case, so the stories went, the Marines had been called on to save the situation. It was, and is, fruitless to point out to such otherwise decent men that most of what was taken by them as fact was nothing but the worst scuttlebutt. But it was believed not only by the rank and file, but also by senior Marine officers, who spread the story of the 27th's cowardice far beyond the Central Pacific. The earlier attitudes of the hard-pressed Marines who had managed only a slight foothold and sustained heavy casualties on D day + 1 and had welcomed the Army, had changed irrevocably. Robert Sherrod, one of the Corps' staunchest defenders, gave a good example of such hostility when he reported a conversation he overheard on the day after the *gyokusai*. He recalled:

Feeling was intense, I observed. In line for breakfast on the morning of July 8 I noted the conversation of two Marine Corps officers: "I wonder if they are going to court-martial any of these 27th officers for neglect of duty? The Japs got through without a shot being fired."[30]

Such attitudes were not surprising given that the overall commander of the Saipan operation publicly characterized the men of the 105th RCT as "yellow" and hoped that his Marines would not call them "yellow bastards." By his intemperate words and actions, H. M. Smith had made certain that the men of the 27th Division would be so remembered. Robert Sherrod, despite his later affirmation that the soldiers of the 27th had fought bravely, had been as guilty as H. M. Smith in branding the unit. Historians of the Pacific War, including some of the most famous, such as E. B. Potter and Samuel Eliot Morison, have been content to repeat H. M. Smith's accusations against the 27th Division without adequately checking their veracity.[31] The 27th Division bore the stigma to Okinawa and beyond. Although the division carried out its combat duties on Okinawa adequately, the rumors of poor performance, carried over from Saipan, were magnified in this later operation. It is no exaggeration to state that over forty years later, the surviving officers and men of the 27th Division still live with the malicious rumors and fundamentally incorrect reporting that date to the relief of General Ralph Smith.

Perhaps the man least scarred by H. M. Smith's sudden decision to do his duty on 24 June was Ralph Smith, the man who in many stories has been cast as one of the antagonists. His reluctance to be an active participant in the ongoing controversy has already been noted. That does not mean that behind his stoic behavior he was unaffected by his summary dismissal, or by the later accusations made against the performance of the men of the 27th Division. He had been surprised and shocked by the timing and method of his removal, but had accepted it. General Richardson's continued confidence in him and the subsequent favorable report by the

Buckner Board on his actions had buoyed his spirits. Soon after arriving in Hawaii, he had been assigned to replace General Griner as commander of the 98th Division. The 98th was stationed in the outer islands with headquarters in Kauai. Although he held that position for only a very short period, Gen. Ralph Smith's style had seemingly not been altered by the events on Saipan. An account from an article in the 98th Division newspaper remarked that he made a practice of eating in the ordinary mess halls and constantly chatted with enlisted men, either individually or in groups. The Army correspondent remarked that he got things done despite being well liked and recalled meeting wounded veterans of the 27th from Saipan who had "an almost fierce loyalty for General Smith . . . They did not talk about General Smith, the man with two stars, but about the man who was up front in the battalions with them."[32]

Gen. Ralph Smith's tenure with the 98th Division was short-lived because General Marshall had concurred with his subordinates that the two main actors in the Saipan drama should not remain in the same theater. The Marine Corps obviously had no intention of removing H. M. Smith from the Central Pacific. Therefore, true to his word, Marshall had orders issued for Ralph Smith to proceed to the mainland to await further assignment. He arrived in San Francisco in early September 1944, and he and his wife drove to Tucson to visit other members of the family. While there, Smith received orders from Ground Forces Headquarters to proceed to Little Rock, Arkansas, to take command of the huge Infantry Replacement Center at Fort Robinson. The Army higher command was making good on suggestions of the Buckner Board. The new assignment, however challenging, was also to be of short duration. Before the war, it was well known within a limited circle in the Army that Ralph Smith was one of the few senior officers who could qualify as an expert in European affairs. The scramble for commanders of the rapidly expanding Army in the months following Pearl Harbor had meant that only in rare instances could the strengths of general officers be matched with the pressing requirements of that tense period. The 27th Division, already in the Pacific theater, had needed a commanding officer, and Ralph Smith, a newly promoted Major General, had needed a division. Thus, for over two years, his knowledge of Europe and particularly France had been subordinated to the major effort of defeating the Japanese. In early 1945, perhaps as a result of the unasked-for publicity attending his relief and Marshall's decision to transfer him out of the Pacific, he was given probably the most satisfying position in his long Army career.

France, after the rapid advance of the Allies and the fall of Paris, had experienced a strange, chaotic system of government. Officially its status was that of a liberated state, but this term cannot adequately describe the overlapping jurisdictions of the non-French military authorities, the Gaullist forces, and the still functioning civilian authorities. By the late fall of 1944, although the postwar government of France had yet to be determined, the French clearly deserved to govern themselves. This dictated a change in status from a liberated to an associated state, under the guidance of General de Gaulle and his associates. Although the war continued to rage on its borders, France was considered as a fully functioning independent state. Diplomatic amenities had to be observed and an embassy created and staffed in Paris. Jefferson Caffery was selected as the first United States ambassador to the new provisional government of France. The post of Military Attache during this period was most important. The man who filled it had to be senior enough not to offend de Gaulle's sensibilities, and be able to confer officially and unofficially with officers of other nations without always being of inferior rank. Ideally he should speak the language well and understand the history and culture of France. He should be gregarious and at ease with the most important people in both an official and unofficial capacity. No more qualified officer could have been selected than Ralph Smith.

Gen. Ralph Smith's career in France forms another interesting chapter in an extraordinary life, but it is extraneous to the main concerns of this book. It is sufficient to note here that, in the course of his many duties, Smith dealt with most of the important men in French affairs, including de Gaulle, Charles Bidault, Generals Juin and de Lattre de Tassigny (the last mentioned became a very good friend). Smith's post also brought him in contact with General Eisenhower and his Chief of Staff

Walter B. Smith and a host of other American and Allied officers, as well as many visiting American dignitaries. There is every indication that General Smith and his staff, among whom was Capt. David Rockefeller, performed their difficult but generally pleasurable tasks brilliantly. One such task was connected with the negotiations leading to the signing of an agreement whereby a private agency, the Cooperative for American Remittances for Europe (CARE) took over distribution of food packages in France.

When Gen. Ralph Smith's tour of duty ended on 1 July 1946, he could look back on a job well done. He had fully justified General Marshall's faith. Having completed thirty years of service, he decided to retire at the end of his four-month leave in October 1946 and then moved immediately to take over the organization and direction of all CARE activities in France and the Low Countries, an obviously vital work for war-torn Europe. Once again this difficult post was mastered, and the fact that many in Western Europe did not go hungry during the winter of 1946–47 was due in part to Ralph Smith's organizational ability.[33] In all the positions he held in Europe and the United States after 1947, Smith was equally successful and left behind not only solid accomplishments, but also a host of friends. In his retirement in Palo Alto, even at the age of 91, Smith remains a positive force in a variety of civil and intellectual activities. Although denying vehemently that the events on Saipan in any way damaged his career or preyed on his mind, he is aware that the only black mark on his career was his summary relief on Saipan. The conventional wisdom concerning the events of June 1944 has been accepted, in part due to Ralph Smith's understandable reticence. He never attempted to defend himself publicly, which, combined with the War Department's shelving of the investigations during the war and the active propaganda campaign waged by Gen. H. M. Smith, meant that he and his division continue to be vilified.

What, then, are the major conclusions to be drawn from this study, undertaken forty years after the events it describes occurred? The most obvious is, without prejudice, to put in perspective the decision-making processes and activities of Gen. H. M. Smith and his staff of the NTLF by weighing other evidence against what H. M. Smith said was done. A second and interconnected result has, one hopes, also emerged—the reconstruction, as far as possible, of the events before and after Ralph Smith's relief. In the course of this study, certain generalizations also emerge, many of which are as valid today as then. Some of these are:

1. The Marine Corps then and now is a specialized organization whose greatest strength is its elite quality. Few units of the Army can measure up to the Corps' general standards. It is strongest when given specialized small unit tasks. Herein lies the strength of the Corps' training and the expertise of its officers.

2. Army divisions in time of war draw their recruits from a different segment of the civilian population than does the Marine Corps. The Army selection process is not as rigorous, nor the training as intense. When different philosophies of attack and defense are factored into these differences, when Army and Marine units are mixed in a campaign there is always the possibility of problems, unless each units' commanders have wide general experience and a sympathy with the officers and men, and the training of their counterparts.

3. Personalities always play a crucial role in command situations. Likes and dislikes cannot be waved away to leave clones of perfect commanding officers with no potentially destructive emotions. However, every effort should be made to curb such tendencies in order to ward off personality conflicts. To select as a commander of joint forces a man such as Gen. Holland M. Smith with an overpowering attachment to his own branch of service is to introduce a major divisive force at the outset on the highest level of command.

4. War by its very nature tends to be chaotic. Senior commanders should be aware of the illogical nature of combat. Once units are committed to battle, the plans so carefully drawn up are modified by circumstances. One of the major factors in altering most good staff planning is the very human characteristic of making errors. This does not mean that incompetence should be ignored, much less rewarded, but that a senior commander should be able to discern the difference between minor and major mistakes and react accordingly.

If this study of command relationships has meaning in a

more direct specific sense, beyond the recitation of what happened on a faraway island long ago, it is that Marine Lt. Gen. Holland M. Smith, entrusted with command of troops from two different services, managed to ignore or violate all of these truisms. A comment by H. M. Smith's longtime antagonist, General Richardson, summed this up when he wrote: "War is a series of mistakes. Everyone makes them, but Holland Smith held up to ridicule and disparagement only those of the Twenty-Seventh Division."[34] The evidence points conclusively to the fact that the relief of Ralph Smith certainly was uncalled for, and the substitution of a new untried commander to bring about a quicker victory on Saipan may even have lengthened the campaign. In any case, the slurs cast upon the officers and men of the 27th Division then and later by H. M. Smith in his articles and books were totally unwarranted and unconscionable. Those who gave a part of themselves to gain victory in the conquest of this important island bastion deserved better—from their commander and from their nation.

NOTES

CHAPTER 1:

[1]Holland M. Smith's brief account of the dismissal of Ralph Smith is in H. M. Smith and Percy Finch, *Coral and Brass* (New York: Charles Scribner's Sons, 1949), pp. 171–175.

[2]General Richardson's position on the inadequacy of Marine training for Corps command is best stated by his answer to H. M. Smith's article which appeared in *The Saturday Evening Post*, 11 December 1948 and was reprinted as an adjunct to Robert Sherrod's "Answer & Rebuttal to Smith vs. Smith, The Saipan Controversy," *Infantry Journal*, January 1949, p. 28.

[3]There are so many examples in Smith, *Coral and Brass*, that it is difficult to cite all of them. For examples, see his comments on Turner, p. 117, Richardson, pp. 125 and 177, and Nimitz, pp. 157 and 178.

[4]Transcript of interview by author with Gen. Ralph Smith, 1 February 1984, and Ralph Smith, "Preliminary Report on Operations of the 27th Division at Saipan" dated 11 July 1944.

[5]*San Francisco Examiner*, 8 July 1944, p. 1.

[6]*New York Journal-American*, 17 July 1944, p. 10.

[7]*New York Journal-American*, 18 July 1944, p. 12.

[8]*New York Times*, 10 September 1944, p. 25.

[9]Ibid.

[10]Ibid.

[11]*New York Herald-Tribune,* 14 September 1944, pp. 1 and 15.

[12]Ibid.

[13]"The Generals Smith," *Time,* 18 September 1944, p. 66, and Robert Sherrod, *On to Westward* (New York: Duell, Sloan and Pearce, 1945), pp. 88–93.

[14]Ibid., p. 161.

[15]*Time,* 18 September, 1944, p. 66.

[16]Ibid.

[17]The technical and as some claim petty charge against Ralph Smith concerned overlapping jurisdiction over the 2nd Battalion, 105th Infantry at Nafutan Point.

[18]Sherrod, "Answer & Rebuttal," *Infantry Journal,* January 1949, p. 26.

[19]Ibid.

[20]Norman V. Cooper, "The Military Career of General Holland M. Smith," Ph.D. thesis, University of Alabama, 1974, University Microfilms, Ann Arbor, Mich., pp. 402–408.

[21]Edmund Love, "The 27th's Battle for Saipan," *Infantry Journal,* September 1946, p. 8.

[22]Fletcher Pratt, "Spruance, Picture of an Admiral," *Harpers Magazine,* August 1946, p. 153.

[23]Cooper, "Holland Smith," p. 458.

[24]Ibid., pp. 430–433.

[25]Ibid., p. 434.

[26]Ibid., pp. 449–450 and Smith, *Coral and Brass,* pp. 12–13.

[27]Cooper, "Holland Smith," p. 459.

[28]Ibid., pp. 459–460.

[29]Ibid., p. 464.

[30]Benis Frank, Oral History Transcript, General Clifton Cates, Marine Corps Historical Archives, 1967, pp. 222–223.

[31]Holland M. Smith and Percy Finch, "Howlin' Mad's Own Story," three parts, *Saturday Evening Post,* 6, 13, and 20, November 1948.

[32]Cooper, "Holland Smith," p. 470.

[33]Love, "Smith vs. Smith," *Infantry Journal,* November 1948, pp. 3–13.

[34]Sherrod, "Answer & Rebuttal," *Infantry Journal,* January 1949, pp. 14–28.

35William Manchester, *Goodbye Darkness* (Boston: Dell Books, 1982), p. 314.

CHAPTER 2:
1The early years and pre-World War II career of Gen. Holland M. Smith are abstracted from Cooper, "Holland Smith" and Smith, *Coral and Brass*.

2Smith, *Coral and Brass*, pp. 48–49.

3Ibid., p. 52.

4Ibid., pp. 60–61 and Transcript of interview by author with Brig. Gen. Harold O. Deaken, USMC (ret.), Los Altos Hills, Ca., 13 September 1983, p. 1.

5Smith, *Coral and Brass*, pp. 72–73, 88, 96.

6Ibid., pp. 75–77.

7Ibid., pp. 100–102.

8Undated handwritten note by Adm. Raymond Spruance to Brigadier General Youndall, USMC, commenting on an Historical Monograph, p. 4 in Spruance Papers, Hoover Institution of War and Peace, Stanford, Ca., and Cooper, "Holland Smith," pp. 199–202.

9Smith, *Coral and Brass*, pp. 104–105.

10Vice Adm. George C. Dyer, *The Amphibians Came to Conquer*, Vol. I (Washington, D.C.: U.S. Government Printing Office), pp. 218–223.

11Cooper, "Holland Smith," p. 203.

12Ibid., p. 205.

13Oral History Transcript, Rear Adm. Charles Moore, USN, 1970, Naval History Archives, pp. 825–827.

14Smith, *Coral and Brass*, p. 114 and Dyer, *Amphibians*, Vol. II, p. 618.

15Smith, *Coral and Brass*, p. 115.

16Edmund Love, *The 27th Infantry Division in World War II* (Washington: Infantry Journal Press, 1949), p. 25.

17Cooper, "Holland Smith," pp. 207–208, and Command Chart in War Department Historical Division, *The Capture of Makin* (Washington, D.C.: War Department Historical Division, 1946), pp. 32–33 and Transcript of interview by author with Gen. Ralph Smith, Palo Alto, Ca., 7 October 1983, pp. 4–5.

CHAPTER 3:

[1]The details of Ralph Smith's early life and career are taken from a transcript made by the author of six tapes recorded by Gen. Ralph Smith between 26 August 1982 and 14 August 1983.

[2]William P. Snyder, "Walter Bedell Smith: Eisenhower's Chief of Staff," *Military Affairs*, Vol. XLVIII, No. 1, January 1984.

[3]Transcript of interview by author with Col. Henry Ross, USA (ret.), 20 April 1984, La Mesa, Ca., p. 7.

[4]Transcript of interview by author with Gen. Ralph Smith, Palo Alto, Ca., 7 October 1983, p. 7.

[5]For the best example of this myth see Smith, *Coral and Brass*, p. 173.

[6]S. L. A. Marshall, *Bringing Up the Rear, A Memoir*, ed. Cate Marshall (San Rafael, Ca.: Presidio Press, 1979), p. 62.

[7]The most detailed account of the Division's history is Love, *The 27th Infantry Division*.

[8]Ibid., pp. 7–8.

[9]Smith, *Coral and Brass*, pp. 168–169.

[10]Transcript of interview by author with Maj. Theodore Baltes, USA (ret.), San Jose, Ca., 24 June 1984.

[11]*Life*, 18 August 1941, and undated notes of Robert Sherrod in Sherrod's Miscellaneous Papers, Syracuse University.

[12]Love, *The 27th Infantry Division*, p. 15.

[13]Ibid., p. 21.

[14]Ibid., pp. 18–19.

[15]Ibid., p. 21.

[16]Transcript of interview by author with former Capt. Bernard Ryan, USA, San Jose, Ca., 27 February 1984, p. 2.

[17]Transcript of interview by author with Col. James Mahoney, USA (ret.), Los Altos Hills, Ca., 28 January 1984, p. 5.

[18]This is confirmed by interviews with Colonel Mahoney, Colonel Ross, Major Baltes, and Captain Ryan and Edmund Love.

[19]Transcript of interview with Colonel Ross, p. 16.

[20]Transcript of interview with Colonel Mahoney, p. 6.

CHAPTER 4:

¹Philip Crowl & Edmund Love, *Seizure of the Gilberts and Marshalls* (Washington, D.C.: Department of the Army, 1955), pp. 11–21; E. B. Potter, *Nimitz* (Annapolis: Naval Institute Press, 1976), p. 295; Dyer, *The Amphibians,* Vol. II, p. 613; and Samuel Eliot Morison, *The Two-Ocean War* (Boston: Little, Brown & Co., 1963), pp. 295–296.

²Dyer, *The Amphibians,* Vol. II, pp. 613–614; Morison, *Two-Ocean War,* pp. 297–298; and Philip Crowl, *Campaign in the Marianas* (Washington, D.C.: Department of the Army, 1959), pp. 7–8.

³W. S. Le Francois, "Carlson's Makin Raid," in S. E. Smith (ed.), *The United States Marine Corps in World War II* (New York: Random House, 1969), pp. 237–256.

⁴Smith, *Coral and Brass,* p. 114.

⁵This is fully covered in a long letter from Admiral Spruance to Col. Warren Hoover, 14 January 1949, pp. 4–5, Spruance Miscellaneous Papers, 1937–63, Hoover Institute Archives. See also Potter, *Nimitz,* pp. 305–306 and Dyer, *The Amphibians,* Vol. II, pp. 617–619.

⁶Spruance letter to Col. Warren Hoover, p. 7 and Vice Adm. E. P. Forrestel, *Admiral Raymond A. Spruance, USN* (Washington, D.C.: U.S. Government Printing Office, 1966), p. 72; and Historical Division, U.S. War Department, *The Capture of Makin* (Washington, D.C.: Historical Division U.S. War Department, 1946), p. 7.

⁷Edwin P. Hoyt, *Storm Over the Gilberts* (New York: Mason/Charter, 1978), p. 46.

⁸Transcript of interview with Gen. Ralph Smith, 7 October 1983, pp. 4–5. See line of command chart in GALVANIC Operations Plan A2–43 contained in Ralph Smith Papers, Box 23, Hoover Institute Archives, Stanford, Ca. Also duplicated in War Department, *Makin,* pp. 32–33.

⁹Transcript of interview, Colonel Ross, pp. 3–6.

¹⁰Transcript of interview with Captain Ryan, p. 4.

¹¹Smith, *Coral and Brass,* p. 118.

¹²Transcript of interview with Colonel Ross, p. 5.

¹³Crowl and Love, *Seizure of the Gilberts and Marshalls* and War Department, *Makin.*

14 War Department, *Makin,* p. 15 and Crowl & Love, *Seizure of the Gilberts and Marshalls,* p. 71.

15 Ibid., pp. 8–9.

16 Love, *27th Infantry,* pp. 25–26.

17 War Department, *Makin,* pp. 12–15, 21.

18 Ibid., pp. 16–21.

19 The firing schedule for all ships and also charts and landings and transport staging areas are in Plan A3–43, Ralph Smith Papers, Box 23, Hoover Institute Archives, Stanford, Ca.

20 Transcript of interview with Colonel Mahoney, p. 8.

21 Transcript of interview with Captain Ryan, pp. 6–7.

22 Ibid., p. 8.

23 S. L. A. Marshall, *Bringing Up the Rear* (San Rafael, Ca.: Presidio Press, 1979), p. 64. See also transcript of S. L. A. Marshall's Report on Makin Operation, Ralph Smith Papers, Box 26, pp. F20–F21, Hoover Archives, Stanford, Ca.

24 Crowl & Love, *Seizure of the Gilberts and Marshalls,* p. 97.

25 Transcript of interview with Captain Ryan, p. 6.

26 War Department, *Makin,* pp. 115–118.

27 Ibid., pp. 118–120 and 125–126.

28 Ibid., pp. 126–127, 132.

29 John Costello, *Pacific War, 1941–1945* (New York: Quill, 1982), p. 436.

30 Transcript of interview with Gen. Ralph Smith, 7 October 1983, pp. 2, 9.

31 Dyer, *The Amphibians,* Vol. II, pp. 677–680.

32 See chart in Henry I. Shaw, Jr., *Tarawa, A Legend is Born* (New York: Ballantine Books, 1968), p. 130.

33 Smith, *Coral and Brass,* p. 125.

34 Ibid., p. 128.

35 Ibid.

36 Ibid.

37 War Department, *Makin,* p. 70.

38 Transcript of interview with Colonel Ross, p. 11.

39 War Department, *Makin,* pp. 126, 128.

40 Transcript of interview by author with Gen. Ralph Smith, Palo Alto, Ca., 9 July 1984.

41 Smith, *Coral and Brass,* pp. 127–128.

42 Transcript of interview with Colonel Ross, p. 7.

[43]Smith, *Coral and Brass,* p. 127.

[44]Transcript of interview with Gen. Ralph Smith, 7 October 1983, p. 7.

[45]Letter Capt. Charles E. Coates to Commanding General 27th Infantry Division dated 31 October 1944 reproduced in Sherrod, "Answer and Rebuttal," *Infantry Journal,* January 1949, p. 25.

[46]Transcript of interview with Captain Ryan, p. 5.

[47]Smith, *Coral and Brass,* p. 126.

[48]Transcript of interview with Gen. Ralph Smith, 7 October 1983, p. 7. See also Crowl & Love, *Seizure of the Gilberts and Marshalls,* p. 97.

[49]Letter from James Roosevelt to author, 30 November 1983.

[50]Copy of letter from John A. Lynch to Mr. Paul Kiniery, c/o *America,* 1 August 1949 in General Ralph Smith's private files. See also transcript of S. L. A. Marshall's report on Makin, Ralph Smith Papers, Box 26, pp. F19–F21, Hoover Institute, Stanford, Ca.

[51]Transcript of interview with Colonel Mahoney, p. 11.

[52]Marshall, *Bringing Up the Rear,* p. 69.

CHAPTER 5:

[1]Transcript of interview by author with Gen. Ralph Smith, Palo Alto, Ca., 9 July 1984, pp. 4–5.

[2]Hoyt, *Storm Over the Gilberts,* p. 152.

[3]Transcript of interview with Gen. Ralph Smith, 9 July 1984, p. 2 and transcript of interview by author with Gen. Robert Hogaboom, USMC (ret.), St. Mary's City, Md., 4 October 1984, p. 1.

[4]Richardson's lengthy memorandum is reproduced in Cooper, "Holland Smith," pp. 259–260.

[5]Admiral King reported that Marshall had expressed misgivings about Marines handling Corps command many times. Cooper, "Holland Smith," p. 261. Forrest C. Pogue in *George C. Marshall, Organizer of Victory* (New York: Viking Press, 1973) does not mention this, but in a brief conversation at Colorado Springs on 9 October 1984 with the author, he indi-

cated that Marshall had serious doubts about Marines handling large units.

[6]Details of planning for and execution of FLINTLOCK are taken from Robert Heinl, Jr. & John Crown, *The Marshalls: Increasing the Tempo* (Washington: Historical Branch, U.S. Marine Corps, 1954), pp. 9–116 and Crowl & Love, *Seizure of the Gilberts and Marshalls,* pp. 167–332.

[7]Cooper, "Holland Smith," p. 267.

[8]Marshall, *Bringing Up the Rear,* pp. 77–78.

[9]Crowl & Love, *Seizure of the Gilberts and Marshalls,* p. 334.

[10]Details of planning for and execution of CATCHPOLE are taken from Heinl & Crown, *The Marshalls,* pp. 117–160 and Crowl and Love, *Seizure of the Gilberts and Marshalls,* pp. 333–334.

[11]Smith, *Coral and Brass.*

[12]Decorations are a touchy subject to many cynical combat soldiers who expect that major awards will be passed around freely to senior commanders at the end of an operation. Klein's case is typical of higher headquarters passing over a person for reasons extraneous to the events for which one was to be cited. If ever any infantryman deserved the Congressional Medal it is Artie Klein. Details confirmed by interview by author with Edmund Love, Flint, Michigan, 6 August 1984, p. 12 and Edmund Love, "Omak," *Army,* September 1981, pp. 36–41.

[13]Heinl & Crown, *The Marshalls,* pp. 140–141.

[14]Transcript of interview with Edmund Love, p. 19.

[15]Heinl & Crown, *The Marshalls,* p. 151. These published figures are the same reported in RCT Operations Report, File 327–0.3, National Archives, Suitland, Md. Those given by Crowl & Love, *Seizure of the Gilberts and Marshalls,* p. 360 of thirty-seven dead and ninety-four wounded are incorrect. They were taken from Samuel Eliot Morison, *History of United States Operations in World War II,* Vol. VII, *Aleutians, Gilberts and Marshalls* (Boston: Atlantic, Little Brown, 1951), p. 304.

[16]Heinl & Crown, *The Marshalls,* p. 151.

[17]John T. Mason, Jr., Oral History Transcript, Admiral Harry Hill, Navy Department Historical Archives, 1966, Vol. 1, p. 447.

[18]Letter H. M. Smith to A. A. Vandegrift, 8 March 1944 as cited in Cooper, "Holland Smith," p. 276.

[19]Mason, Oral History Transcript, Admiral Harry Hill, Vol. 1, pp. 447–448.

[20]Transcript of interview with Colonel Ross, p. 16.

[21]Transcript of interview with Edmund Love, p. 14.

[22]Ibid., p. 2.

[23]Mason, Oral History Transcript, Admiral Harry Hill, Vol. 1, p. 448.

CHAPTER 6:
[1]Carl Hoffman, *Saipan: The Beginning of the End* (Washington, D.C.: Headquarters U.S. Marine Corps, 1950), pp. 13–18.

[2]Ibid., p. 22.

[3]Ibid., p. 23.

[4]Operations Plan 3–44 in NTLF, VAC Marianas, Phase I, (Saipan) Operations Report, File A1–2, Marine Corps Archives.

[5]Hoffman, *Saipan,* p. 26.

[6]Hdq. NTLF, Marianas, Phase I, (Saipan), G–2 Report, Enclosure D, File I–5, p. 6, Marine Corps Archives.

[7]Lt. Col. John Lemp, Secret Memorandum, "Observer Report on the Marianas Operation (FORAGER)" to Commanding General Army Ground Forces, 11 July 1944, pp. 13–14; and transcript of interview with Colonel Mahoney.

[8]Love, *27th Infantry,* pp. 116–117; and Lemp, "Observer Report," p. 6.

[9]Hoffman, *Saipan,* p. 32.

[10]Lemp, "Observer Report," p. 10.

[11]Hoffman, *Saipan,* p. 34.

[12]Lemp, "Observer Report," p. 8.

[13]Ibid., pp. 12–13.

[14]Hoffman, *Saipan,* pp. 3–6; and 1:62,500 and 1:20,000 scale maps prepared for JICPOA by Engineers dated May 1944.

[15]Hoffman, *Saipan,* p. 13.

[16]Samuel Eliot Morison, *History of United States Operations in*

World War II, Vol. VIII, *New Guinea and the Marianas,* pp. 167–169.

[17]Headquarters NTLF, Marianas, Phase I, G–2 Report, Enclosure D, pp. 6–9.

[18]Ibid., p. 6.

[19]Ibid., pp. 9–10.

[20]Ibid., p. 10.

[21]Morison, *New Guinea and the Marianas,* pp. 174–185.

CHAPTER 7:

[1]Details of Marine Corps planning and landings of 2nd and 4th Marine Divisions are taken from Hoffman, *Saipan,* pp. 17–76 and "4th Division Operations Report, Saipan, 15 June–9 July," File A14–1 and "2nd Marine Division, Special Action Report, Phase I, Saipan," File A11–1, Marine Corps Archives.

[2]Hoffman, *Saipan,* pp. 48–55.

[3]Major Yoshida's Report in "Headquarters NTLF, Marianas, Phase I, G–2 Report, Enclosure D," pp. 9–10.

[4]Morison, *History,* Vol. VIII, pp. 197–198.

[5]"4th Division Operations Report, Saipan," File A14–1, Annex J., pp. 1–6.

[6]"2nd Marine Division, Special Action Report, Saipan," File A11–1, pp. 1–13.

[7]Hoffman, *Saipan,* p. 69. Lemp, "Observer Report," p. 18 indicated a figure of 2000 for two days fighting.

[8]Hoffman, *Saipan,* p. 82.

[9]Headquarters NTLF, Marianas, Phase I, Report, p. 11. See Lemp, "Observer Report," p. 18 for contrasting figures.

[10]Hoffman, *Saipan,* pp. 86–90.

[11]Morison, *History,* Vol. VIII, pp. 202–203.

[12]Ibid., p. 203.

[13]327-03, "Operations Report, Battle for Saipan, 27th Division, 17 June–6 August 1944," National Archives, Suitland, Md. and Love, *27th Infantry,* pp. 128–130.

[14]Transcript of interview with Colonel Ross, p. 14.

[15]Love, *27th Infantry,* p. 132.

[16]Transcript of interview with Colonel Ross, pp. 14–15.

[17]Transcript of interview by author with Gen. Jacob Herzog (ret.), Albany, N.Y., 17 September 1984, p. 12.

[18]Transcript of interview with Captain Ryan, p. 12.

[19]Ibid., pp. 13–14.

[20]Love, *27th Infantry,* pp. 153–154.

[21]327-INF (165) 0.3 Report of Saipan Action, 165th Infantry Regiment, 16–17 June 1944, National Archives, Suitland, Md.

[22]Hoffman, *Saipan,* p. 98.

[23]Love, *27th Infantry,* p. 158.

[24]Ralph Smith, Top Secret, "Report on Operations, 27th Division, Saipan," 15–24 June 1944, p. 3, Ralph Smith's private papers.

[25]Lemp, "Observer Report," p. 25.

[26]Extract from Ralph Smith's radio recording, 19 June 1944, General A. A. Vandegrift File, PC 465, April–June 1944, Box 4, Folder 41.

[27]Headquarters NTLF, Marianas, Phase I, G–2 Report, Enclosure D, pp. 16–18.

[28]Love, *27th Infantry,* p. 167.

[29]Benis Frank, Oral History Transcript, Gen. Robert Hogaboom, 1972, Marine Corps Archives, p. 208 and Transcript of interview by author with General Hogaboom, St. Mary's City, Md., 4 October 1982, p. 2.

[30]Love, *27th Infantry,* pp. 168–175.

[31]Ibid., pp. 184–185.

[32]Ralph Smith, "Report on Operations," p. 6.

[33]NTLF Operations Order 9–44 in NTLF, V AC, Marianas, Phase I, Operations Report, F16A1–2, Marine Corps Archives and 327–2.1 Operations Report, Saipan, National Archives, Suitland, Md.

[34]Robert Sherrod, "Some Reports on 27th Division at Saipan," Sherrod Notes from Notebooks, May–Dec. 1944, p. 2.

[35]Love, *27th Infantry,* p. 222.

[36]FO #45, Able, 327.0.3 "Operations Report, 27th Division," National Archives, Suitland, Md. Italics are the author's.

[37]Love, *27th Infantry,* p. 190.

[38]Ibid., p. 193.

[39]Transcript of interview with Captain Ryan, p. 16.

[40]Ralph Smith, "Report on Operations," p. 9.

[41]Ibid., p. 11.

42Love, *27th Infantry,* p. 194.

43Ibid., pp. 209–213.

44Col. Geoffrey M. O'Connell to Lt. Gen. R. C. Richardson, 12 July 1944, Exhibit WW, "Proceedings of a Board of Officers Appointed by Letter Order Serial AG 333/3, 4 July 1944, H. Q. U.S. Army Forces in Central Pacific Area, 31 July 1944," hereafter referred to as Buckner Board Report. Copies of this report are in the National Archives, Washington, D.C. and Box 035, Robert C. Richardson, Jr. Papers, Hoover Institution of War and Peace, Stanford, Ca.

45Love, *27th Infantry,* pp. 219–222.

46Smith, *Coral and Brass,* p. 171.

47Colonel O'Connell to General Richardson, 12 July 1944, Exhibit WW, Buckner Board Report, Richardson Papers, Box 035.

48Ibid.

49Extract from Ralph Smith's radio recording, 19 June 1944, p. 4.

CHAPTER 8:

1Details of action on Saipan are based upon the narratives from Hoffman, *Saipan,* pp. 126–148 and Love, *27th Infantry.* Additional materials taken from NTLF Special Action Report of Marianas, Phase I, Saipan, 12 August 1944, Marine Corps Archives, "Operation Report Battle for Saipan, 27th Division, 17 June–6 August 1944," 4th Division Operation Report, Saipan, 15 June–9 July 1944 and 2nd Marine Division, Special Action Report, Phase I, Saipan.

2Hoffman, *Saipan,* p. 127.

3Ibid., pp. 126–128.

4Ibid., p. 128.

5NTLF Operations Order 10–44 in NTLF Special Action Report, duplicated in Love, *27th Infantry,* pp. 658–659 and Love, "Smith vs. Smith," *Infantry Journal,* November 1948, p. 6.

6Ralph Smith, "Report on Operations," p. 10.

7Ibid., p. 11.

8Ibid., p. 13 and Love, *27th Infantry,* p. 657.

9Love, *27th Infantry,* p. 660.

10Benis Frank, Oral History Transcript, General Graves Erskine, 1975, p. 325.

11Ibid., pp. 325–326.

12Transcript of interview with Colonel Ross, p. 21.

13Love, *27th Infantry*, p. 227.

14Transcript of interview with Captain Ryan, pp. 18–19.

15Ibid., p. 20.

16Transcript of interview with Colonel Mahoney, p. 16.

17327-INF 1(106)-0.3 After Action Report 106th Infantry, p. 4, National Archives, Suitland, Maryland.

18Transcript of interview with Colonel Ross, p. 19.

19Love, *27th Infantry*, p. 227 and Hoffman, *Saipan*, pp. 127–128.

20Love, *27th Infantry*, pp. 231–232.

21Ibid., pp. 239–240.

22Ibid., pp. 233–239.

23"Troop Locations, Overlay to Japanese Northern Marianas Group Operations" in Hdqs. Northern Troops Landing Force, Marianas, Phase I, Saipan, G–2 Report, Enclosure D, Marine Corps Archives.

24Hoffman, *Saipan*, p. 138.

25Ibid., p. 136.

26Ibid., pp. 137–138. Author's italics.

27Love, *27th Infantry*, pp. 243–244.

28Cooper, "Holland Smith," p. 334.

29Frank, Oral History Transcript of General Erskine, p. 319.

30Benis Frank, Oral History Transcript, Lieutenant General John McQueen, 1973, pp. 86–92 and Oral History Transcript, General Joseph Stewart, 1973, pp. 30–33, Marine Corps Archives.

31Cooper, "Holland Smith," p. 312.

32Statement by Gen. Ralph Smith quoted in Sherrod, "The Saipan Controversy," *Infantry Journal*, January 1949, p. 19. General Smith has also restated the lack of liaison between Corps and his division a number of times in various interviews with the author.

33Report Maj. Gen. Sanderford Jarman to Lt. Gen. R. C. Richardson, 23 June 1944, Exhibit K, Buckner Board Report, Richardson Papers, Box 035.

34Cooper, "Holland Smith," pp. 335–336.

[35]Transcript of interview with Gen. Ralph Smith, 1 February 1984, p. 7.

[36]File A14–3, 4th Marine Division Operations Reports, p. 42, Marine Corps Archives.

[37]Robert Sherrod Notebook, Saipan 1944, 17 June–2 July, p. 57, Sherrod Private Papers, Washington, D.C.

[38]Frank, Oral History Transcript of General Erskine, p. 322.

[39]Ibid., p. 318.

[40]Ibid., p. 322.

[41]Ibid.

[42]NTLF Operational Despatches, Despatch from CTG 56.1 to CG 27th Infantry Division, 24 June 1944, Marine Corps Archives. Telegram is duplicated in Love, "Smith versus Smith," *Infantry Journal,* November 1948, p. 10.

[43]Transcript of interview with General Hogaboom, p. 5 and Columbia University Oral Histories, Rear Adm. Charles Moore, 1970, p. 1044.

[44]Frank, Oral History Transcript of General Erskine, p. 323.

[45]For Spruance's reactions see handwritten letter Spruance to Jeter Isley, 14 January 1949, p. 9 in Spruance Miscellaneous Papers, 1937–1963, Hoover Institution Archives, Stanford, Ca.

[46]Sherrod Notebook, Saipan 1944, 17 June–2 July, p. 57.

[47]H. M. Smith to A. Vandegrift, 18 July 1944, HMS papers, Auburn as quoted in Cooper, "Holland Smith," p. 341.

[48]Written comment to author by Joseph Sykes, Palo Alto, Ca., 15 January 1985.

[49]Love, *27th Infantry,* pp. 249, 261.

[50]Ibid., pp. 249–252.

[51]327–0.3, 27th Division, G-3 Periodic Reports, 23 June 1944, National Archives, Suitland, Md.

[52]Love, *27th Infantry,* pp. 254–258.

[53]Ibid., p. 259 and Hoffman, *Saipan,* pp. 137–138.

[54]Transcript of interview with Edmund Love, pp. 8–9.

[55]Transcript of interview with Jacob Herzog, p. 18.

[56]Transcript of interview with Edmund Love, p. 13.

[57]Transcript of interview with General Ralph Smith, 1 February 1984, p. 10.

[58]Love, *27th Infantry,* p. 263.

[59]Ibid., p. 264.

60Frank, Oral History Transcript of General Erskine, p. 324.
61Ibid., pp. 324–325.
62Ibid., p. 325.
63Ralph Smith, "Report on Operations," pp. 15–16.
64Transcript of interview with General Ralph Smith, 1 February 1984, p. 10.
65Ibid., p. 10.
66Ralph Smith, "Report on Operations," p. 16.
67Pilot's Flight Log Book, 25 June 1944, of Navy Captain (Ret.) Frank Harris, Angels Camp, Calif.

CHAPTER 9:
1Smith, *Coral and Brass,* p. 173.
2The combat portions of this chapter are based upon Love, *27th Infantry,* pp. 263–472; Hoffman, *Saipan,* pp. 157–243; Crowl, *Campaign in the Marianas,* pp. 203–265; and 327–INF (105) 0.3 Operations Report, 105th Infantry, Saipan; 327–INF (165) 0.3 Report of Action of 165th Infantry, Saipan; and 327–INF (106) After Action Report, 106th Infantry, in National Archives, Suitland, Maryland.
3Love, *27th Infantry,* pp. 263–273.
4Lemp, "Observer Report," p. 31.
5Love, *27th Infantry,* p. 299.
6Ibid., or Hoffman, *Saipan,* p. 287.
7Love, *27th Infantry,* p. 279 and Lemp, "Observer Report," p. 31.
8Love, *27th Infantry,* pp. 280–284.
9Lemp, "Observer Report," p. 31 and Hoffman, *Saipan,* p. 150.
10Love, *27th Infantry,* pp. 271–275 and 106th Infantry After Action Report.
11Gen. Sanderford Jarman's Report to General Richardson, 30 June 1944, Buckner Board Report, Exhibit QQ.
12Ibid. and transcript of interview with Colonel Ross, p. 17.
13Insert of Ayers' statement in Sherrod, "Answer and Rebuttal," *Infantry Journal,* January 1949, p. 17.
14Love, *27th Infantry,* p. 293 and Crowl, *Campaign in the Marianas,* pp. 213–214.
15Ibid., p. 298.

16Ibid., pp. 299–315 and Crowl, *Campaign in the Marianas,* pp. 217–220.

17Cooper, "Holland Smith," pp. 332–333.

18Crowl, *Campaign in the Marianas,* p. 211.

19Love, *27th Infantry,* p. 325.

20Smith, *Coral and Brass,* p. 175.

21Secret Memorandum, Major General Griner to Lieutenant General Richardson, 11 October 1944 in Richardson Papers, Box 035.

22Ibid.

23Ibid.

24Transcripts of interviews with General Herzog, Colonels Ross and Mahoney, and Captain Ryan.

25Crowl, *Campaign in the Marianas,* p. 224.

26Brigadier General E. B. Colladay to Island Commander, 5 September 1944, Richardson Papers, Box 035.

27Cooper, "Holland Smith," p. 269.

28Crowl, *Campaign in the Marianas,* p. 232.

29Ibid., p. 230.

30Ibid., p. 248.

31Smith, *Coral and Brass,* p. 194. Perhaps it is only a proof-reading error, but H. M. Smith on p. 195 confuses the Army regiments, having the "300 yard" gap existing between the 1st and 3rd Battalions of the 106th Infantry.

32The exact size of the gap is not known with any accuracy. Most commentators use the figure of 400 yards although H. M. Smith in *Coral and Brass,* p. 195 indicates it was only 300 yards wide. As to coverage, see statement by Col. Leslie Jensen, insert in Sherrod, "Answer and Rebuttal," *Infantry Journal,* January 1949, p. 20.

33NTLF Report, Marianas, Phase I, G–2 Report, Enclosure D, pp. 57–58. Saito's message is also duplicated in Hoffman, *Saipan,* pp. 222–223 and Crowl, *Campaign in the Marianas,* p. 257.

34Transcript of interview with Col. Benjamin Hazard, 5 January 1985, p. 1 and statement by Lt. Col. W. M. Van Antwerp, insert in Sherrod, "Answer and Rebuttal," *Infantry Journal,* January 1949, pp. 20–21.

35Love, *27th Infantry,* p. 436.

36For the detailed action of the Japanese attack see 327 INF

(105) 0.3 Operations Report, 105th Infantry, Saipan and Historical Division, War Department, "The Fight on Tanapag
Plain," *Small Unit Actions* (Washington, D.C.: War Department, 1946); Crowl, *Campaign in the Marianas,* pp. 256–264;
and Love, *27th Infantry,* pp. 440–450.

37Love, *27th Infantry,* p. 443 and Hoffman, *Saipan,* p. 223.

38Hoffman, *Saipan,* pp. 224, 228 and Love, *27th Infantry,*
pp. 455–456.

39Memorandum Major General Griner to Commander
NTLF (Maj. Gen. Schmidt), 16 July 1944, Richardson Papers,
Box 035. Marine Major W. P. Oliver gives a different story
claiming that Griner was informed. Hoffman, *Saipan,* p. 224.

40A copy of General Smith's citation is in Richardson Papers, Box 035 and Love, *27th Infantry,* p. 484; the Presidential
Unit Citation signed by Secretary of the Navy James Forrestal
is in Hoffman, *Saipan,* Appendix X.

41"World Battlefronts," *Time,* 19 July 1944.

42Love, *27th Infantry,* footnote 1, p. 429, states that he had
affidavits of over 50 officers and men attesting to this. General
Griner also stated this in his Memorandum to Commander
NTLF, 16 July 1944, in Richardson Papers, Box 035. The
G–1 of the 27th Division, Colonel C. Oakley Bidwell, in a
letter to Dr. June Hoyt, 30 July 1984, confirms this.

43C. Oakley Bidwell to Dr. Hoyt, 30 July 1984.

44Hoffman, *Saipan,* pp. 224–225 and Love, *27th Infantry,* p.
461.

45Hoffman, *Saipan,* pp. 228–229.

46Major General Griner's Certificate dated 12 July 1944 to
Buckner Board, Exhibit ZZ.

47Love, *27th Infantry,* p. 519.

48Insert in Sherrod, "Answer and Rebuttal," *Infantry Journal,* January 1949, p. 27.

49Memorandum General Griner to Commander NTLF, 16
July 1944, Richardson Papers, Box 035.

50Love, *27th Infantry,* p. 440.

51The number and location of the Japanese casualties in the
gyokusai attack caused quite a minor controversy between the
27th Division and Corps. For further details see Ibid., p. 452;
Memorandum General Griner to Commander NTLF, 14 July

1944 and Memorandum Col. Oakley Bidwell, 12 July 1944 in Richardson Papers, Box 035.

[52] Transcript of interview with Colonel Hazard, 5 January 1985 and transcript of telephone interview with Howard Cook, Palo Alto, Ca., 18 January 1985.

[53] Sherrod, *On to Westward,* p. 140.

[54] Letter C. Oakley Bidwell to Dr. Hoyt, 30 July 1984.

[55] *Time,* 18 September 1944, p. 66 and Smith, *Coral and Brass,* p. 179.

[56] Statement by General Griner, Insert in Sherrod, "Answer and Rebuttal," *Infantry Journal,* January 1949, p. 22.

[57] Sherrod's Notebooks, 7 July 1944.

[58] Memorandum General Griner to Commander NTLF, 14 July 1944, Richardson Papers, Box 035.

[59] Ibid.

[60] Memorandum NTLF to Commander 27th Division, 15 July 1944, Richardson Papers, Box 035 and General Griner's statement, insert in Sherrod, "Answer and Rebuttal," *Infantry Journal,* January 1949, p. 222.

[61] Admiral R. A. Spruance, "Report on Japanese Counterattack at Saipan on Morning of July 1944," dated 19 July 1944. Part of this part is duplicated in Cooper, "Holland Smith," p. 358.

[62] Sherrod Notebooks, 7 July 1944.

[63] Sherrod's notes on a conversation with Gen. H. M. Smith, 29 August 1944, Sherrod Papers.

[64] Transcript of interview with Gen. Ralph Smith, 1 February 1984, p. 12.

[65] Major Gen. Ralph Smith, "Report on Operations."

[66] Memorandum from Brig. Gen. Thomas North to General Handy, 11 August 1944, p. 1, National Archives, Suitland, Maryland.

[67] Cooper, "Holland Smith," pp. 385–386.

[68] Quoted in article by James Minife, *New York Times,* 12 November 1948.

[69] Letter from Gen. Ray Blount to General Richardson, 15 November 1948, Richardson Papers, Box 036.

[70] Buckner Board Report, p. 1.

[71] Lt. Gen. H. M. Smith to Com TF51, 24 June 1944 in Buckner Board Report, Exhibit D.

72Buckner Board Report, p. 3.

73Memorandum North to Handy, p. 2.

74Transcript of interview with General Hogaboom, p. 5.

75Memorandum North to Handy, p. 2.

76Buckner Board Report, p. 10.

77Memorandum North to Handy, p. 2.

78Buckner Board Report, p. 10.

79Memorandum General Jarman to General Richardson, 30 June 1944; Ibid., Exhibits I and J.

80Smith, *Coral and Brass,* pp. 177–178 and Cooper, "Holland Smith," pp. 382–383.

81Details of Turner's conversation with Richardson are from Admiral Turner to Commander 5th Fleet, 16 July 1944. Spruance's complaint is in Admiral Spruance to Admiral Nimitz, 18 July 1944. Admiral Nimitz to General Richardson, 19 July 1944, Richardson Papers, Box 036.

82General Richardson to Admiral Nimitz, 23 July 1944, Richardson Papers, Box 036.

83*New York Times,* 3 November 1948.

CHAPTER 10:

1Memorandum General Richardson to General Marshall, 4 August 1944, Richardson Papers, Box 036.

2Crowl, *Campaign in the Marianas,* p. 195.

3Memorandum Maj. Gen. Thomas T. Handy for the Chief of Staff, 16 August 1944, p. 4, appended to Buckner Board Report, National Archives.

4Memorandum for General Handy by Lt. Gen. Joseph T. McNarney, 19 August 1944, p. 1, Richardson Papers, Box 036.

5Ibid., p. 2.

6Letter General Griner to General Richardson, 30 September 1944, Richardson Papers, Box 035.

7Letter General Richardson to Judge Advocate General's Department, 19 October 1944 and Col. E. H. Snodgrass to General Richardson, 23 October, Richardson Papers, Box 035.

8Smith, *Coral and Brass,* p. 179.

9Potter, *Nimitz,* p. 374.

[10]Admiral Nimitz to Chief of Naval Operations, 27 October 1944, p. 1, Richardson Papers, Box 036.

[11]Ibid., p. 2.

[12]Transcript of interview with Edmund Love, p. 2.

[13]Memorandum CNO to Chief of Staff, U.S. Army, 6 November 1944, War Department, Chief of Staff Army File (WDCSA) 000.7, National Archives.

[14]Memorandum for General Handy by General McNarney, 19 August 1944, p. 2.

[15]Memorandum General Marshall to Admiral King, 22 November 1944, WDCSA file 000.7, National Archives.

[16]Memorandum COMINCH for General Marshall, 23 November 1944, WDCSA file 000.7, National Archives.

[17]*New York Times,* 12 November 1948.

[18]Love, *27th Infantry,* p. 670.

[19]Cooper, "Holland Smith," p. 410.

[20]Ibid., 402.

[21]Ibid., pp. 410–11.

[22]Ibid., p. 412.

[23]Memorandum General Ralph Smith to General Richardson, 28 August 1944, Richardson Papers, Box 035.

[24]Memorandum General Jarman to General Richardson, 6 September 1944, Richardson Papers, Box 035.

[25]Memorandum General Griner to General Richardson, 11 October 1944, p. 4, Richardson Papers, Box 035.

[26]Memorandum Brig. Gen. Redmond Kernan to General Richardson, 16 August 1944, Richardson Papers, Box 035.

[27]Memorandum Brig. Gen. Clark Ruffner to General Richardson, 23 October 1944, Richardson Papers, Box 035.

[28]Letter Gen. H. M. Smith to Gen. A. Vandegrift, 11 October 1944 as quoted in Cooper, "Holland Smith," p. 403.

[29]Memorandum Maj. Stephen McCormick to General Richardson, 2 September 1944, Richardson Papers, Box 035.

[30]Sherrod, "Answer and Rebuttal," *Infantry Journal,* January 1949, p. 23.

[31]See Potter, *Nimitz,* pp. 370–375 and Morison, *New Guinea and the Marianas,* pp. 330–332.

[32]Copy of undated article from 98th Division Newspaper appended to private letter from Mrs. Williston Wirt (General

Ralph Smith's sister), 29 September 1944, Ralph Smith Private Papers.

[33] Details of Ralph Smith's later career are taken from a transcript made by the author of six tapes recorded by Gen. Ralph Smith between 26 August 1982 and 14 August 1983.

[34] *New York Times*, 12 November 1948.

BIBLIOGRAPHY

PRIMARY SOURCES

Archives, Hoover Institute of War & Peace, Stanford, Ca.

Richardson, General Robert E., Papers, Boxes 035 and 036.

Smith, Major General Ralph C., Papers, Boxes 23–26.

Spruance, Admiral Raymond, Miscellaneous Papers, 1937–1963, 1 box.

Marine Corps Historical Archives, Washington, D.C.

CINCPAC-CINCPOA Operations Plan 13–43 (Makin), 5 October 1943.

CINCPAC-CINCPOA Operations Plan 3–44 (Marianas), 23 April 1944.

Fourth Marine Division, Operations Report, Saipan, 15 June–9 July, File A14–1.

Northern Troops & Landing Force (NTLF) V AC, Marianas, Phase I, Saipan, File A1–2.

Second Marine Division, Special Action Report, Phase I, Marianas, Saipan, File A11–1.

Smith, Lieutenant General Holland M., Papers, File 3B41.

Vandegrift, General A. A., Papers, File PC 465.

Frank, Benis (interviewer), Oral History Transcript, "General Clifton Cates," 1976.

Frank, Benis (interviewer), "General Graves Erskine," 1975.

Frank, Benis (interviewer), "General Robert E. Hogaboom," 1972.

Frank, Benis (interviewer), "Lieutenant General John Mc-Queen," 1973.

Frank, Benis (interviewer), "Brigadier General Joseph Stewart," 1973.

National Archives, Washington, D.C.

Army Chief of Staff, Decimal File, 1944–45, Record Group 165, "Proceedings of a Board of Officers Convened Pursuant to Letter Orders AG 333/3 Hqs. U.S. Armed Forces, Central Pacific Area, 4 July 1944" [Buckner Board Report]. A copy is also in Richardson Papers, Hoover Institution, Stanford, Ca.

Army Chief of Staff, Decimal File, 1944–45, Record Group 165, Miscellaneous letters between Generals Marshall, Handy, McNarney, and Admiral King.

National Archives, Suitland, Maryland

Record Group 407, File 327–0.3.

Operations Report, GALVANIC, Makin Operations, TF 52.6, 16–25 November 1943.

Operations Report, Marshall Islands, Kwajalein & Eniwetok.

27th Infantry Division Operations Report, 17 June–6 August 1944, "Battle for Saipan."

105 RCT Operations Report, FORAGER Operation, Saipan, June–August 1944.

106 RCT Operations Report, FORAGER Operation, Saipan, June–July 1944.

165 RCT Operations Report, FORAGER Operation, Saipan, June–July 1944.

Naval Archives, Washington, D.C.

Columbia University, Oral Histories:

Transcript, "Admiral Harry Hill, USN," Vol. I, 1969.

Transcript, "Rear Admiral Charles Moore, USN," 1970.

Miscellaneous:

Interviews by author:

Maj. Theodore Baltes, USA, San Jose, Ca., 24 June 1984.

Brig. Gen. Harold O. Deakin, USMC, Los Altos Hills, Ca., 13 September 1983.

Capt. Frank Harris, USN, Angels Camp, Ca., 14 July 1984.

Col. Benjamin Hazard, San Jose, Ca., 14 July 1984 and 5 January 1985.

Gen. Jacob Herzog, USA, Albany, N.Y., 17 September 1984.

Gen. Robert Hogaboom, USMC, St. Mary's City, Md., 4 October 1984.

Col. Russell Honsowetz, USMC, Alamo, Ca., 3 September 1983.

Edmund Love, Flint, Michigan, 6 August 1984.

Col. James Mahoney, USA, Los Altos Hills, Ca., 28 January 1984.

Col. Henry Ross, USA, La Mesa, Ca., 20 April 1984.

Capt. Bernard Ryan, USA, San Jose, Ca., 27 February 1984.

Robert Sherrod, Washington, D.C., 12 August 1944.

Maj. Gen. Ralph Smith, USA, Palo Alto, Ca., 24 August 1983, 1 February 1984, 9 July 1984.

Maj. Gen. Ralph Smith, USA, transcript of six tapes recorded at Palo Alto, Ca. between 26 August 1982 and 14 August 1983.

Letters from:

C. Oakley Bidwell to Dr. June Hoyt, 30 July 1984.

Gen. Charles B. Ferris (Ret.) to author, 31 January 1985.

Copy of draft letter Brig. Gen. Redmond Kernan to Professor E. B. Potter, 23 April 1979.

Copy of letter John A. Lynch to Reverend Robert Hartnett, S. J., editor *America*, 1 August 1949.

James Roosevelt to author, 30 November 1983.

Joseph Sykes to author, 15 January 1985.

Letter & enclosure (98th Division Newspaper) from Mrs. Williston Wirt, 29 September 1944.

BOOKS

Costello, John. *The Pacific War.* New York: Quill Press, 1982.

Department of the Army, *U.S. Army in World War II, The War in the Pacific.* Washington, D.C.: U.S. Government Printing Office.

Crowl, Philip. *Seizure of the Gilberts and Marshalls.* 1955.

Crowl, Philip. *Campaign in the Marianas.* 1960.

Dyer, Vice Admiral George C. *The Amphibians Came to Conquer: The Story of Admiral Richmond Kelley Turner.* Washington, D.C.: Government Printing Office, N.D.

Forrestel, Vice Admiral E. P. *Admiral Raymond A. Spruance, USN, A Study in Command.* Washington Navy Dept., 1966.

Heinl, Lt. Colonel Robert D. Jr., and Lt. Colonel John A. Crown. *The Marshalls: Increasing the Tempo.* Washington, D.C.: Historical Branch, U.S. Marine Corps, 1954.

Hoffman, Carl W. *Saipan, The Beginning of the End.* Washington, D.C.: Historical Division, U.S. Marine Corps, 1950.

Hough, Frank O. *The Island War: The United States Marine Corps in the Pacific.* New York: J. P. Lippincott Co., 1947.

Hoyt, Edwin P. *Storm Over the Gilberts.* New York: Mason/Charter, 1978.

Hoyt, Edwin P. *To the Marianas.* New York: Avon Books, 1983.

Isley, Jeter A., and Philip Crowl. *The U.S. Marines and Amphibious War.* Princeton, N.J.: Princeton University Press, 1951.

Johnston, Richard W. *Follow Me: The Story of the Second Marine Division in World War II.* New York: Random House, 1948.

King, Admiral Ernest J. *Fleet Admiral King, A Naval Record.* New York: W. W. Norton & Co., 1952.

Love, Edmund G. *The 27th Infantry Division in World War II.* Washington, D.C.: Infantry Journal Press, 1949.

Love, Edmund G. *War is a Private Affair.* New York: Harcourt Brace & Co., 1959.

Manchester, William. *Goodbye Darkness.* New York: Dell Books, 1979.

Marshall, Brigadier General S. L. A. *Battle at Best.* New York: William Morrow & Co., 1963.

Marshall, Brigadier General S. L. A. (ed. Cate Marshall). *Bringing Up the Rear, A Memoir.* San Rafael, Ca.: Presidio Press, 1979.

Marshall, Brigadier General S. L. A. *Island Victory.* Washington, D.C.: Infantry Journal Press, 1944.

Morison, Samuel Eliot. *History of Naval Operations in World War II.* Boston: Atlantic, Little Brown. Vol. VII, *Aleutians, Gilberts & Marshalls,* 1951; Vol. VIII, *New Guinea and the Marianas,* 1962.

Morison, Samuel Eliot. *The Two Ocean War.* Boston: Atlantic, Little Brown, 1963.

Moskin, J. Robert. *The U.S. Marine Corps Story.* New York: McGraw Hill, 1982.

Pogue, Forrest C. *George C. Marshall, Organizer of Victory.* New York: Viking Press, 1973.

Potter, E. B. *Nimitz.* Annapolis, Md.: Naval Institute Press, 1976.

Proehl, Carl W. (ed.). *The Fourth Marine Division in World War II.* Washington, D.C.: Infantry Journal Press, 1946.

Shaw, Henry I. Jr. *Tarawa, A Legend is Born.* New York: Ballantine Books, 1969.

Shaw, Henry I. Jr., Bernard C. Nalty, and Edwin Turnbladh. *History of U.S. Marine Corps Operations in World War II,* Vol. III, *Central Pacific Drive.* Washington, D.C.: Government Printing Office, 1966.

Sherrod, Robert. *On to Westward.* New York: Duell, Sloan and Pearce, 1945.

Smith, General Holland M. and Percy Finch, *Coral and Brass.* New York: Charles Scribner's Sons, 1949.

Smith, S. E. (ed.). *The United States Marine Corps in World War II.* New York: Random House, 1969.

U.S. Naval History Division. *U.S. Naval History Sources in the United States.* Washington, D.C.: Government Printing Office, 1979.

War Department. *The Capture of Makin, 20 November–24 November 1943.* Washington, D.C.: Government Printing Office, 1946.

UNPUBLISHED WORKS

Cooper, Norman Varnell. "The Military Career of General Holland M. Smith, USMC." Ph.D. dissertation, University of Alabama, 1974.

Lemp, Colonel John. "Observer Report on the Marianas Operation (FORAGER)" in Ralph Smith's private files, Palo Alto, Ca.

Sherrod, Robert. "Notebooks, May–December 1944" in Robert Sherrod's private files, Washington, D.C.

Smith, Major General Ralph. "Report on Operations, 27th Division, Saipan, 15–24 June 1944" in General Ralph Smith's private files, Palo Alto, Ca.

PERIODICALS

Donovan, James A. Jr. "Saipan Tank Battle," *Marine Corps Gazette*, October 1944.

Heinl, Robert D. Jr. "Naval Gunfire Support in Landing," *Marine Corps Gazette*, September 1945.

Love, Edmund G. "Omak," *Army*, September 1981.

Love, Edmund G. "Smith versus Smith," *Infantry Journal*, LXIII, November 1948, pp. 3–13.

Pratt, Fletcher. "Spruance, Picture of an Admiral," *Harpers Magazine*, August 1946, p. 153.

Richardson, Lieutenant General Robert C. Jr. "Letter to the Editor," *Saturday Evening Post*, 11 December 1948.

Sherrod, Robert. "An Answer & Rebuttal to 'Smith versus Smith': The Saipan Controversy," *Infantry Journal*, LXIV, January 1949, pp. 14–28.

Sherrod, Robert. "Battalion on Saipan," *Marine Corps Gazette*, October 1944.

Sherrod, Robert. Unsigned articles on Saipan. *Time*, 19 July and 18 September 1944.

Smith, Holland M., and Percy Finch. "My Troubles with the Army on Saipan," *Saturday Evening Post*, 13 November 1948.

Snyder, William P. "Walter Bedell Smith: Eisenhower's Chief of Staff," *Military Affairs*, Vol. XLVIII, No. 1, January 1984.

Stockman, Captain James R. "The Taking of Mount Tapotchau," *Marine Corps Gazette*, October 1948.

NEWSPAPERS

New York Journal American, 17 July and 18 July 1944.

New York Times, 10 and 14 September 1944, 3 November 1948, 28 November 1948.

New York Herald Tribune, 14 September 1944.

San Francisco Examiner, 8 July 1944.

INDEX

The National Bestseller!

GOODBYE, DARKNESS

by WILLIAM MANCHESTER

author of *American Caesar*

The riveting, factual memoir of WW II battle in the Pacific—
and of an idealistic ex-marine's personal struggle to understand
its significance 35 years later.

"A strong and honest account, and it ends with a clash of
cymbals."—*The New York Times Book Review*

"The most moving memoir of combat in World War II that I
have read. A testimony to the fortitude of man. A gripping,
haunting book."—William L. Shirer

A Laurel Book   **$5.95**   **32907-8**